Aboriginal™

Aboriginal™

The Cultural and Economic
Politics of Recognition

JENNIFER ADESE

UNIVERSITY OF MANITOBA PRESS

Aboriginal™: The Cultural and Economic Politics of Recognition
© Jennifer Adese 2022

26 25 24 23 22   1 2 3 4 5

All rights reserved. No part of this publication may be reproduced or transmitted in any form or by any means, or stored in a database and retrieval system in Canada, without the prior written permission of the publisher, or, in the case of photocopying or any other reprographic copying, a licence from Access Copyright, www.accesscopyright.ca, 1-800-893-5777.

University of Manitoba Press
Winnipeg, Manitoba, Canada
Treaty 1 Territory
uofmpress.ca

Cataloguing data available from Library and Archives Canada
ISBN 978-1-77284-005-6 (PAPER)
ISBN 978-1-77284-006-3 (PDF)
ISBN 978-1-77284-007-0 (EPUB)
ISBN 978-1-77284-008-7 (BOUND)

Cover design by Sébastien Aubin
Cover image: David P. Lewis/Shutterstock.com
Interior design by Jess Koroscil

The University of Manitoba Press acknowledges the financial support for its publication program provided by the Government of Canada through the Canada Book Fund, the Canada Council for the Arts, the Manitoba Department of Sport, Culture, and Heritage, the Manitoba Arts Council, and the Manitoba Book Publishing Tax Credit.

Funded by the Government of Canada | Canadä

To Oghogho—for the past, present, and future.

Contents

ix	Preface
1	Introduction
33	Chapter 1 – Aboriginal, Aboriginality, Aboriginalism, Aboriginalization: What's in a Word?
71	Chapter 2 – Aboriginalized Multiculturalism™: Canada's Olympic National Brand
109	Chapter 3 – Selling Aboriginal Experiences and Authenticity: Canadian and Aboriginal Tourism
141	Chapter 4 – Marketing Aboriginality and the Branding of Place: The Case of Vancouver International Airport
177	Conclusion – Thoughts on the End of Aboriginalization and the Turn to Indigenization
195	Notes
225	Bibliography
247	Index

Preface

As a child I was fascinated with words. I knew from a very young age the power that they could have. I remember that at the age of eight, while sitting in my mother's chair with our thesaurus, I would pore over words in an endless search for other words that could say more and do more than those I already had in my vocabulary. This pursuit arose not out of a desire to show off or be obnoxious, but rather out of an innate sense that the words I had been exposed to growing up could not do enough of what I needed them to do to convey the things I often thought and felt. I often wonder if it is because, out of the three different languages my grandparents spoke (and the many more than that my ancestors could speak), I can only speak one.

When languages themselves are lost entire worlds disappear with them. And so I have often had to "make do" with what I have and to try to be both critical and precise in my usage of the English language. This is why this book—while it is about so much more—is at its heart the study of a word. More than this, and as I discuss later, it is about what words are made to mean. To acknowledge those who have contributed to this work and to my thinking, then, it is a tall order. In some way or another, almost every Indigenous person I have ever met has impacted my thinking about the terms under study in this book. This book is very much the result of walking through life alongside other Indigenous peoples and thinking about the terms used by us and for us, both from within Indigenous languages and within English.

This book is the culmination of over a decade's worth of work, that began under the careful guidance of my doctoral supervisor, Susan Searls at McMaster University. Susan, you are and have always been an inspiring thinker, writer, and mentor, and I am so grateful that our paths were brought together. Your quiet brilliance has always been a source of inspiration to me. I as well would like to extend my gratitude to other members of my doctoral thesis committee—Chandrima Chakraborty and Rick Monture. I would also like to extend my gratitude to other friends and mentors I met during my time at McMaster University.

There are numerous colleagues, friends, and mentors whom I have had the pleasure of meeting and working with/learning from closely at various points over the long lifetime of this project: Daniel Coleman, Daniel Heath Justice, Nadine Attewell, Rob Innes, Kaitlin Debicki, Peter Thompson, Peter Hodgins, Pauline Rankin, Pat Gentile, Kahente Horn-Miller, Hayden King, Heather Dorries, Darren O'Toole, Zoe S. Todd, Chelsea Gabel, Paul Gareau, Daniel Voth, Daniel Sims, Tricia McGuire-Adams, Melody McKiver, Erin Konsmo, Cheslea Vowel, Jerry Flores, and as well my dear friends Chris Andersen, Karen Andersen, Geraldine King, Malissa Phung, Thu Nguyen, and Stacia Loft. To the Métis women who inspire me and keep me motivated, thank you: Melanie Omeniho, Linda Boudreau, Lorelei Lanz, Lisa Pigeau, Victoria Pruden, and Annette Maurice. Thank you as well to the early years educators that have taken care of my child while I undertook this work. This is not by any means an exhaustive list and if I am remiss in not naming someone here—I extend both my gratitude and my apologies!

I would be remiss if I did not extend my most heartfelt thanks to Jill McConkey. What else is there but to say that you are absolutely brilliant and amazing (and patient)? You are all of that and more. My deepest thanks to Glenn Bergen for our first conversation outside of the Mohegun Sun, way back in 2012, that put UMP on my radar for this project. I knew in my heart then that I wanted this work to be published by UMP—so thank you. Thank you as well to the rest of the UMP team. Thank you as well to Darcy Cullen at UBC Press. Portions of this project were written with the aid of the Social Sciences and Humanities Research Council and during my tenure as a Canada Research Chair. I thank both SSHRC and the Canada Research Chairs program for their support.

Last, but most certainly not least, thank you to my family for your emotional and intellectual support. My deepest debt of gratitude to Sampson Adese for your dedication to helping me see this project through by being the present parent while I worked to finish it up, for acting as a constant sounding board for ideas, and for believing in the project in the times when I had given up hope on its completion. Kinanaskomitin.

Aboriginal™

Introduction

On 20 May 2020, the Canadian government's chief/manager of the Library of Parliament, Tonina Simeone, uploaded a new HillNotes blog post directed towards (primarily) civil servants, titled "Indigenous peoples: Terminology Guide." In it, Simeone wades into what they refer to as "terminological complexities," and makes a strong statement against the use of the term Aboriginal when referring to First Nations, Métis, and Inuit: "the term 'Aboriginals' should be avoided. 'Aboriginal' should be used as an adjective, rather than a noun."[1] Simeone's blog and directions to federal public service workers is merely a reflection of a growing societal shift. A few years earlier, in 2017, the Indigenous-led digital agency Animikii published a short online article, wherein the staff at Animikii outlined their preference for the term Indigenous over the term Aboriginal. The piece, titled #MakingIndigenousHistory, appeared as a part of the company's web series for (what was then called) National Aboriginal History Month (now National *Indigenous* History Month). In the article the authors encapsulate the core criticism launched towards the term Aboriginal by Indigenous peoples: that it presents us with a "flawed construction."[2] The "Aboriginal" in National Aboriginal History Month, they argue, "reflects an archaic understanding that fails to recognize Indigenous peoples in Canada as distinct, separate Nations."[3] While they do not clarify how the term Indigenous speaks to nationhood in a way that the term Aboriginal does not, they nevertheless make a number of key arguments.

First, the authors of the Animikii piece contend that *unlike* the term Aboriginal, the usage of the word Indigenous comes "from within the Indigenous communities themselves."[4] The implication here is that the term Aboriginal has been imposed on Indigenous peoples by outsiders—by non-Indigenous peoples. By contrast, the word Indigenous is positioned by Animikii as self-selected; Indigenous is thus a term that Indigenous peoples adopt of their own free will and with their own purposes and intent. Their second thread of critique concerns the etymology of the word Aboriginal. According to Animikii's research, Aboriginal is "not only an English word but also . . . The 'ab' in Aboriginal is a Latin prefix that means 'away from' or 'not,' so in that sense, Aboriginal can actually mean 'not original,'" which they argue, in essence, contradicts the fact that Indigenous peoples are "original to" the land.[5] Echoing the work of the late Canadian writer Don Marks in his 2014 article, "What's in a Name: Indian, Native, Aboriginal or Indigenous," Animikii contends that the word Aboriginal, as an English word, is woefully inadequate to the tasks of recognizing and thus describing "the diversity within the Indigenous Communities of Canada."[6]

While the intent behind the argument is significant—to push back against the legacy of terminological misrecognition and generalization of hundreds of distinct Indigenous nations—the gaps in these arguments are immediately apparent. For one, the word Indigenous is as much an English word as Aboriginal is, with both deriving from Latin. According to the Merriam-Webster dictionary they both appear in common English language usage in the mid-1600s; the word Indigenous (as an adjective) has a notable association with ecology, referring to that which is "produced, growing, living, or occurring natively or naturally in a particular region or environment."[7] The word Aboriginal likewise first appeared as an adjective, as a descriptive word intended to signal a state of being as "the first or earliest known of its kind present in a region" and/or of "relating to the people who have been in a region from the earliest time: of or relating to *aborigines*."[8] By the middle of the next century, however, Aboriginal had come to also be used as a noun, denoting a person, place, or thing. In most cases the two are synonymous with one another, with little etymological difference.

To the other concern raised by Animikii (and Marks), that the Latin prefix "ab" in Aboriginal means "away from" or "not," their interpretation is not exact. Animikii states that "away from" and "not" are synonymous. Yet the equation of the two is a matter of colloquial speech and interpretation, and not necessarily etymological fact. This thus muddies our thinking regarding the term because of its perceived inherent negativity—as Animikii writes, our thinking of it as meaning "*not* original."[9] Such narrowed interpretation ignores that "ab," when combined with another word, more accurately means *either* "from," "away," or "off."[10] To be "*ab*normal" is to be away from the normal or to be "off" from the normal. As educational website Membean cogently outlines, to be *absent* is to be away from a place; to *abdicate* is to move away from power; and to *abvolate* is to fly away.[11] In this sense, it implies deviation rather than negation ("not" normal). If understood in this way, then, as meaning away or away from, Aboriginal has a clear association with *place*; Aboriginal refers to being original to, being *from*, away from, or even derived from a place. If we take this as an exact interpretation of the definitional nuances of the terms, then it becomes much harder to embrace Animikii's third point, that the word Aboriginal is *inherently* reductive because it does not recognize the diversity and complexity of Indigenous peoples and communities. There may be more to the thinking regarding this claim than what is presented online, but Animikii offers little explanation of how the word Indigenous, by contrast, allows for a diversity of existence that Aboriginal forecloses upon.

For whatever challenges exist in trying to sufficiently account for Aboriginal's origins at a definitional level, it is clear that although the term is entrenched within section 35 of the Constitution of Canada, 1982 in relation to the recognition of Aboriginal and treaty rights (something I will discuss in greater detail later on), it has evoked stark responses from Indigenous and non-Indigenous peoples alike.[12] Given the complex history of terminology used to refer to Indigenous peoples of Turtle Island, the Métis Homeland, Inuit Nunangat, and so on, and the continuing struggle by Indigenous peoples to compel non-Indigenous peoples to use the words Indigenous peoples use for ourselves, it is no wonder Indigenous peoples view terminological choices with deep skepticism, distrust, and outright disgust. If it is a term that is entrenched within Canada's Constitution and holds some significant legal and political weight, what is *wrong* with Aboriginal? In casual conversations that I have had with other Indigenous peoples over the past twenty years or so, I have heard each of the points raised by Animikii first-hand. Some people have insisted, as Animikii does, that the prefix "ab" implies that Indigenous peoples are "not normal" and that Indigenous peoples are *not* original; others, by contrast, have been more concerned with the way that it is a stifling and constraining term that favours generality over distinctiveness. In one conversation with an acquaintance, they made it clear that they would much rather be referred to, and to refer to themselves, as Indian, than to go anywhere near the word Aboriginal. Many First Nations, Métis, and Inuit have grappled with the meaning and significance of the term Aboriginal *and* of Indigenous and our relationship to those terms.

Linguistics researcher David Wilton argues that "the origin of a word does not determine its meaning. A word's meaning comes from usage, not etymology."[13] It is precisely because a word's meaning comes from its *usage* and *not* its etymology, that we see the word Aboriginal go from being a descriptive placeholder in the Constitution to a now contentious label. As such, this book is concerned with what the word Aboriginal has been made to mean since its deployment in section 35(1) and (2) of the Constitution Act of Canada as a marker of Aboriginal and treaty rights recognition.

It is here that the book's line of argumentation draws on the conceptual framings advanced by Michel Foucault and Stuart Hall with respect to discourse, discursive formations, and regimes of truth. Hall writes, "discourses are ways of talking, thinking, or representing a particular subject or topic. They produce meaningful knowledge about that subject."[14] Further to this when multiple statements converge, they create a "discursive formation."[15] The production of knowledge through discourse in turn "influences social practices, and so has real consequences and effects"; this is because discourse invariably operates "in relation to power" and is rarely, if ever, a neutral exercise.[16] As I argue in the forthcoming chapters, what we say and how we say it has power. When a particular discourse is effective at "organizing and regulating relations of power" as in the case of Aboriginality, it in turn produces a "regime of truth."[17] As a potent discursive formation, Aboriginality perpetuated a particular regime of truth regarding the state of relations between Indigenous peoples and Canada—placing a positive veneer overtop an insidiously harmful and toxic exercise of neoliberal state power and influence.

For a time, Aboriginality was ubiquitous in cultural and economic sites. As a pre-eminent brand in the 1990s, 2000s, and the early part of the 2010s, Aboriginality is a hallmark of the rise of neoliberal colonialism. In the chapters that follow, I trace its emergence through socio-economic and cultural sites, sites that overlap with politics and the politicized meaning of the term. By 2010 Aboriginal emerged as Canada's brand of "Aboriginalized" liberal multiculturalism, showcased that year for the world during the Canadian-hosted Vancouver Winter Olympic Games. It also appeared in the context of corporate branding in the for-profit tourism industry where a discourse of authentic Aboriginality emerged as a valuable economic aspect of both Indigenous peoples' and Canada's economies. Lastly, the term Aboriginal served as a potent label for the marketing of place—for the exercise of place-branding; in airport terminals such as that of the Vancouver

International Airport (YVR), the incorporation of "Aboriginal art" lends visual credence to claims to the legitimacy of Canadian sovereignty on unceded and unsurrendered Indigenous lands.

When I was a teenager in the 1990s, the term Native was everywhere. My high school's programming for urban Indigenous kids called *Native* Circle, I frequented the *Native* Centre, and I attended numerous conferences, programs, and gatherings organized for the *Native* community. As well, I, along with some of my friends, self-identified as *Native*. When I applied to university in the late 1990s, I applied to the *Native* Teacher Education Program (NTEP) at Lakehead University. It was there, when I arrived in the fall of 1999, that I began to see and hear the word Aboriginal, and occasionally Indigenous, used in lieu of Native. For example, I enrolled in my first year in the course Introduction to *Indigenous* Learning, where our professor asked us, on behalf of the university, to (if applicable) voluntarily self-identify as *Aboriginal* students. In another instance, I became involved in the university's *Native* Students Association, while at the same time attending university administration meetings for the *Aboriginal* Management Council.

By the time I left university in 2003, the word Aboriginal was finally emerging as popular public terminology. Twenty years after it was entrenched in Canada's Constitution, it was hitting its peak use—universities renamed programs and initiatives, conference organizers were adopting the term for their events, both for-profit and non-profit corporations rushed to adopt the term, and government entities strategically shuttled Indian and Native in favour of Aboriginal. The shift would be most noticeable in urban areas where heterogeneous Indigenous communities would leave government officials, educational institutions, and other organizations grasping for all-encompassing terminology to respond to calls from Indigenous peoples and organizations for greater inclusivity. A consequence of this shift also meant that, as with Native, Aboriginal became a form of one's self-identification—a person could suddenly *be* Aboriginal; the federal government significantly contributed to this by creating, through Statistics Canada, an enumerable category through which people could situate Aboriginal as a form of self-identification. As

I discuss in Chapter 1, it was irrelevant to Statistics Canada as to whether a person was accepted by the communities that the term Aboriginal in section 35 was intended to speak to (First Nations, Métis, or Inuit); given that recent censuses take self-identification as a legitimate foundation on which to base their records, Aboriginal became an identity unto *itself*.

Statistics Canada's creation of an Aboriginal identity category undoubtedly contributed to the extension of the term Aboriginal beyond legal and political realms. It is, however, the central argument of this book that the rapid rise of neoliberal globalization through the 1980s, and the associated socio-cultural, economic, and political shifts it brought to bear within Canada, have led to the most significant expansion of the term. Rather than staying fixed as a constitutional proxy for the rights of First Nations, Métis, and Inuit, through the 1990s and 2000s the term Aboriginal became a beacon for the emergence of neoliberal colonialism. In the wake of the constitutional era, Indigenous peoples would be offered the promise of freedom via inclusion in the neoliberal market—instead of the self-determination they had been demanding through the 1980s. As a result, Aboriginal became invaluable to, and within, Canada, as state and non-state actors rushed to incorporate it, quite literally, as a brand identity that *said something* about the state of relations between Indigenous peoples and Canada. It gave a prettied-up face to a nation grappling with growing public knowledge (and attendant embarrassment) related to its ongoing legacies and effects of colonization. Aboriginal, as a brand identity, marketed the state of relations with Indigenous peoples as entirely reconciliatory. Bad things (such as residential schools) were positioned as in the past (although the last school did not close until 1996), and the contemporary nation alleviated of responsibility for enacting violence against Indigenous peoples. When mobilized by state and corporate actors, it detracted attention away from ongoing questions about the legitimacy of Canadian sovereignty; assimilatory policies; free, prior, and informed consent; and repressive tactics in response to Indigenous resistances.

For Indigenous peoples who adopted the language of Aboriginal, who mobilized Aboriginal as a brand identity, or who inhabited the term as one in which they closely identified with, in many ways it reflects the continued and constant struggle to intervene in narratives constructed by others; to this end it cannot be read without a consideration of Indigenous agency. That Indigenous peoples adopted the term at all, beyond the bounds of the Constitution, is demonstrative of a conscious decision to do so. Given that the aftermath of constitutional negotiations revealed that the Canadian state would continue to ignore calls to accept Indigenous self-determination, however, it is little wonder those who continued to engage with the Canadian state, its institutions, and with Canadians more widely, would end up doing so upon a terrain of "Aboriginal-making."

To be sure, my fascination with the word Aboriginal and my interest in how Indigenous and non-Indigenous peoples have used the term (the subject of which is the main focus of this book) stem in large part from watching how it gradually displaced the term Native to become the lingua franca of Indigenous identification in the 2000s. But it also connected to a firm belief that Aboriginal is best understood as a dog whistle for a reorientation, or intensification, of Indigenous encounters with Canada and Canadians under the auspices of neoliberal colonialism. Although intended to function in a bounded manner as a placeholder for the rights of First Nations, the Métis Nation, and Inuit, and the attendant responsibilities of the Canadian state, the term Aboriginal's uptake in socio-economic life transformed it into a banner of Indigenous peoples' inclusion (and thus accession) to Canada and its liberal multicultural vision. This vision was central to Canada's work in the looping global competition for human resources that is neoliberal globalization. For Indigenous peoples continuously oppressed by Canadian settler colonialism, this in turn manifested in the extension of settler colonialism to neoliberal settler colonialism or neoliberal colonialism.

To be sure, settler colonialism has always been about resources and building national economies. Yet neoliberal colonialism transformed the terrain upon which the dispossession of Indigenous peoples takes place. Neoliberalism has led to a wholesale restructuring of the world, and thus of how states relate to and communicate with their citizens and with one another. This has had a direct impact on the nature of Indigenous peoples' experiences with past and current settler-colonizing nation-states like Canada. To further trace the contours of such a shift, it is necessary at this stage to define more precisely what neoliberalism is and to discuss the relationship between neoliberalism and colonialism.

American political economist Robert McChesney writes that neoliberalism "refers to the policies and processes whereby a relative handful of private interests are permitted to control as much as possible of social life in order to maximize their personal profit."[18] Māori political scholar and theorist Maria Bargh likewise surmises that the extension of the market involves a threefold emphasis on "'free' trade and the 'free' mobility of capital, accompanied by a broad reduction in the ambit and role of the state."[19] The state's primary role is to "ensur[e] military, police, and legal infrastructures are in place, thereby allowing the market to operate freely and without state intervention."[20] Neoliberalism, then, is "essentially a totalizing economic machine that transforms whole communities" leading to the corporatization of everyday life.[21] Successive Canadian governments have likewise adopted neoliberal ideology over the past four decades, with politicians working alongside corporations and economists to naturalize market language into the everyday lives of its population. In an effort to help the free flow of capital and define everything in market terms, the state has gradually dismantled social and welfare programming in favour of the privatization of social services under the pretext of the nation being perpetually in debt.

In Ontario, for example, under the Progressive Conservative premiership of Mike Harris (1995–2002), social services experienced an unprecedented gutting and public services became increasingly privatized. Harris's "Common Sense Revolution" used provincial debt as a rationale to issue substantive (and in some cases irreparably) harmful cuts to public spending and for the enactment of anti-homelessness legislation such as the Safe Streets Act (1999), something to which I will return to in the later pages of Chapter 2.[22] To put this in a different perspective, I offer the following short narrative. As a child I bore direct witness to the harm caused by Harris's cuts. My mother received social welfare benefits from the Mother's Allowance program, which operated in Ontario from 1920 until 1997, when it was cut by the Harris government. While the program was rife with problems (it was a tool of what anti-poverty activist and scholar Margaret Little critiques for "moral regulation of single mothers in Ontario"),[23] it was also a vital lifeline for families like mine. I have very vivid memories of my mother going hungry while we eked out an existence on Mother's Allowance; even under the program there was rarely enough to make sure that we would all be fed. Yet as Little has pointed out, the termination of the program led to even greater devastation; it drove my mother and me into even greater poverty and precarity. Cuts to such social spending without a consideration of the "human costs," language that is itself evidence of the intrusion of the corporatization of everyday language, were devastating.[24] But this is precisely how neoliberal ideology works. The interests of corporations and capital trump the on-the-ground realities and needs of human beings. Paradoxically, the market is situated as the only mechanism capable of improving human well-being.[25] The government's job thus becomes one of encouraging the flow of capital, which in turn contributes to the liberalization of market forces.

Within this, nations compete for the attention of multinational corporations, looking to promote the image that they offer a genial and welcoming climate for unfettered capitalist expansion. Branding and the notion of "the brand" are central to corporate operations and as such, with the rise of neoliberalism, nation-states engage in branding exercises. The practice of nation-branding is not, however, new. In the early years of Canada's formation as a nation-state, nation-branding appeared as linked to municipal and regional branding for the purposes of settlement and national population growth. This was acute relative to the Prairies and the Pacific coast as promoters and boosters worked to attract new settler Canadians would then in turn contribute to both settlement and the growth of regional, provincial, and federal economies.[26] Cultural historian Daniel Francis writes that in the late 1800s, major railway companies, along with both federal and provincial governments, engineered a series of major campaigns to "sell Canada."[27] Through the use of propaganda and promotion, Canadian governments actively sought to expand the Anglo-Saxon population within Canada who would help to shore up its territorial claims in the so-called Northwest by inhabiting rural areas and who would help to financially regenerate and sustain the nation.

This was in turn tied to the belief that western expansion through settlement would foment Canada's status as a nation on the world stage. The "need for immigrants, based on [the] notion that Canada's future within the British Empire, was dependent on western expansion to lift Canada 'from colony to nation' in not simply legal terms but in terms of its global power."[28] Promotional materials targeted towards immigrants from the British colonial metropole, for example, expounded on the potential of immigrants to help build a new empire in contributing to the formation of Canada's national identity.[29] Canada's imperial aspirations also meant that it both saw and cultivated an image of Indigenous peoples as a threat—one that would be subdued by a supposedly superior society. In order to market the Prairies as safe and Indigenous peoples as non-threatening, the young Canadian nation actively worked to both pacify and subjugate Indigenous peoples; it did so to secure its claims to sovereignty and to legitimate its efforts to assert authority over Indigenous lands and resources. The suppression of Indigenous peoples was "an integral, if not always explicit, component of the Tory government's program of development" in the late 1800s.[30] This was considered vitally important to Canadian nation-building following the Northwest Resistance, when First Nations and Métis actively defended themselves and their lands from Canadian dispossession. In response, as will be discussed later in greater detail, the Canadian government enacted punitive measures to control Indigenous nations on the Prairies.[31]

Meanwhile, Indigenous peoples were being drawn into the marketing of Canada's early iteration of its national identity. As will be discussed in greater detail in Chapter 3 of this book, boosters and other promoters, particularly those working in regional tourism but also on behalf of the nation itself, drew on representations of Indigenous peoples and, where possible, actively engaged Indigenous peoples to perform for tourists.[32] An infantile conceptualization of "reconciling" Indigenous peoples' existence to the nation—primarily via assimilation but also through limited and highly managed forms of inclusion—was then central to expanding Canada's territorial claims and shoring up its identity as a distinct nation. The expansion and elaboration of capitalism through the development of both new and pre-existing industries and markets was undoubtedly a major contributor to the view that Canada had potential as a future empire; in the late 1800s and into the early 1900s, boosterism and other ways of marketing regions of Canada (and therefore Canada itself) served as a precursor to the rise in branding that would appear later and under which Indigenous peoples would become even more strategically important to the nation (Figure 1).

With the emergence of neoliberal globalization in the 1980s, corporatized rhetoric contributed to a notable change in the articulation of nation-state identities.[33] Through the 1990s and 2000s, states such as Canada have rushed to reframe national identity—through the language of neoliberalism—as Canada's brand. Under neoliberalism, what it is to be Canadian is not so much about identifying what connects people within Canada for the purpose of fomenting national unity; instead it is about engendering the nation-state with its own unique image/personality so that it holds appeal to national and international

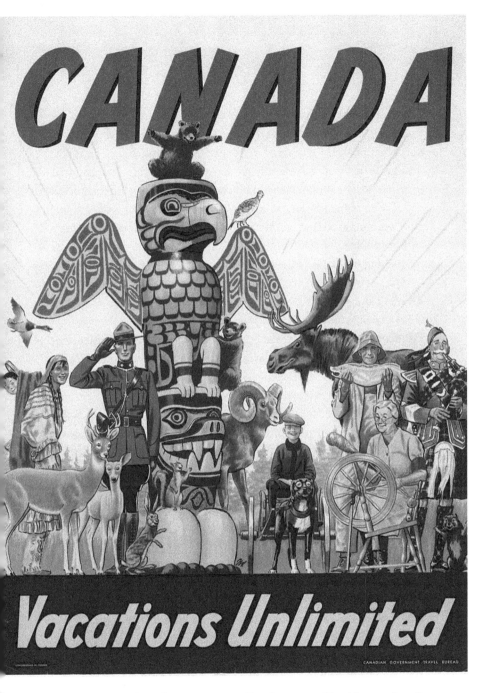

Figure 1. Canada Vacations Unlimited, c. 1930–50, Canadian Government Travel Bureau. One of many travel advertisements that promoted Canadian national identity as connected to settler perceptions of Indianness. Source: R1409 – Library and Archives Canada.

markets. Older marketing approaches are tweaked and Canada itself becomes a product, inasmuch as it is imagined as a place.

Branding is an important part of corporate marketing due to increased regional, national, and global competition between corporations, particularly among those that were once locally rooted and have become multinational in their reach. Multinational corporations have expanded beyond their original national borders and are caught up in a global competition for economic dominance, a competition that sees the privileging of the interests of the market over those of citizens and communities. The contemporary globalization of economic and social life has meant that nations have become intently focused on seeing the expression of national identity as part of a branding exercise. Boosterism and early forms of promoting Canada did so from a foundation that saw Canada's future as expressly British-Canadian. While other European constituents might be tangentially represented within Canadian national identity, its core was envisioned by early expansionists as unabashedly British-Canadian.[34] By the time neoliberalism surfaced, cracks had long begun to show in that Anglocentric vision for Canada.

Through resilience in the face of assimilation and attempted eradication, Indigenous peoples have resisted and disrupted the British-Canadian hegemony on these lands. In response Canadian politicians have grappled with how to work Indigenous peoples into the national narrative. The development of neoliberal ideology and its reach into all corners of everyday life provided a pathway for the state to endeavour to do so. In light of growing public consciousness over its treatment of Indigenous peoples the state actively sought to repackage the nation's image "for commercial consumption and nostalgic re-narration purged of historical responsibility."[35] The amplification, incorporation, and marketing of *Aboriginal* cultural difference (a vision of Indigenous existence as imagined as being separate from *politics*) was thus one way, other than outright denialism, that politicians and corporations worked to cover over colonialism.

Neoliberalism in settler colonial contexts transforms Indigenous peoples from liabilities into resources—which can likewise be consumed. This has led to rampant expansion in the commodification and branding of Indigenous peoples, bodies, identities, cultures, lands, spirituality, craftwork, and so on. Waitaha professor Makere Stewart-Harawira, a leading scholar on Indigenous experiences under capitalism and globalization argues that, "in the face of increasing globalization, indigenous cultures and identities are being increasingly threatened by the commodification of indigenous culture that is occurring at multiple levels."[36] Throughout the 1990s and 2000s, Canada sought to distinguish itself in the global marketplace in part by turning the outcome of constitutional rights entrenchment via section 35 into a packageable product itself that effectively said something positive about the nature of Indigenous-Canada relations. Aboriginal, intended as a touchpoint for rights was incorporated, both figuratively and literally, as a revenue-generating product that has co-opted a form of Aboriginal material and spiritual cultures and knowledges into the Canadian economy.

As I discuss throughout the following chapters, Canadian governments and corporations promote market solutions for colonial problems. Even scholars working with Indigenous communities have adopted neoliberal models and position them as a pathway towards (albeit limited) self-determination, contending that in some ways economic development under neoliberalism can provide the best pathway for the realization of self-determination. For example, Canadian professor of politics Gabrielle Slowey writes that "neoliberal globalization may be a remedy to First Nations dispossession, marginalization, and desperation because it opens up space for First Nations self-determination . . . in terms of increased political authority and overall improved economic status."[37] Howard-Wagner et al. likewise write that neoliberal globalization has the potential to "chang[e] the relationship Indigenous peoples have with the state."[38] They argue that some Indigenous peoples pursue economic development as a result of "a growing indigenous anti-statism in the context of funding dependency," that is, those who have grown weary of being placed into a state of dependency and who believe that states that lack the will to "deliver on Indigenous rights" turn towards "market strategies to achieve self-determination. Economic development is a means to an end: it provides a pathway to financial sustainability."[39] At the same time, they argue, Indigenous peoples continue to insist on their distinctiveness and thus demand that states recognize "their rights to self-determination and community development."[40] In any event, many of these market strategies are simply not viable. For example, models of Aboriginal tourism as a branch of ecotourism (discussed in Chapter 3) cannot be equalizers because they rely on access to land bases that hold visual and/or socio-cultural appeal for tourists. Given that part of colonization's reordering of Indigenous nations involved the tactical relocation of select communities and bands to remote (and in most cases barely habitable) regions or reserves, and that many still lack access to clean drinking water, not all communities *can* find workable neoliberal models that allow them to engage in such development.[41]

As Bargh writes, neoliberalism functions "as a new form of colonisation" in that it has a "past and a history which is filled with particular kinds of attitudes towards Indigenous people and indigenous cultures" that are consistent with those at the heart of colonization.[42] Both colonization and neoliberalism rely on a preoccupation with forcing all humans into one way of living. For Indigenous peoples broadly, neoliberal practices and policies are those "practices and policies which seek to extend the market mechanism into areas of the community previously organised and governed in other ways."[43] Crucially, Anishinaabe scholar Darrel Manitowabi points out that neoliberalism "is particularly damaging to collectivities because it transforms communities into individuals linked to an economic engine."[44] Neoliberalism, with its emphasis on individualism and the economic growth of individuals and corporations, ultimately sees Indigenous peoples "and cultures as obstacles to economic development which must be eliminated."[45] As such, neoliberal practices such as privatization and corporatization threaten Indigenous peoples' ways of understanding resources through a paradigm of relationality, as "diverse and holistic, rather than market based."[46]

Under neoliberalism, market solutions are considered to be both necessary and naturally superior ways for resolving the problem of poverty because "all individuals are equal in the eyes of the market."[47] If the market is inherently neutral it is, so the arguments in favour of neoliberalism go, the best mechanism for addressing/preventing inequality. If neoliberal policies and practices can further economic growth, which then leads to development, this will in turn enhance the "wellbeing of all people" through giving rise "to better standards of living."[48] Meanwhile, neoliberal practices and policies are thus also lauded as effective tools for the regulation and social management of citizens, and for civilizing populations and encouraging peace.[49] It is here where we see the points of interconnection between the two. As I will discuss in Chapter 2, Indigenous peoples who refuse to be socialized into neoliberal market dynamics are cast as "bad Indians." In turn, those positioned as "bad Indians" are subjected to a renewed set of racist tropes that allude to their savagery, their irreconcilability with Eurowestern values, and their failure to properly civilize. Indigenous peoples are seen as obstacles to economic development "which must be eliminated, or, more prevalent recently, as obstacles which can nonetheless acquire a greater level of civilisation through the right kind of training."[50] Neoliberalism is a renewed modality of settler colonialism—neoliberal colonialism or neoliberal settler colonialism—albeit one that actively tries to conceal its colonial tenets.

Neoliberalism's management techniques and its approaches to the civilization process work more covertly than the civilizing projects did in the early colonial nation-building era.[51] The central way in which it entrenches itself in Indigenous peoples' lives is by promising resolution of grinding poverty caused by centuries of dispossession and oppression. In the context of this book, the Canadian state's only apparent solution for the poverty it has engineered is to try to force Indigenous peoples to embrace neoliberalism and neoliberalism's goal of economic growth.[52] As such the state consistently pushes Indigenous peoples towards individualized, corporatized economic development (take, for example, the relentless pushing of communities away from communal land ownership towards the privatization of reserve lands with the state's express interest in increasing non-Indigenous corporations' access to on-reserve resources). Again, economic development (in terms of corporate development and ownership) and privatization propose market solutions for colonial problems—particularly highlighted in attempts to eradicate Indigenous ties to lands that the Canadian state wants to claim as its own. Those who stand in the way of corporations, media, government, and everyday Canadian citizens are cast as failures to properly civilize and/or are criminalized, like the Wet'suwet'en and the Unist'ot'en Camp in their struggle against the Coastal GasLink pipeline and the Haudenosaunee of Six Nations at 1492 LandBackLane.[53]

Under neoliberal colonialism, *all* exchanges between Canada and Indigenous peoples are filtered through a market lens under the promises of a truer freedom. Meanwhile, in terms of its national brand identity, the Canadian state generates a new cover under which to try and hide its paternalism. It stops far short of relinquishing its colonial stranglehold on Indigenous peoples, wanting instead to "be seen to allow people the 'freedom' and 'empowerment' to govern themselves, but at the same time distrusting the abilities of some peoples, particularly Indigenous peoples, to do so."[54] Yet neoliberal colonialism promises a kind of freedom via the market that Indigenous peoples could and will never be able to occupy. The Canadian state occupied, and continues to occupy, a position of domination in relation to Indigenous peoples; even if Indigenous peoples *want* to be neoliberal subjects, the situation is thus that (particularly for those still governed by the Indian Act of 1876) they are not the free actors that the neoliberal ethos is founded upon.[55] It is precisely this situation, along with the innate tensions between neoliberalism and what it is to "be Indigenous" that sits at the heart of neoliberal colonialism. While neoliberalism is touted as neutral, for Indigenous peoples it is anything but. The way that neoliberalism functions, and the rationale for it, produce systems of domination that are at times indistinguishable from colonization: in effect neoliberalism, especially for Indigenous peoples living within settler colonies like Canada, *is* colonialism.[56]

It is important to note here that the entrenchment of Aboriginal/Aboriginality as Canada's national brand was neither wholly successful nor ubiquitous; as is discussed in the chapters that follow, inasmuch as there are those who inhabited the term Aboriginal for their own purposes, there were those who rejected the decontextualization of the term and its broad application. As Kahnawà:ke Mohawk author Taiaiake Alfred and Tsalagi scholar Jeff Corntassel highlight, a binary was established between those who were co-opted by the state (*Aboriginal*) and those who continued to stand outside of it (*Indigenous*). For those Indigenous peoples who resisted inclusion by "being Indigenous" (to borrow from Alfred and Corntassel again), they interrupt the work of neoliberal governments and multinational corporations by asking what is being hidden in the underbelly of Aboriginality. As I discuss later and return to in greater depth in the Conclusion, they continue to pose questions of ethics, critique the limits of Canadian sovereignty, and insist on an alternative way of being in the world that sees land as a relation rather than a commodity.

Theorizing Aboriginal in the Politics of Recognition

This book is organized into four chapters and a substantive Conclusion. Chapter 1 examines the emergence of the term Aboriginal in the context of Indigenous-Canadian state relations, discussing how, through law and political organization, the term enters Indigenous peoples' lexicon, appearing as a preferred term for constitutional entrenchment. While there is not an expansive body of literature placing the term Aboriginal and its associated meanings under examination, Indigenous theorists have grappled with its use considering the implications of the constitutional moment. The most well known of these took aim at the problems arising from legal-political entrenchment and the extension of Aboriginal to cultural discourse. In "Being Indigenous: Resurgences against Contemporary Colonialism," Alfred and Corntassel contend that "'aboriginalism' is a legal, political, and cultural discourse designed to serve an agenda of silent surrender to an inherently unjust relation at the root of the colonial state itself."[57] The authors take the view that engagement in the very processes leading to constitutional recognition sees Indigenous peoples acquiesce to Canadian colonization. Aboriginalism is then a discursive formation that masks relations of domination and subjugation. The authors elaborate on this, arguing that "the acceptance of being 'aboriginal' (or its equivalent term in other countries, such as 'ethnic groups') is a powerful assault on Indigenous identities. It must be understood that the aboriginalist assault takes place in a politico-economic context of historic and ongoing dispossession and of contemporary deprivation and poverty; this is a context in which Indigenous peoples are forced by the compelling needs of physical survival to cooperate individually and collectively with the state authorities to ensure their physical survival."[58] Alfred and Corntassel contend that negotiating with the state on an already colonized and deeply unequal terrain, and entering political relationships that are already skewed such as to deny Indigenous self-determination, is highly problematic. Furthermore, they argue, because of centuries of colonial violence, Indigenous peoples are forced to engage in political negotiations to survive.

Glen Sean Coulthard (Yellowknives Dene), scholar and author of *Red Skin, White Masks: Rejecting the Colonial Politics of Recognition* (2014), extends Alfred and Corntassel's analysis through the work of famed Martinican scholar Frantz Fanon and his seminal work *Black Skin, White Masks* (1952). Coulthard produces a more focused analysis of the inner workings of the politics of recognition in colonial contexts. In his cogent critique of the politics of (Aboriginal) recognition he writes that "instead of ushering in an era of peaceful co-existence grounded on the ideal of reciprocity or mutual recognition, the politics of recognition in its contemporary liberal form promises to reproduce the very configurations of colonialist, racist, patriarchal state power that Indigenous peoples' demands for recognition have historically sought to transcend."[59] Coulthard also builds from the work of political theorist Richard Day, contending that the politics of recognition refers "to the now expansive range of recognition-based models of liberal pluralism that seek to 'reconcile' Indigenous assertions of nationhood with settler-state sovereignty via the accommodation of Indigenous identity claims in some form of renewed legal and political relationship with the Canadian state."[60] Coulthard asserts that Indigenous peoples firmly assert and reassert their nationhood but the settler-state framework is only ever willing to reconcile this to its own claim to sovereignty through a watered-down process of accommodation. For Alfred and Corntassel, this is akin to what Kiera Ladner refers to in her work on the Royal Commission on Aboriginal Peoples (RCAP) as creating a position of "negotiated inferiority."[61]

While each of these scholars focuses more on the legal and political, this chapter and this book are primarily interested in the way that the term Aboriginal (and as such what Alfred and Corntassel call Aboriginalism) becomes a hallmark of not only legal and political relationships but also socio-economic ones. Without entrenchment of clear definitions of Aboriginal rights and of Aboriginal, their definition and interpretation have been left not only to the courts, but to governments, Indigenous peoples, and the general Canadian public, who put the term to work in ways that would be both coterminous and at times wildly at odds. This is not to imply that these can be discretely discussed. As detailed in Chapter 1, these things are in fact deeply interwoven. However, in an era of neoliberal colonialism, Aboriginal, Aboriginalism, Aboriginality, and Aboriginalization are the manifestation of such deeply striated socio-economic relationships. It is in fact the decontextualization of Aboriginal, from the political-legal purposes in which it was mobilized, and its subsequent extension into socio-economic life, that lead us down the path whereby we might see it as a kind of acculturated (rather than negotiated) inferiority.

As far as I concur with Alfred and Corntassel, in Chapter 1 I also argue that it is important to understand how in some ways Aboriginal/Aboriginalism are co-constituted—and that analyzing such encounters solely through a lens of impoverishment does not do justice to those Indigenous activists involved in entrenching the term in the Constitution. Alfred and Corntassel write, "There are many 'aboriginals' (in Canada) or 'Native Americans' (in the United States) who identify themselves solely by their political-legal relationship to the state rather than by any cultural or social ties to their Indigenous community or culture or homeland. This continuing colonial process pulls Indigenous people away from cultural practices and community aspects of 'being Indigenous' towards a political-legal construction as 'aboriginal.'"[62] While this may well be the case for some people, in Chapter 1 I contend that Indigenous activists and organizations agitating for constitutional recognition did so from a powerful sense of their place within Indigenous community contexts. Such activists and community organizers consistently struggled for a vision of Aboriginality that was more expansive and tied to self-determination. This is particularly notable as Indigenous political activists recommended both "aboriginal people" and "Indigenous people" for constitutional usage; as such it is not so much the term itself but the dynamics at work that are covered over by terminology. While "aboriginal rights" and "aboriginal people" are used within the Constitution, the term Aboriginal was chosen because it was both broad and inclusive of First Nations (as "Indians" in the Constitution), Métis, and Inuit. As such we need to redirect our attention away from a hyperfocus on the term itself to look at what it has been *made* to mean. Chapter 1 details how Indigenous peoples pushed for a constitutional document that established legal recognition of/for Indigenous self-determination. No such document materialized, and what later appeared were, at best, fractured commitments to self-government on the part of the state that would create the conditions for the concretization of neoliberal colonialism.

Aboriginal Multiculturalism: Canada's Brand

Immediately following constitutional entrenchment, the federal government, via Statistics Canada, laid the groundwork for the contortion of "aboriginal rights" and "aboriginal peoples" by creating a statistical category—and a socio-cultural category—known as "aboriginal identity."[63] The nationhood of "aboriginal peoples" was effectively de-emphasized by state categorization and tabulation and in its place processes of/for self-identification were created. The construction of Aboriginal and thus Aboriginal peoples as a rights-holding collective was summarily transformed; the term was instead repositioned as an individual claim to a self-situated Aboriginal identity.

This exportation of an individualistic articulation of Aboriginal identity bound Indigenous peoples to non-Indigenous peoples' expectations of readily assimilable Aboriginal people, primed for inclusion within the Canadian liberal multicultural framework. As I discuss in Chapter 2, Aboriginal identity was incorporated as a central part of Canada's brand identity. Inasmuch as it stood on its own, it was nevertheless drawn into Canada's "core brand" identity—as multicultural Canada. Multiculturalism finds its origins as governmental policy with the 1963 Royal Commission on Bilingualism and Biculturalism. Convened to address Québécois contributions to Canadian culture and national identity, the commission issued a report in response to these concerns, recommending, among other things, the official declaration of Canada as a bilingual (English and French) nation—resulting in the Official Languages Act of 1969. The federal government soon faced pressure by other European ethnic Canadians (primarily Prairie-based Ukrainians, Poles, and Germans and their associated labour unions) to recognize their contributions to Canada; this in turn led to the establishment of multiculturalism policy in 1971 (formalized in 1988 as the Multiculturalism Act), whereby multicultural policy recast these and other non-British and Québécois populations as "diversities." These and other "ethnic minority" populations fell outside of the narrative of the two founding nations and were given recognition within the national fabric based on their having immigrated to the nation post-Confederation.

First Nations, Métis, and Inuit, on the other hand, effectively dodged inclusion as ethnic minorities within multicultural policy precisely because, as anthropologist Sandra Lambertus writes, "multiculturalism and Native relations and their respective policies, and connections to Canadian society have developed along different trajectories."[64] In the period from which multiculturalism would emerge, the Canadian government was in the process of attempting to finalize the assimilation of Indigenous peoples holding various legal statuses vis-à-vis Canada. In the mid-twentieth century, Inuit (who were only briefly included under the Indian Act) were subjected to various "experiments" alongside forced attendance at residential "schools." Inuit families were forcefully relocated to the High Arctic;[65] the federal government instituted the dehumanizing practice of forcing Inuit to wear dog tags with numbers (in lieu of government officials learning Inuktitut names);[66] Inuit were removed from communities and sent to tuberculosis sanitoriums in the south, and were never returned home (or were returned to the wrong homes/families);[67] and according to Inuit, the Royal Canadian Mounted Police (RCMP) killed many sled dogs in order to restrict movement of Inuit across their territories and to force them into "settled" living. Sled dogs were vital to Inuit as a mode of transportation, but they were also meaningful members of Inuit families—the impact of this was devastating for families.[68]

The Canadian government also made concerted efforts to assimilate Métis in the nineteenth century—via armed military suppression in Red River (present-day Winnipeg) in 1870 and again in Batoche, Saskatchewan, in 1885, and the Manitoba and Northwest Halfbreed Scrip Commissions (1870s–1920s), wherein Métis were induced to sign away their claims to land as Indians in exchange for a scrip certificate that could be redeemed (in theory) for land or money (during which Métis were swindled out of their scrip via settler Canadian land speculators).[69] However, in the twentieth century the government adopted a policy of neglect. Métis, as the Canadian government saw it, did not exist as distinct Indigenous people. As Prime Minister John A. Macdonald famously stated, "If they are Indians they go with the tribe; if they are half-breeds they are whites."[70] This attitude would give rise to, as mentioned, a policy of neglect, whereby agreements made to secure land bases for Métis via the Manitoba Treaty (a.k.a., the Manitoba Act of 1870) went unfulfilled. The attitude that Métis were not a distinct people *or* a nation, and the attendant lack of regard for Métis land rights, forced many Métis to eke out a marginal existence in road allowances (narrow strips of unused land claimed by the Crown that ran alongside roadways).[71] Much of the policymaking as it pertained to Métis would then stem from provincial and municipal governments as they sought to "manage" deeply impoverished marginal Métis communities. In Alberta, after fierce activism on the part of Métis people in the province, what are today known as the provincially overseen Métis settlements were established.[72] In Manitoba, Métis who lived in small communities on the fringe of urbanized areas, such as Rooster Town and Turkey Town, saw their homes razed for urban development,[73] while Métis in more rural areas, such as Ste. Madeline, were likewise displaced.[74] In Saskatchewan, under the leadership of Tommy Douglas, Métis were forcibly relocated to farming colonies and made to work in menial jobs to benefit non-Métis enterprises and the government.[75]

For First Nations in that time period, in light of a growing global human rights movement following the Holocaust and the conclusion of the Second World War, some oppressive parts of the Indian Act were removed. These included prohibitions on cultural and spiritual expression through ceremonies, sexist bans prohibiting Indian women from voting in band council elections, and restrictions on First Nations bringing land claims issues forward to the courts.[76] In spite of these changes, however, the Indian Act remained a deeply paternalistic and oppressive document; for instance, provisions regarding enfranchisement (the removal of someone's status as an Indian) remained, in particular those that created deep inequality for Indigenous women who continued to lose their status, and future entitlement of their children to status, if they married a non-Indian or non-status Indian man.[77]

By 1960, as the Bill of Rights, the first document addressing equal rights of Canadians, was unveiled, the government endeavoured to repeal the "portions of Section 14(2) of the *Canada Elections Act* . . . in order to grant the federal vote to status Indians. First Nations people could now vote without losing their status."[78] In spite of this and other amendments, as discussed in Chapter 1, First Nations continued to mobilize politically around the repressiveness of the Indian Act and of federal, provincial, and municipal governments. Then, in 1963 the Canadian government commissioned an anthropologist named Harry Hawthorn to study the situation of Indigenous peoples. The late political theorist Alan Cairns cogently summarizes Hawthorn's report, writing that Hawthorn ultimately argued that status Indians "should be given the educational and other tools they need to make meaningful choices of how they wished to live. It was assumed that sufficient numbers would choose a contemporary version of Indianness that Indian communities would persist into the indefinite future."[79] Hawthorn writes that status Indians were "citizens minus" because of failed government policies and recommended assimilation policies be ended and that Indigenous peoples be recognized as "citizens plus."

Hawthorn's work would continue to frame debates around policy into the next decade. Cairns states that Hawthorn's framing of Indigenous rights and existence sits in tension with that of people like James (Sakej) Youngblood Henderson, a widely regarded human rights lawyer and legal scholar, who in 1994 issued what he termed a "treaty federalism" approach to Indigenous activism.[80] Cairns ultimately critiques the treaty federalism approach outlined by Henderson for creating division between Indigenous peoples and Canadians, and for its view of Canada "as a multinational polity in which we relate to each other through the separate nations we belong to."[81] For Cairns this would keep people apart rather than build unity between them. This tension would continue to sit at the heart of policymaking through the 1960s, as Canadians continued to ignore demands for respecting nation-to-nation relations with First Nations in favour of attempts to negotiate the assimilation of First Nations into the Canadian polity.

There is no greater evidence of this than the "Statement of the Government of Canada on Indian Policy, 1969," colloquially known as the 1969 White Paper. A culmination of loose interpretations of the Hawthorn Report, alongside limited consultations with reserve communities, the White Paper sidestepped First Nations' tangible concerns about Aboriginal and treaty rights, title to land, self-determination, and access to education and health care; instead, in June of 1969 the federal government, under then prime minister Pierre Elliott Trudeau, sought to push through the White Paper. Building on the notion that status Indians were already "citizens plus" and thus at an *unfair* (dis)advantage, the White Paper proposed dissolving the Indian Act and removing the "special status" of First Nations.[82] Much of this was also premised on Trudeau's own political platform—that of creating a "just society" in which all Canadians had equal rights. If status Indians remained subject to the Indian Act, then, according to Trudeau's just society vision, they were discriminated against and thus unequal. At the same time "special status" elevated them "above" other Canadians—a further inequality.[83] The federal government's intention, as described in the White Paper, was to achieve equality among all Canadians by eliminating *Indian* as a distinct legal status and by regarding Aboriginal peoples simply as citizens with the same rights, opportunities, and responsibilities as other Canadians. In keeping with Trudeau's vision of a just society, the government proposed to repeal legislation that it considered discriminatory. In this view, the Indian Act was discriminatory because it applied only to Aboriginal peoples and not to Canadians in general. The White Paper stated that removing the unique legal status established by the Indian Act would "enable the Indian people to be free—free to develop Indian cultures in an environment of legal, social and economic equality with other Canadians."[84] The Canadian government received an extraordinarily strong response in the form of Harold Cardinal's *The Unjust Society*, in which he condemned what he argued was another of Canada's many attempts to assimilate status Indians.[85] On behalf of the Indian Chiefs of Alberta he also authored "Citizens Plus," also known as the Red Paper.[86] The document was a direct response to the White Paper and reiterated the importance of honouring treaties between First Nations and the Crown.

It is within this history, which I have briefly outlined here, where we find credence to Lambertus's point that part of the reason Indigenous peoples wind up outside of multicultural policy is that Indigenous policymaking and multiculturalism move on different trajectories. But in this period, I would argue, they are branches of the same tree—a Canadian governmental policy tree that, according to Trudeau's vision, would be one in which diversity would be valued insofar as all were equal. At the same time Indigenous peoples were contending with assimilatory policymaking couched in a language of equality, and they were, as legal scholar Douglas Sanders notes, having to make clear that they were not ethnic or cultural minorities; Indigenous leaders were clear that they were not akin to other Canadian communities being knitted together under the banner of multiculturalism. Sanders writes, "Indian leaders have rejected the terms ethnic or cultural minority as inadequate to describe the special situation of Indigenous peoples. They assert a uniqueness which they feel is denied by terms which equate them to Irish Catholics or Chinese."[87] More precisely, however, the application of the terms ethnic and cultural minority to Indigenous peoples does not merely deny a belief in their uniqueness, but rather the inclusion of Indigenous peoples in Canada's multicultural vision is a direct denial of their nationhood. As federal civil servant Barbara Jill Wherrett asserts, it is a denial of Indigenous peoples' "status as nations,"[88] for even Métis and non-status First Nations "deny that they are 'citizens like any others'. . . they think of themselves as cultural collectivities and not simply as aggregates of individuals. They have a much more organic view of the community. They see themselves as a distinct cultural group and they explicitly reject the efficacy of the liberal value of equal opportunity as a means of dealing with them."[89]

    Lambertus suggests, however, that recognition of Indigenous nations as founding nations "affords Aboriginal people the legitimacy and rights not available to minorities and ethnic groups."[90] This modified version of "equitable inclusion" would be tantamount to obliteration, however, in two ways. First, subsuming Indigenous nationhood in any way within the model of liberal inclusion that is multiculturalism would mean the complete (at least in the eyes of the state) disappearance of distinctive Indigenous nationhood; wherein it might be propped up as a "third pillar" (as Canadian author and public intellectual John Ralston Saul has suggested) of Canada's founding, it at minimum erases the pervasive implications of past and ongoing colonization.[91] What I mean by this is that Indigenous nations have not been willing participants in the construction of Canada as it stands. Canada's founding narrative is not one of a triumphalist, unified vision, but of suppression, repression, oppression, and genocide. The relegation of Indigenous peoples to minority status via any form of inclusion in the founding narrative would have profound impacts on the ongoing fiduciary responsibility of the Canadian government—providing the government with an avenue to forgo such responsibility altogether.[92]

It is from the foundation provided by multiculturalism, the self-proclaimed qualities of inclusiveness and tolerance, that Canada has embraced one of its strongest (if not *the* strongest) branding strategies. Sociologist Renisa Mawani suggests that Canada presently draws Indigenous peoples into national narratives to affirm the state's innate multiculturalism, its reflexivity, and tolerance. Canada promotes itself as a nation that "now fully recognizes that First Nations are 'our Communities' who, notwithstanding the effects of Canadian colonialism, now enjoy the full benefits of multicultural citizenship."[93] This move is one way that the nation markets itself as being absolved of "its colonial past, suggesting that we have transcended it."[94] Brimming beneath the surface of this transcendence is the reality that multiculturalism was devised to cope with English Canadians' settler anxieties and fears of national illegitimacy.

While multiculturalism's primary stated purpose is to reflect the nation's diversity, tolerance, equality, and multicultural harmony, it also provides a "discursive rhetorical structure that smooths over social anxiety regarding the solidity of national boundaries."[95] Canada, driven by settler anxieties and a crisis of whiteness, and by the pressures of increased international market competition, tries to re-narrate its history by invoking the rhetoric of multiculturalism, providing a language for the nation to brand itself "on the global stage as urbane, cosmopolitan, and at the cutting edge of promoting racial and ethnic tolerance among western nations."[96] In spite of the platitudes of (neo)liberal multiculturalism as both policy and brand, it remains contentious; Indigenous peoples have both challenged the bicultural and bilingual "founding myths of settler nationhood" and have resisted being subsumed within multiculturalism, a policy that would position Indigenous peoples as diversities and ethnic minorities.[97] The refusal of Indigenous peoples to subscribe to multiculturalism is based both on the language it uses but also on its very ideological basis—one that would fundamentally negate that Indigenous nations are sovereign nations with which Canada is legally bound, via Indigenous laws, Canadian laws, various treaties, and so forth, to negotiate with on a nation-to-nation basis.

Understanding these concerns, multiculturalism can best be understood as a tool by which the nation seeks to conceal its intolerance while maintaining its core ethnic genus, reinventing itself free of its colonialist past, "obscur[ing] issues of land theft, genocide, sexual conquest, forced assimilation, displacement, the outlawing of religious practices, residential schools, imposed governments and laws, the extreme intrusions on basic human rights."[98] As will be revealed here, Canada's attention to rebranding itself can be understood as an effort to transform the national narrative "in order to present distinctive images in order to attract foreign investment and skilled labour."[99] As nations seek to "justify their existence" they embark "upon a renewed quest for the hearts and minds of 'their' people both at home and around the world," a quest that is explicitly tied to global competitiveness and economic rationales.[100] The state's interest in branding itself and its relationship to Indigenous peoples are increasingly tethered to this neoliberal search for resources.[101]

If we, in light of this, bring this analysis of multiculturalism to bear on Coulthard's critique of the colonial politics of recognition and to our thinking about neoliberal colonialism, it becomes much easier to see the ways in which the watered-down political relationship left in the wake of constitutional negotiations represents little more than the state's attempt to "reproduc[e] through a seemingly more conciliatory set of discourses and institutional practices that emphasize our *recognition* and *accommodation*," as an Aboriginal addition to liberal multiculturalism.[102] Through a comparative analysis of the 1976 Montreal Summer Olympics closing ceremony, the 1988 Calgary Winter Olympics opening ceremony, and the 2010 Winter Olympics opening ceremony, in Chapter 2 I analyze how processes for generating Aboriginal inclusion and securing Aboriginal representation required inducing Indigenous peoples to identify with a highly managed form of Aboriginal identity that wove together rhetoric of multiculturalism, eco-friendliness, sustainability, and "authentic Aboriginality." The central argument presented within this chapter is that in an era marked by the rhetoric of Aboriginal-Canadian reconciliation—beginning with the passage of the Constitution, extended through the Royal Commission on Aboriginal Peoples (1995), and concretized by the Jean Chrétien Liberal government's "Statement of Reconciliation" (1998), multiculturalism came to be marketed as evidence of Canada's successful efforts at reconciliation, concealing the ongoing subjugation of Indigenous peoples.

By contrast, Indigenous peoples' assuming the banner of Aboriginal marked their continued attempt to strategically reclaim the terrain of interaction and refute the at times stifling discourse of Aboriginality. Yet this had profound implications. While some Indigenous bodies (not peoples) were coveted, valued as central performers in Canada's opening ceremonies and as a display of "Aboriginal Canadian nationalism," other bodies, those that could not or would not "play Aboriginal," were rendered problematic, even criminal. The narrative produced at once before and during the Olympics is one that split Indigenous peoples into either good (Aboriginal) national subjects who fell in line with Canada's new Aboriginalized-settler nationalism, or bad ones that needed to be hidden so as not to counter-narrate Canada's benevolent, tolerant, inclusive, multicultural, and ultimately, "post-colonial" brand identity.[103]

Constructing Authentic Aboriginality: Tourism and Corporate Branding

The chapters in this book overlap in significant ways. While Chapter 2 centres nation-branding as an analytic lens, Chapter 3 theorizes the way that Aboriginal has been taken up at the corporate level—as a corporate brand identity. Branding is a central part of corporate marketing strategies that involve the imbuing of a product with its own unique image/personality so that it holds appeal for consumers. Branding has become an important part of corporate marketing due to increased regional, national, and global competition between corporations, particularly among those that were once locally rooted and have become multinational in their reach. Corporations have expanded beyond their original national borders and are caught up in a global competition for economic dominance, a competition that sees the privileging of the interests of the market over those of citizens and communities. In the years leading up to the 2010 Vancouver Winter Olympics, the Canadian Tourism Commission (CTC) and the Four Host First Nations Society (FHFN) signed a "Statement of Cooperation" declaring "their intention to work collaboratively to bring greater awareness of Canada's Aboriginal Tourism Experiences."[104] They outlined a partnership that they claimed was aimed at building "a stronger Aboriginal cultural tourism industry within British Columbia that respects the unique qualities and richness of the First Nations and Aboriginal Peoples of this land."[105] Tied to reconciliatory rhetoric, the Aboriginal in Aboriginal tourism is a symbol of settler imperialist nostalgia for a pre-colonial, untouched, yet more-real-than-Indian Indigenous person.

Whereas Indianness has been prized for its unique qualities and as a foil to British Canadianness, it was never meant to continue into modernity. By contrast, Aboriginality is positioned as the ideal articulation of Indigenous existence. It promises enough difference so as to be appealing to the market but is devoid of the threat that the difference of Indianness signalled. In Chapter 3 I therefore address the complex interplay of Indigenous participation in corporate articulations of Aboriginality via the Canadian tourism economy. The chapter also examines the role of tourism in shaping Canadian national brand identity through the marketing of Aboriginality. It is important to clarify at the outset that this is not a criticism of Indigenous peoples who elect to engage in either what becomes Aboriginal tourism *or* Canadian tourism. Métis scholar Howard Adams has argued that Indigenous peoples who participate in these forms that give in to Euro-tourist demands as simply "playing Indian," an example of "white oppressors and Indian and Métis [who] collaborate with each other portraying the archaic culture in public spectacle."[106] It is undoubtedly the case, however, as settler historian Paige Raibmon writes in the context of her research on Indianness and the construction of the notion of authenticity, that Indigenous peoples are not naïve to the significance of the concept of authenticity—and to its value in the changing landscape wrought by colonization. To plainly refer to Indigenous peoples' deployment of the concept of authenticity as "strategic essentialism," Raibmon argues, is reductive and allows colonial interpretations to overdetermine our understanding of such engagement. Instead, it is important to acknowledge the complexity of Indigenous engagements with authenticity: Raibmon writes, "Aboriginal people did not draw colonial authenticity around themselves like a curtain and continue on behind it with timeless 'real' lives. There was no single, unified Aboriginal experience of true 'authenticity.'"[107] This is very much the case in the context of constructions of Aboriginality. The chapter's (and indeed the book's) principal focus is thus intended to critically assess the nuanced ways in which the state, via the fostering of the creation of "Aboriginal tourism," furthers the project of neoliberal colonialism. In observing the twinning of Aboriginal with tourism, we can more clearly see the ways that an entity such as Aboriginal tourism was promoted as leading to a proper form of neoliberal socialization and alleviation from poverty. But this was not a process in which Indigenous peoples were merely passive victims.

If Aboriginal tourism as an "Indigenous-friendly" form of economic development became a magic salve for the intergenerational impacts of colonization, it would become much easier to sidestep public accountability for the legacies of colonization and ongoing questions about Aboriginal and treaty rights. The commodification of the tourism industry, along with state intervention within tourist relationships, prevents any possibility that tourism can function as a project that leads Indigenous peoples towards greater self-determination. The challenge is, as Jessica Francis identifies, that "tourists have come to desire these popular and damaging Aboriginal images over more accurate and authentic portrayals."[108] Such observations arise precisely because even as Indigenous peoples engage in a sort of "Indigepreneurialism" (a term used colloquially to refer to Indigenous entrepreneurialism), the inclusion of such endeavours within a larger rhetoric of Aboriginality (in Aboriginal tourism) serves a state-driven nationalist and economic pedagogy.

The Canadian nation is, to borrow from performance studies scholar Margaret Werry, "imagineered" through tourism as a multicultural, settler-Indigenized state. Werry posits that nations are "not so much imagined as *imagineered*," meaning that the state engages in the production or participatory drama of its national identity, drawing on the work of "culture agents across business, civil society, policy, and entertainment."[109] In the context of Canada, then, this imagineered national brand (and to be sure the collusion which Adams critiques) is used to minimize the state's hand in racism and colonialism, and in perpetrating the physical, cultural, environmental, and spiritual genocide of Indigenous peoples. Responsibility for Indigenous peoples' struggles are thus placed on people themselves, this time as failures to heal themselves through the market; failures because they have been given the opportunity to do so on an equal playing field.

However, the selection and representation of Aboriginality within cultural and eco-tourism spaces is not cut and dried. Aboriginalism in these spaces does serve (somewhat) different ends than Aboriginalism or Aboriginality does in legal and political spaces. In the absence of Indigenous-run tours that correspond with market demand, non-Indigenous companies gladly fill the void and often do more harm than good. In many ways it is thus necessary as a form of protection that Indigenous peoples enter the circulation of tourism and touristic image production. Considering this, I theorize the challenges to claiming Aboriginal tourism as a site of Indigenous possibility in the face of enterprises trading in racist representations coded in a language of reality and authenticity. This is the function of Aboriginality—the promise of freedom in deeply bounded form. Representations within these sites, although delivered to more limited audiences than those of the Olympics (that is, broadcast around the world), still worked in such a way as to create a general temporally significant discourse about Canadian nationalism as an Aboriginalized multicultural country.

"Our Home and Aboriginal Land": Place-Branding in the Era of Aboriginality

In Chapter 4 I turn my attention to the politics of place through a focused discussion on the way Aboriginality is mobilized for the work of crafting a discernable place brand for the Vancouver International Airport. According to George Allen, veteran Canadian brand and design consultant and researcher, "the idea that physical places can be branded is a natural extension of corporate brand theory. It is generally accepted that places, as defined by culture, politics, and geography, are increasingly seen to be products, as subject to brand management practices as a cup of coffee or a car."[110] Neoliberalism transforms place into a marketable commodity. The work to brand place involves consideration of *location*, "which is the geographical area that provides the interactions; the second is *locale*, which is the setting for informal and institutional social relations; the third is 'sense of place,' which is the local social structure of feeling that subjectively and emotionally attaches people to places."[111] This work requires that the brand of a place be developed in close alignment with place identity—that there is an express link between identity, experience, and image familiar to those already there and that resonates with those who might consider travelling to a place.[112]

The analysis in Chapter 4 intersects in a number of ways with the preceding chapters. The airport is a departure and arrival point vital to tourism operations, and during the Vancouver Olympics the airport served as a massive hub for international travel. It was, in fact, the airport's job to give arrivals to Vancouver for the Olympics their first exposure to that which defined the city beyond its walls. The Vancouver International Airport Authority (VIAA) was charged with creating a multi-layered narrative to serve as an appealing introduction to Vancouver's, and thus Canada's, Olympic brand. The chapter opens by placing the emergence of air travel, and thus the later development of passenger airport terminals, into context with the broader story of colonization. An overlooked site for analysis, airports are themselves crucial technological developments that have been tools of colonialism and continue to play a central role in Canada's ongoing nation-building project.

The discussion then turns to consider the implications of the development of passenger terminals and the gradual introduction of Indigenous-made artwork into terminals, with a focus on Vancouver. Through an analysis of the possibilities and problems of YVR's Art Foundation and its approach to "Aboriginalizing" the airport, I identify some central tensions with respect to the way Aboriginal (framed in terms of Aboriginalized multiculturalism, as discussed earlier) is made to speak to and enhance the place brand of the airport and the City of Vancouver. Here, I ultimately argue that the Aboriginalization of YVR was furthered by a strong desire for a unique identity that simultaneously had to be managed and carefully packaged to draw attention away from potential questions about the airport's—and Vancouver's—existence on unceded xʷməθkʷəy̓əm land.

From Aboriginalization to Indigenization and Beyond

In the book's final chapter, I offer some reflections on what it means now that Aboriginality has been largely supplanted by Indigeneity, and Aboriginalization by Indigenization. As discussed in the book's opening pages, Aboriginal is now often seen as dated, as politically incorrect, and as clear evidence of one's co-optation by the Canadian state. Indigenous/Indigeneity has undoubtedly emerged as the preferred "pan" term of the day. In light of this, in the Conclusion I revisit each of the chapters to consider the implications of the terminological shift and the shifting dynamics that underpin the shift; I argue that while Indigenous, Indigeneity, and Indigenization have been positioned by people as markedly distinct from Aboriginal, Aboriginality, and Aboriginalization, marking a kind of liberatory catch-all terminology, cracks have begun to show in its widespread acceptance. In particular, the term has become a calling card of a supposed "new era" of relations between Indigenous peoples and the current Canadian federal government under the leadership of Liberal prime minister Justin Trudeau. Yet a careful analysis of some of the tenets underpinning the current state of affairs reveals that while the move towards Indigenous portends a move out from under Aboriginalism (as Alfred and Corntassel label it), it more accurately offers repackaged rotten fruit from the same rotting tree of neoliberal colonialism.

Aboriginality, and what I argue are processes of Aboriginalization, became a guiding ethic of Aboriginal inclusion, one that masked the violence of colonization that the later emphasis on *Indigenization* (rather than a material manifestation of *decolonization*) would be positioned as bringing to light. Canada has actively sought to bury its legacy of colonialism and genocide through the propping up and facilitation of the discourse of Aboriginal/Aboriginality, a discourse whose "primary function is [still] to sustain the foundation myth."[113] Whereas Aboriginalization speaks to the surface-level and often symbolic inclusion of Indigenous peoples, Indigenization proclaims its ability to right the course of Indigenous–non-Indigenous relationships by taking seriously calls for *meaningful* engagement. This book concludes with some final probing of Aboriginal in light of the turn towards Indigenous discussed in Chapters 2 and 3. Indigenous may be itself as much of a "flawed construction," as Animikii argued, that Aboriginal was/is if we focus solely on the etymological implications of Indigenous. Yet as is argued throughout this book, each terminological shift marks much more than a simple move towards whatever is politically correct at a given moment. It is far more useful to see that these terminological shifts mark significant signposts in Indigenous peoples' navigation of relations with Canada as a colonizing, neoliberal nation-state.

1

Aboriginal, Aboriginality, Aboriginalism, Aboriginalization: What's in a Word?

The word Aboriginal has been used so widely by anglophones that tracking its every twist and turn would likely lead one on an endless journey. As previously discussed, Aboriginal and Indigenous can be traced back to the 1600s and appears across a number of sites in Anglo-European writing—most frequently in philosophy, literature, politics, anthropology, natural sciences, and law. A cursory scan of digitized texts available via Google shows that between 1625 and 1867 (the year Canada became a country), in most cases, the word Aboriginal was used in reference to humans and in the context of place. It was primarily used to refer to, as its definition suggests, people who were "original to a place," irrespective of whether they were indigenous to places such as Turtle Island, Inuit Nunangat, Aztlán, and Abya Yala.[1] An increase in encounters between Indigenous peoples and British colonists gave rise to the conceptualization of what was variously referred to as *"native title, Indian title,* and *aboriginal title."*[2] Brian Slattery, an expert in Aboriginal rights discourse and Canadian constitutional law and a senior adviser to the Royal Commission on Aboriginal Peoples (RCAP), writes that

> Aboriginal title was the creature of a distinctive body of common law that was generated by the policies and practices of the British Crown in its intensive relations with Indigenous American nations during the seventeenth and eighteenth centuries. Aboriginal title was not a right known to English common law or any Indigenous system of law; it flowed from the distinctive set of rules that bridged the gap between English and Indigenous legal systems and provided for their interaction. This body of law passed into British colonial law—the largely common law system that governed the Crown's relations with its overseas colonies and

furnished their basic constitutional frameworks. In this manner it came to operate in all the nascent British colonies in America, and subsequently in Australia, New Zealand and other British possession. This distinctive or *sui generis* body of law is known as the *common law of aboriginal rights*.[3]

While Slattery notes that in regard to the concept of title the word Aboriginal was used interchangeably with "native" and "Indian," his observations reflect the gradual concretization of the word's salience to British colonial law, a system that provided the foundation for Canadian common law. Slattery highlights the implications of this relative to the development of Canada's constitutional framework, something I will return to later on.

Towards the late 1700s and into the early 1800s, the natural sciences and the attendant emergence of scientific racism introduced a third conceptualization whereby the term became explicitly associated with the bodily identification of those designated as part of the "Aboriginal race." As natural scientists sought to extend work on the classification of flora and fauna to humans, to the fracturing of human populations into racial categories, there emerged references to Aboriginal Americans or Aboriginal North Americans, or aboriginals from the Americas, or the "aboriginal race," each tinged with a latent belief in Indigenous peoples' innate biological inferiority to those designated as Caucasian and/or white.[4] One of the most well-known proponents of scientific racism, Samuel Morton drew heavily on the term in his work in ethnography and craniology to position Indigenous peoples as racially inferior on the basis of a range of physical and mental characteristics.[5] Morton distilled tens of thousands of distinct Indigenous nations, quite plainly, into the singular "aboriginal race."[6] The transition from referring to people in relation to place to the formulation of a concept of Aboriginal title, and the assertion that Aboriginal people existed as part of a distinct and discrete (and inferior) race, irreversibly recast the word Aboriginal; from its relatively neutral origins it became tied to racism and the dispossession and colonization of Indigenous peoples.

While non-Indigenous peoples readily embraced the notion of the existence of an "aboriginal race" and its purported inferiority, in Canada the word Indian was more commonly used. Although Aboriginal continued to discursively circulate in relation to "aboriginal rights,"[7] the word Indian was foregrounded in British and Canadian policymaking; it therefore became both the colonial lingua franca and the epistemological framework through which Indigenous existence was interpreted, understood, and articulated by settler colonists. Indeed, the word Indian was so prevalent that, in 1939, the Quebec, provincial and the federal government tussled over whether Inuit (then referred to by Canada as "Eskimos") were Indians for the purposes of federal legislation and responsibility and whether "Indian" and "Eskimo" were, in fact, coterminous.[8] In the decision related to the dispute, the Supreme Court ruled that Inuit (as Eskimos) were Indians for the purposes of federal responsibility. The question re-emerged in the latter decades of the twentieth century as Métis and non-status First Nations fought the Canadian government in court to affirm that they, too, were to be counted as Indians under section 91(24) of the Constitution. As with the Supreme Court's ruling in 1939, in 2016, the Court ruled in *Daniels v. Canada (Indian Affairs and Northern Development)* that, for the purposes of federal responsibility, Métis and non-status First Nations *are* Indians under section 91(24).[9] Canada's model for addressing the rights of Indigenous peoples has consistently been based on ideas about Indianness.[10]

The word Indian has held such force that it has survived well over two hundred and fifty years of British and Canadian colonial policymaking regarding Indigenous peoples: from England's first British Indian Department, in operation from 1755 to 1860; to the 1763 Royal Proclamation, whereby a system for the extinguishment of lands belonging to and reserved for "the said Indians" was established;[11] to the Indian Act of 1876, Canada's first consolidated legislation directed towards those it defined as Indians; to section 35 of the 1982 Constitution, whereby Indians are classed as one of three Aboriginal peoples; and to Indian Affairs and Northern Development, the recently renamed Canadian federal policymaking arm responsible for those designated as status Indians (1966–2017).[12] Because of its deep entrenchment within Canadian law and policy, the term Indian is still very much in use.

The most enduring piece of legislation to use the word Indian, the Indian Act, has also produced an enduring *definition of* Indian (as to whom the federal government recognizes as Indian). A consolidation of two prior legislative acts, section 3(3) of the Indian Act defined "Indian" as follows: "Firstly. Any male person of Indian blood reputed to belong to a particular band; Secondly. Any child of such person; Thirdly. Any woman who is or was lawfully married to such person."[13] This definition led to generations of enfranchisement whereby so-called Indian women lost their status under the Indian Act. While the sexism inherent in the Indian Act has been (at least partially) addressed through advocacy work of enfranchised First Nations women and their descendants, successful court challenges, and revisions, it remains that the word Indian plays a significant role in the lives of Indigenous peoples today.[14]

Aboriginal and Pre-Constitutional Law

By contrast, outside of elite scholarly circles, from the late 1800s and until the time of constitutional negotiations and debates, the word Aboriginal was used far less often in everyday life than much more derogatory words such as savage, half-breed, and Eskimo, and far less than Indian and Native, both words also seen by some as derogatory but as less immediately racist than the former three.[15] As previously mentioned, its primary use was in relation to the concept of Aboriginal title and thus Aboriginal rights. Yet from Canada's founding to the adoption of the Constitution, the Canadian government was not particularly interested in accepting, in any serious way, the ongoing existence of Aboriginal rights and Aboriginal title; given the dearth of legal challenges to colonial dispossession, alongside the entrenchment of the word Indian in longstanding British colonial policy approaches, it tracks then that Aboriginal remained tightly associated with the legal context and was largely absent from common usage.

This situation would change as a result of the *Calder* decision. In 1973, the ground-breaking Supreme Court case heard representatives of the Nisga'a nation assert that "the aboriginal title, otherwise known as the Indian title, of the Plaintiffs . . . has never been lawfully extinguished."[16] The basis of the claim was such that Aboriginal title arose directly out of "aboriginal occupation; that recognition of such a title is a concept well embedded in English law; that it is not dependent on treaty, executive order, or legislative enactment."[17] In the decision, the justices recounted, "Once aboriginal title is established, it is presumed to continue until the contrary is proven. When the Nishga people came under British sovereignty they were entitled to assert, as a legal right, their Indian title."[18] The Supreme Court acknowledged that the Nisga'a held Aboriginal title to their lands prior to the formation of British Columbia as a province. In the first clear declaration by a Canadian court as to the existence of Aboriginal title to land, the Supreme Court justices of the time affirmed that the Nisga'a held "Aboriginal title" to land prior to Britain's first declaration of autonomy on Indigenous land via the Royal Proclamation of 1763—that "such title existed outside of, and was not simply derived from, colonial law."[19] What is significant to the discussion here is that while Indian and Aboriginal are used interchangeably by both the Nisga'a and the Canadian Supreme Court (and indeed indigenous—small "i"—is also deployed, though with far less frequency), there is a far more consistent reference, and appeal, to such rights as *Aboriginal* rights.

The Language of Political Organization

The term Aboriginal thus serves as important language signalling the inherent rights of Indigenous peoples as *original* inhabitants of the land—something that the word Indian is incapable of speaking to. But what is also interesting here is the way that, in spite of its importance, it appears to have had little relevance to/for Indigenous *self-identification* even with the rise of pan-Indigenous political organizing in the twentieth century.[20] Indigenous peoples—though primarily First Nations and Métis—mobilized against the Canadian government through coordinated efforts that gave rise to pan-Indigenous organizing. This served as an extension of politicized expression that nevertheless adopted and adapted Eurowestern political organizational structures.[21] As Canadian historian J.R. Miller has succinctly written, Indigenous peoples "had not acquiesced in the increasingly paternalistic and authoritarian policies that were put in place from the 1850s onward."[22] Rather than acquiesce, Indigenous peoples continued to challenge Canada's assimilatory agenda, forming new alliances across nations. These alliances in turn gave rise to different articulations of Indigenous political formulations organized regionally and provincially—the Indian Tribes of the Province of British Columbia, the Allied Tribes of British Columbia, the Native Brotherhood of British Columbia, the Indian Association of Alberta, the Federation of Saskatchewan Indians, the Métis Association of Alberta, the Saskatchewan Métis Society, along with a number of others.[23]

Indigenous women also formed a number of organizations that would form the basis for their political involvement—such as the Indian Homemakers' Association of British Columbia. Between 1965 and 1975, Indigenous women formed over fifteen distinct local and provincial organizations.[24] For the most part, organizations formed separately around status Indian and non-status and Métis concerns as Métis did not have reserved land bases and non-status Indians were often those enfranchised from the Indian Act. F.O. Loft formed the League of the Indians of Canada in 1918 and Andrew Paull the North American Indian Brotherhood in 1945;[25] both organizations represent early attempts to develop large cross-provincial organizations, yet neither drew on the word Aboriginal as a term of collective identification. In a similar vein, national organizations developed specifically with Indigenous women's rights in mind opted for other terminology as well—the National Committee on Indian Rights for Indian Women (NCIRIW) in 1971–72 and the Native Women's Association of Canada (NWAC) in 1974.

The creation of the National Indian Council in 1961 and the creation of the National Indian Brotherhood (NIB) in 1967 solidified a separate "pan-status Indian" organizational structure; a few years later, in 1971, Inuit Tapirisat of Canada (now Inuit Tapiriit Kanatami) was founded, with a focus on Inuit land claims, self-government, and rights for Inuit from across the fifty-three communities within Inuit Nunangat.[26] In Saskatchewan, the formation of the Association of Métis and Non-Status Indians of Saskatchewan (AMNSIS) brought together both Métis and non-status Indigenous peoples in the province; those involved with AMNSIS, along with some off-reserve status Indians, in turn contributed to the development of a national organization covering a wider array of positions in relation to Canada's recognition categories by forming, in 1971, the Native Council of Canada (NCC).[27] What remains consistent across these organizations—and most of those not mentioned—is that in their titles they all draw from a pool of words that include Indian, Métis, Inuit, and Native—but not Aboriginal.[28]

Bringing Aboriginal into Focus: From Rights and Title to Constitutional Recognition Politics

If Indigenous peoples in the pre-constitutional era did not generally adopt the word Aboriginal in the names of collective organizations, and if it appeared far less often in governmental policymaking, how did it come to be the place-holding word of choice in the Constitution? The expanded usage of the term was a significant subject of debate. In spite of concerns about the term, in the constitutional wake, it quickly moved to the foreground of governmental policymaking, occupying the interstices between Indigenous peoples and Canadian governments, and flooding outward more generally to Indigenous and non-Indigenous peoples. Organizations did not change their formal titles to include Aboriginal either in the run-up to or in the immediate aftermath of the adoption of the Constitution, in the constitutional era the word Aboriginal was used with frequency to speak to the urgency of constitutionally entrenching Aboriginal rights.

Through the late 1960s and the 1970s, the Trudeau government continued to push forward discussion of constitutional patriation. George Manuel, then president of the NIB, appeared alongside representatives from organizations such as the Manitoba Métis Federation and the Committee for Original Peoples' Entitlement (COPE) at the Special Joint Committee of the Senate and the House of Commons on the Constitution of Canada held from 1970 to 1972.[29] The NIB's brief outlined the organization's preliminary thinking on the matter: "We feel it would be premature at this time to take a positive position in relation to our stand. However, we do outline that we were the original people of this country and as such there were special provisions mentioned in the Constitution of Canada; that the Indians were recognized through the Indian Act of Canada; that there were treaties negotiated with the various tribes across Canada; and that there were territories definitely recognized and controlled by Indian people in the days when Indian people were the ruling people in Canada."[30] Of central importance to the NIB's developing position was that section 91(24) of the British North America Act (BNA Act) affirmed Indians as a federal responsibility. Other provincial First Nations representatives expressed similar sentiments. For Métis and Inuit, the conversation was somewhat different. While Inuit focused on land and development, the entrenchment of Aboriginal rights, and the significance of the Royal Proclamation of 1763, Tom Eagle's submission on behalf of the Manitoba Métis Federation noted that while Métis also have a "strong Indian identity" they have not been traditionally recognized as being included in section 91(24).[31] Because of this narrow interpretation of section 91(24), Ethel Deschambault, a spokesperson for the Manitoba Métis, "called for the word aboriginal [which was applied as a given to both First Nations and Inuit] to be redefined to include Metis."[32]

Although they had scarcely had time to consider the significance of their exclusion/inclusion, representatives from the various organizations were clearly (and rightly) concerned that the patriation of a new Constitution without any input on their behalf would nullify inherent and pre-existing rights, or at the very least make it that much more difficult to challenge Canada's domination. The federal government of the time also had as its core objective the elimination of "special rights," and the Trudeau government was poised to off-load "federal responsibility for Indigenous peoples to the provinces."[33] Some form of entrenched rights recognition thus quickly moved front and centre for many Indigenous organizations. Two months after Deschambault's call for Métis inclusion, at a meeting on 17 November 1970, Christopher Lafontaine, a member of the Saskatchewan Métis Society, indicated that to his knowledge Métis had not been given access to funding, as First Nations had, for engaging in a research process in order to clarify their rights and their position on the Constitution and in relation to both Aboriginal rights and treaty rights.[34] Recommendations arising from the Special Joint Committee meetings of late 1970 indicate that Indigenous organizations needed time to research "treaty and aboriginal rights," that there should be affirmation of the "special place of native peoples, including Métis, in Canadian life," that provincial governments should recognize "Indian languages as regional languages," and that there should be "no jurisdictional changes . . . made in administrative arrangements concerning Indians and Eskimos without consultation with them."[35]

Throughout the meetings of the early 1970s and the rest of the decade, different Indigenous peoples and organizations continued to refine and refer to "aboriginal rights," and insisted that they needed time to discern what that precisely meant. In the summer of 1978, the NIB, NCC, and ITC "were invited on an observer basis to the October 1978 First Ministers' Conference, and at the February 1979 First Ministers' Conference, an item on 'Canada's Native People and the Constitution' was placed on the agenda of future conferences."[36] Throughout, the federal government repeatedly referred to "native people," in a climate increasingly oriented towards articulating Aboriginal rights. First Nations leaders, such as Paul Williams with the Union of Ontario Indians (UOI) rejected the use of "native" for its overly general nature. He was concerned that, unlike words "like nations and tribes" that had "historic status," the word "native" did not speak to anything at all: "Status Indians feared that policies based on the all-inclusive term native could erode their special rights."[37] The more direct concern was that an overly general term might fail to uphold the responsibilities of the federal government vis-à-vis those referred to as "Indians" in section 91(24).

By contrast, representatives of Métis and non-status Indians sought to ensure that the present and future understanding of who held rights under the section would be consistent with its true spirit and intent. To this end, Harry Daniels, a Métis political activist and then president of the NCC, preferred native because Indian was imposed terminology, but also argued that Canada's early Constitution had been misinterpreted so as to deprive Métis and non-status Indians of "rights they possessed at the time of Confederation."[38] Daniels saw this struggle to clarify terminology as a vital exercise that had to be resolved before any discussion regarding what Aboriginal rights meant: "We will negotiate whatever special rights we have after that fact. I think it is redundant to argue now what special rights there will be; we have to first of all negotiate the redefinition of that term and the acceptance of our people of that term and what it means, the generic term 'Indian' or 'native.'"[39] Therefore, while First Nations activists like Williams found Native overly generalizing, for Métis and non-status people a more general word offered the potential for more inclusive terminology. This expansive terminology *would* be important, however, as *all* parties recognized that there were four peoples to be included: "Indian, Inuit, . . . Metis and nonstatus."[40]

Indigenous organizations continued to debate the most appropriate terminological placeholder; meanwhile, government agents sought clarity for the purpose of subverting a more robust recognition of Aboriginal rights that might have otherwise been consistent with what Indigenous organizations were calling for. In spite of the fact that organizations had different perspectives on the most appropriate terminology, Wherrett observes that "there were increasing similarities in the discourse between 1978 and 1980, a reflection of common feeling of injustice, and shared perceptions of the problems of the Canadian system."[41] By 1980, the NCC indicated to government representatives that through discussions with the NIB and Inuit Committee on National Issues the organizations had agreed on the collective terms they wished to see used in the Constitution, namely "'aboriginal rights,' 'aboriginal peoples,' and 'Indigenous peoples.'"[42] The agreed-upon terminology represented a compromise most significantly for First Nations but ensured that Inuit, Métis, and non-status Indians were represented through a less specific and narrow term. Of significant note here is that, with the determination of "aboriginal peoples" and "aboriginal rights" as the chosen collective terminology, "Indigenous peoples" was also included. The close association of "aboriginal" with "rights" established its constitutional entrenchment. Yet this raises interesting questions, given what I discuss in the Conclusion of this book—that the turn *away* from Aboriginal *to* Indigenous is seen by many as a way of signalling autonomy from the Canadian state and existence outside of the bounded politics of Aboriginal recognition.

While agreed-upon terminology was addressed early on, Indigenous organizations still struggled to find firm footing within constitutional negotiation processes.[43] As Indigenous communities and organizations continued to discuss, research, question, prod, and strategize among themselves regarding the next stages of involvement with the constitutional process, Indigenous activists also worked to refine their definition of Aboriginal rights; in doing so they drew on the aforementioned pieces of British colonial legislation, but also continued to ground it in an understanding of their distinctive nationhood and of their own laws and teachings regarding their innate responsibilities as original peoples of the land.[44] The political discourse mobilized by Indigenous organizations saw a move away from the language of "citizens plus" and to language focused on nationhood and self-determination. For First Nations this discourse was framed through referencing their relationships to their respective Creators. Métis consistently reiterated the distinctive political status of the Métis Nation and Inuit drew from language consistent both with traditional knowledge tied to their existence and with a sense of a distinctive political status.[45] At the heart of the evolving definition of Aboriginal rights for all parties, however, sat a clear sense of nationhood, self-determination, and inherent rights. This is particularly evident in the language used by the Union of British Columbia Indian Chiefs (UBCIC) as they initiated the largest mass action campaign in relation to the Constitution. In April 1980, the UBCIC issued their "Aboriginal Rights Position Paper," which included the following statement: "Traditionally, as aboriginal people, we had uncontested, supreme and absolute power over our territories, our resources and our lives. We had the right to govern, to make laws and enforce laws, to decide citizenship, to wage war or make peace and to manage our lands, resources and institutions. We had our own political, legal, social and economic systems. The power to govern rests with the people and, like our aboriginal rights, it comes from within the people and cannot be taken away."[46] The UBCIC affirmed that as inherent rights, "Aboriginal rights cannot be bought, sold, traded or extinguished by any government. Our responsibilities and our right to be who we are can never be relinquished."[47] Not only does the UBCIC's position paper reflect that a burgeoning conceptualization of

Aboriginal rights hinges on that which is inherent to First Nations as original *collectives* and *nations* of the land—an innate *right* to exist as *nations*—they are not actually contingent on Canada's (and in this era the Trudeau government's) willingness to recognize them.

Nevertheless, recognition comes to play a significant role, as previously mentioned, in the context of engagement with a federal government eager to extinguish Indigenous nations' distinct existence. While we see clear delineation as to the explicit contextual meaning of Aboriginal rights, we also begin to see how Aboriginal, more generally, is conceptualized by Indigenous peoples within a political terrain oriented towards Indigenous elimination. In the early stages of the Special Joint Committee meetings held through 1980-81, the Trudeau government avoided engaging in a discussion of Aboriginal rights in relation to the Constitution. However, the strength of organized resistance led to a massive refocusing of constitutional dialogue. The UBCIC and other Indigenous peoples' activist movements rejected Canada's attempts to "decolonize" itself from Britain while retaining an ongoing commitment to the colonization of Indigenous peoples.[48]

Then president of UBCIC George Manuel chartered two trains to take the organization's leaders, along with community members, from Vancouver to Ottawa. On 24 November 1980, the trains departed for Ottawa from Vancouver.[49] Known as the Constitution Express, the UBCIC trains picked up more people along the way to Ottawa, arriving with roughly one thousand people in tow.[50] From there, activists carried on to New York City, where they presented a petition to the United Nations, and then travelled onward to Europe.[51] By that point, the federal government had grudgingly begun inviting different Indigenous peoples to Special Joint Committee meetings at which the federal *and* provincial governments would be told in no uncertain terms that they would have to reckon with Aboriginal rights. At the meeting on 9 December 1980, Rob Milen, legal counsel for AMNSIS, likely in recognition that time would not be on the side of Indigenous communities, argued that in putting the word "aboriginal" as a placeholder in the Constitution, it would "sufficiently ope[n] the door for us to go and do our homework, to prove to the government of Canada, or if necessary to the courts, what rights we have. We feel that would sufficiently open the door for the Indian, Inuit, Metis or nonstatus peoples, whatever, to then convince the government to go sit down with their people community by community, provide all the historical research . . . We ask you, we believe, a very simple thing, by putting the word 'aboriginal' there."[52] After a few weeks of statements and briefs in the final weeks of 1980, the Special Joint Committee reconvened in January 1981, at a meeting in which then Minister of Justice Jean Chrétien presented a package of revised amendments. The amendments for the proposed Canadian Charter of Rights and Freedoms (CCRF) (not the Constitution) included in section 25 recognition of "existing Aboriginal rights." Marlee Pierre-Aggamaway, from the Native Women's Association of Canada, soundly reminded the committee members that Aboriginal rights belonged in the Constitution, not the Charter, because Indigenous peoples "belong to sovereign nations" and exist "as a third order of government."[53] Pierre-Aggamaway and others rejected Charter inclusion because the Charter's focus on *human* rights stood apart from the assertion of sovereign *Aboriginal* rights. The attempt to situate Aboriginal rights within the Charter failed to meaningfully address the concerns of Indigenous organizations in a manner consistent with Indigenous visions for constitutional entrenchment.[54]

Against the suggestion that the entrenchment of Aboriginal rights in the Constitution could wait until after it was patriated, Donald Rosenbloom, acting as legal counsel for the then-named Nishga Tribal Council argued that doing so "ignores the history of the provincial government and its relationship to the native people of Canada . . . There will never be consent from the provinces to enshrine the principle and it is for that reason that we use our words cautiously when we say that the suggestions of the Prime Minister and that of the present Minister of Indian Affairs that Indian people should patiently wait until patriation, is, indeed, a suggestion which has to be a sham. There will be no entrenchment after patriation."[55] This assertion became important because those opposed to entrenching Aboriginal rights in the Constitution often relied on a lack of clarity as to the meaning of Aboriginal rights in their attempts to negate them. Rosenbloom challenged the attempts to stall entrenchment on the basis of definitional questions, arguing that other concepts (which were equally unclear), such as "freedom of assembly," were left to the courts to define and determine.[56] Opposition on the part of Indigenous organizations and, later, the New Democratic Party, forced Chrétien to abandon his opposition, delay, and diversion tactics, and pushed the federal government to fully commit—at least in principle—to work on developing what would become section 35.[57]

Conceptualizing the Aboriginal in Aboriginal Rights

As constitutional engagement intensified through the 1980-81 meetings, Indigenous organizations faced persistent questioning from many committee members as to the definitions of "Aboriginal, Indian, Métis, and Inuit" and the notion of Aboriginal rights.[58] When faced with language that indicated that Aboriginal (and thus Aboriginal rights) would be extended to "every person of aboriginal descent," Senator Duff Roblin, a Conservative from Manitoba, asked what "every person of aboriginal descent" meant and if there would be a "cut-off line" to determine who would qualify as Aboriginal for the purposes of Aboriginal rights.[59] In response, Pierre-Aggamaway responded, "To be of aboriginal descent is to be born of at least one parent who two generations before descended from the first people. Now, that is a first kind of description we are giving you in answer to that. That is not an acceptable definition at this point in time and has not been thoroughly discussed and agreed to by our own nations. But those are some of the offerings."[60] Cree activist Nellie Carlson offered a somewhat firmer response as she spoke to the sexist aspects of the Indian Act regarding status (that would later be addressed, at least partially, through Bill C-31 in 1985) that ignored the central role of First Nations women in the transmission and survival of First Nations cultures.[61] While many saw the question of Indianness as relatively cut and dried because of the Indian Act—and definitions of Inukness also appeared to be less controversial—the meanings of both Métis and non-status came under intense scrutiny.

Roblin, in particular, prompted participants of the Special Joint Committee to engage in pursuing clarification as to the definition and meaning of both Métis and non-status Indian. He prodded the committee members to consider the question of "where the Metis status begins and takes off, and where the non-status Indian begins and takes off."[62] Roblin grappled with what today we might articulate as the difference between self-identification and collective identification—the difference between a person self-identifying as Aboriginal and a person being identified by their communities of origins and affiliation as Aboriginal for the purposes of Aboriginal rights: "Suppose that the real answer is to say that anyone who says, 'I am an aboriginal' thinks himself to be one and living in that society probably is one way of approaching it, so that it becomes a self-defining term. But I can assure you it is going to cause a lot of trouble in defining that expression in any advance we make to improve this measure; and any help you can give us in clarifying the matter will be most helpful to me."[63]

Indeed, Roblin's concern has proved to be somewhat prescient in the wake of the Constitution, as I will discuss shortly.

There has been a surge in the number of people self-identifying as Métis, people with little association to the Métis Nation; in light of definitions put forward by Métis during the 1980s constitutional talks, such Métis self-identification erroneously interprets Métis as simply meaning "mixed race" rather than Métis being connected to a distinctive national history and thus distinctive Aboriginal rights.[64] Daniels wrote a letter in support of the then-named Labrador Métis in 2010; however, the name was changed to Nunatukavut to recognize that the community is not, in fact, Métis, but of Inuit descent. Identifying as Métis was therefore a political strategy at a time when Métis political activism had gained footing within the constitutional process.[65] By looking at Daniels's response to Roblin we see, first, clear pushback at the imposition of external definitions: "We, Senator Roblin, have stated time and time again that we will decide who aboriginal people are. We have been suffering with artificial definitions for so long and forced to play a silly game of who is an aboriginal person, who is an Indian, who is not an Indian, who is a Metis, a non-status and franchised Indian, a treaty Indian, a non-treaty Indian, a registered Indian or a non-registered Indian. There are about 14 definitions of who we are."[66] Daniels promptly issued a much clearer articulation of Métis identity for the purposes of clarifying how and why the Métis Nation is Aboriginal for the purposes of Aboriginal rights:

> Canadian history records a legal and political tradition of recognition of the aboriginal rights of mixed blood people . . . In the 19th Century the most prominent recognition of our rights was on the prairies where the Metis had emerged as a distinct national group and had asserted national rights against the Selkirk Colony, against the Hudson's Bay Company and, in the Provisional Government of 1869, against the Government of Canada. The Government of Canada met with negotiators representing the Provisional Government and the terms of the Manitoba Act were drafted and agreed to. The Manitoba Act was passed by the Provisional Government, by the Canadian Parliament and confirmed by Imperial legislation. It stands as

part of the Constitution of Canada. The Manitoba Act recognized Metis land rights and provided, in addition to their holdings in 1870, for an additional Metis land base of 1.4 million acres.[67]

Métis, in the context of constitutional rights, is put forth as defined in and through the distinct political consciousness of the Métis as an Indigenous nation with an inherent right to self-determination, self-determination that includes the right to identify one's own people (or citizens, as the language exists in Métis political consciousness today). Yet because of the lack of federal intervention in and oversight of Métis processes of membership and recognition, committee members still questioned how the Métis Nation would proceed with "proving or identifying who the Metis people are."[68] Various Métis representatives asserted that it would be up to the Métis Nation itself to determine who is Métis in the context of Aboriginal rights and the Constitution: "We will identify our own people. We are working on that now, and have been doing research of our own. We are doing it ourselves, and we will present that when the time is right . . . The organization will have to do it, because no one else can."[69] When asked what he would "visualize the Metis nation as being," John Sinclair (AMNSIS) responded that "the Metis nation of course is people . . . What we are saying is that we feel the Metis nation could extend from Northwestern Ontario into Northeastern British Columbia and the people that we talked to are prepared to sit down and negotiate pieces of land here and there."[70] Sinclair reiterates what many organizations stated—that Indigenous peoples would need time to research and evaluate their position vis-à-vis Aboriginal rights and that at the heart of this sits the right of self-determination.

Regarding questions as to the meaning of Aboriginal rights, Daniels, on behalf of the NCC, responded pointedly to one line of questioning:

> Oh well, I must draw on the strength of the Oxford dictionary, which states in respect to aboriginal rights: "Any rights that the people held before the colonists arrived." That implies to me, linguistic rights, land rights, the right of access to resources; cultural rights, social rights, political rights, religious rights. Those are the aboriginal rights; those are the rights of people.

> Those statements or responses by government people to the
> effect that they do not know what aboriginal rights are, are
> an indication of either a great deal of ignorance of the English
> language or their unwillingness to accept that these people, who
> were a nation of people, rich in culture with linguistic differences,
> with a social system, with a very definite political system with
> dealings with each other, and a way of holding land—that is the
> aboriginal right; before the arrival of Europeans on these shores,
> whoever got here first, whether it was the Vikings or Jacques
> Cartier, the people operating within a set mode and in different
> geographical areas, and these people are now saying, "We want to
> continue that." And that is our aboriginal right to do so.[71]

As Daniels's reply reveals, given that committee members know full well *what* Aboriginal rights means, their refusal to acknowledge a definition that arises from within their own linguistic tradition reflects a latent anxiety about Indigenous sovereignty. Such anxiety was heightened by the reminder that whatever terminology was in play was ultimately a placeholder for a great diversity of Indigenous nations. Williams, on behalf of the Union of Ontario Indians, argued,

> We do not have what you call Indian rights. The rights of each
> of these nations, in relation to the Crown, are different; because
> the treaties of each of these nations with the Crown contained
> different terms. Thus the Ojibways do not have Indian rights; they
> have Ojibway rights. The Micmacs do not have Indian rights; they
> have Micmac rights. Canada's Indian Act has been an attempt
> to take a diversity of nations, with a diversity of relationships
> with the Crown, and to generalize, and then in the process of
> this generalization to lose sight of certain rights, certain specific
> relationships, because each of these is different . . . Canada, with
> its European heritage, understands things in terms of relations
> between the individual and his government. The rights we are
> talking about are not individual rights. They are the rights of

groups... What we are discussing here are collective rights and not individual rights.[72]

Williams also highlights a central discord with Canada's conceptualization of Aboriginal rights—one that it is viewed through a Eurowestern lens that only recognizes the rights of individuals relative to rights of collectives.

It is here that it is important to pause on the emphasis placed by different Indigenous peoples and organizations on the fact that Aboriginal rights, as discussed in the context of the Constitution, were and are intended to be seen as collectively held rights. According to Nicholas, representing First Nations of New Brunswick,

> Aboriginal rights include our right to exist as Indians, to govern ourselves and to determine our livelihood, political, cultural, economic, social and legal units. We have these rights and much more, because we have never been conquered, never released or extinguished our aboriginal rights in New Brunswick... Aboriginal rights are much more than a slogan, more than a people, because they include our spiritual, cultural, physical and emotional needs. We hope that you, as honourable representatives of Canada, will act with due faith and freedom of thought to accept the principle that aboriginal rights do exist today in New Brunswick.[73]

However, in the wake of the Constitution, such understandings become increasingly reduced by the wider circulation of Aboriginal. This in turn sees a shift from an affirmation of the inherent nature of Aboriginal rights—and an understanding that they encompass not only the collective rights of a people but also what it means to exist as Indigenous—to an at times uncritical embrace of Aboriginal as a marker of, quite plainly, *individual* identity. At least some of this arises because of the decision to address the precise meaning of Aboriginal rights at a later date. The later refusal of the premiers to accept Indigenous articulations of Aboriginal rights at the First Ministers

Conferences held throughout the 1980s left a great deal of interpretative work up to Canada's judiciary.

Given the explicit ties between Aboriginal rights and the judiciary, the courts' role in defining Aboriginal rights has been the subject of considerable debate. Delia Opekokew, acting as legal counsel for the Federation of Saskatchewan Indians, in putting forth the federation's definition of Aboriginal rights asserted that "Aboriginal rights relates to the right for the Indian people to have their ownership to the lands and people to control those resources and lands, so it is a two aspect answer. Presently in the court system in Canada aboriginal title only recognizes the right to occupancy without recognizing the right to self-determination and the right to control."[74] As previously mentioned, Rosenbloom contended that leaving judicial interpretations open was less of an issue than failing to entrench Aboriginal rights in the first place. Given the rushed timeline for constitution debate, a number of Indigenous peoples and their allies found themselves advocating for entrenchment and, under significant pressure, ceding control over the definition of Aboriginal rights. A number of Indigenous organizations expressed concern that leaving the definition of Aboriginal rights to the courts would be greatly constraining given that Canada's judiciary was, as it is now, primarily made up of non-Indigenous peoples.[75]

Jim Sinclair's statements echo the concern that while relying on the judiciary by no means is a perfect option, it offers a certain measure of stability, relative to relying on the good will of politicians. Sinclair, a non-status Indian activist who had initiated a lawsuit against Prime Minister Trudeau to ensure Métis would be included in the First Conference on Aboriginal Constitutional Affairs, argued,

> The concern that we have, it is like going from the fox to the wolf, who is going to be tougher on us, the courts or the politicians. Like I say, that is going to be another road but I would personally feel that something should be enshrined in the constitution that we could at least take to the court because if we leave it to the whims of the politicians who will change it because the majority says so, and you get elected by the majority, we are in trouble. Again, the other thing that is wrong with the democratic system, and I see it wrong in Canada today, is the fact that in a democracy

the majority seems to trample on the rights of the minority groups and it leaves us out.[76]

In terms of choosing between leaving clarification of Aboriginal rights to politicians or the courts—neither option can be decoupled from its entrenched Eurocentrism—it was felt that the judicial system offers at least an illusion of fairness. This is evidenced in statements made by Wilton Littlechild, acting as legal advisory for the Federation of Saskatchewan Indians (FSI), who reminded committee members that FSI submitted a position paper recommending the establishment of an "Indian rights protection office," expressly charged with clarifying and upholding the proposed "aboriginal rights" provision.[77] Of course, this was not heeded.

By late spring 1981, however, it finally seemed that Canada was on course to entrench provisions around Aboriginal rights within the Constitution. In the face of a counterplan from eight provinces and a "last chance conference" meant to smooth over hostilities held at the beginning of November 1981, Aboriginal rights provisions were abruptly removed from the constitutional agreement between the negotiating parties.[78] Constitutional law scholar Adam Dodek argues that this was because no Indigenous peoples were present in the latter stages of discussion on the Constitution, and none were present in this final meeting. Further, he argues, since Aboriginal rights were not a primary concern for anyone present, section 35 was ultimately "sacrificed 'almost by neglect.'"[79] In the face of renewed opposition—coupled with the uproar created in response to the exclusion of guaranteed protections for women—by late November section 35 was re-added and the following year, on 17 April 1982, the Constitution was patriated. The final text of section 35 reads as follows:

RIGHTS OF THE ABORIGINAL PEOPLES OF CANADA
Recognition of existing aboriginal and treaty rights
35. (1) The existing aboriginal and treaty rights of the aboriginal peoples of Canada are hereby recognized and affirmed.

Definition of *aboriginal peoples of Canada*
(2) In this Act, *aboriginal peoples of Canada* includes the Indian, Inuit and Métis peoples of Canada.

Land claims agreements
(3) For greater certainty, in subsection (1) *treaty rights* includes rights that now exist by way of land claims agreements or may be so acquired.

Aboriginal and treaty rights are guaranteed equally to both sexes
(4) Notwithstanding any other provision of this Act, the aboriginal and treaty rights referred to in subsection (1) are guaranteed equally to male and female persons.[80]

At the time, an additional section, section 37, had been added that bound the government to convene a First Ministers' Conference on Aboriginal Constitutional Matters no later than 17 April 1983 for the purpose of "the identification and definition of the rights of those peoples to be included in the Constitution of Canada."[81] In consideration of this very specific history, and the genesis of both Aboriginal and the concept of Aboriginal rights as thoroughly articulated by Indigenous peoples during the disputes about exclusion and inclusion, how and why does the term become conflated? How did the term slip out of the pages of the Constitution and into everyday life?

Post-Constitutional Uptake and New Aboriginal Articulations

There are significant reasons that Aboriginal, and constitutional references to "Aboriginal people" in particular, stretch beyond the confines of the constitutional moment. Judicial conceptualizations of Aboriginal relative to Aboriginal people and Aboriginal rights would be frustratingly limited in the post-Constitutional era. While the first major post-constitutional legal decision to rule on the precise nature of Aboriginal rights via the Constitution should have established a framework for an expansive definition of Aboriginal rights and thus Aboriginal, the second major decision effectively constrained and contained it.[82] In 1990, in the thick of ongoing negotiations as to the precise meaning of Aboriginal and Aboriginal rights, the Supreme Court of Canada issued its decision in the *R. v. Sparrow* case. While the ruling established a framework for future courts to affirm the existence of Aboriginal rights, it also outlined conditions under which Aboriginal rights could be infringed upon. It established that Aboriginal rights are neither finite nor unlimited rights. Still, and pertaining directly to this book's analysis, the Court held that in terms of the Constitution's reference to "existing aboriginal rights" any interpretation of such rights "must be interpreted flexibly so as to permit their evolution over time," and that in the context of fishing rights specifically as an Aboriginal right, it is necessary to "be sensitive to the aboriginal perspective itself on the meaning of the rights at stake."[83] Here, the Court establishes that there must be a responsive and flexible interpretation of Aboriginal rights. The Court paradoxically entrenches the notion that *Aboriginal* may itself be interpretated in a flexible manner.

The Supreme Court's ruling in *R. v. Van der Peet* (1996) departs from *Sparrow* in a notable way. In their ruling the justices created the "Integral to a Distinctive Culture Test," what is colloquially known as the "Van der Peet Test." This would be the first significant judicial attempt to define precisely what constitutes an Aboriginal right. Of relevance to this analysis, while *Sparrow* promised a wider and Indigenous-infused vision of both Aboriginal and Aboriginal rights, the justices in *Van der Peet* in effect "froze" Aboriginal rights and thus Aboriginal in a pre-contact past by insisting that Aboriginal rights are *only* rights connected to practices that stem from the pre-contact period.[84] Neither ruling tangibly engaged with Indigenous worldviews in spite of the fact that the justices stated in *Van der Peet* that Aboriginal rights constituted a form of "intersocietal law."[85] Neither ruling offered a more precise articulation of Aboriginal or even, really, of Aboriginal rights. A case-by-case basis approach under section 35 would lead to a body of law that would provide an overarching *method* for interpretating who is Aboriginal for the purposes of section 35 Aboriginal rights, and what those rights *may* be, but this approach would be notably different from what Indigenous activists had in mind.

As then law student Anna Zalewski writes, because there was likely little recognition of the "existence of an Aboriginal right to fish in the case of the Musqueam" in *Sparrow*, there was a "lack of precision" as to how the court understood "Aboriginal perspective" in its ruling and on how "that perspective should be expressed in the definition of Aboriginal rights."[86] It would not be until the first Métis rights test case regarding section 35 Aboriginal rights that the Court would have to grapple with *how* it defined Aboriginal for the purposes of determining *who* was Aboriginal and *who* might be entitled to Aboriginal rights protections. In *Sparrow*, as in *Van der Peet*, there was no question as to whether the Musqueam and Stó:lō existed. What was at stake in *R. v. Powley*, inasmuch as the case was about Métis rights, was the question of whether the Métis community that the defendants in the case claimed to be from *existed* as an Aboriginal community.

According to the justices in the ruling decision, in the absence of what they call "formal identification" (presumably state recognition via the Indian Act or as an Inuit Beneficiary), determining Métis identity would need to take place "on a case-by-case basis taking into account the value of community self-definition, the need for the process of identification to be objectively verifiable and the purpose of the constitutional guarantee."[87] In their decision the justices held that the Powleys are from a Métis community, setting a legal precedent as the first Supreme Court case associated with Métis rights within Ontario. However, as leading Métis scholar Chris Andersen writes in his thorough analysis of the Powley decision, the Court did not require any "historical self-identification as Métis in order to launch a contemporary claim as such," instead relying on the illogic that the term Métis simply means mixed.[88] By extension, Andersen argues, the Powleys only needed to "prove their ancestral Indigenous community's separateness from adjacent tribal communities" rather than state precisely how they were Métis—demonstrating lineage connecting a Métis past to a Métis present reality. This became part of the justices' criteria for establishing the existence of Métis Aboriginal rights, in turn developing a test (much as *Van der Peet* had for First Nations and presumably Inuit) for future legal decision-making. The "Powley Test," as it is commonly known, along with the decision itself, in effect produced the judicial category of Métis. While the federal government contends that the Powley decision did *not* create a legal definition of Métis, it most certainly *did* generate a judicial definition that was wildly incongruent with Métis articulations of both Métis and Aboriginal during constitutional negotiations.[89] To wit, the Supreme Court once again failed to produce a true form of intersocietal law that engaged with Métis people's perspectives on their own identities and existence.

Andersen therefore problematizes the way that the Court produced the category of Métis as an erroneously flexible category that had the effect of negating Métis people's distinct existence both as a people and as a nation.[90] In treating Métis, Aboriginal, and Aboriginal rights as malleable categories that would only be defined through problematic and seemingly reductive tests and subsequent court decisions, we see exactly how far from Indigenous peoples' intentions during constitutional processes things were heading. Further, that individual case law tests *individual/individualized* claims, the Court produces, in effect, an articulation of Aboriginal that is palpably separate from the purpose and intent of the term's inclusion in the Constitution—as a signpost of collectively held rights. Inasmuch as the Powley decision generated precedent in theory for future Métis claims, as the justices themselves acknowledged, Métis rights would continue to be evaluated on an individual, case-by-case basis.

Given the issues arising within judicial framings, with respect to the widening of the terminology and their intricacies as broader categories, it makes sense that if parties responding to the Special Joint Committees had been asserting that Aboriginal rights meant more than just a narrow (existing) Canadian judicial interpretation—that it also referred to Indigenous laws, governance, and nationhood, but couched in the language of Aboriginality—that it would eventually reach a wider audience, beyond the legal system. Subsequent to the passage of the Constitution, the definition of Aboriginality was extended by Indigenous organizations themselves. A number of Indigenous-led organizations began to gradually incorporate the word Aboriginal into everything from definitions of membership to policy position papers and cultural programming, in order to connect directly to language now entrenched in the Constitution, in case law, and in other legislation. The way that Aboriginal rights and Aboriginal people were defined and narrated through Constitutional conversations, and the subsequent lack of further clarification in the text of the Constitution itself, enabled loose interpretations of the two terms. At the same time, as organizations began to use the term more expansively, particularly when interacting with the Canadian government, the provinces, and non-Indigenous peoples, its normalization in everyday life set a standard that this was a *preferred* term of reference and suitable for common use.

Just as the term Aboriginal was quickly made malleable so, too, was Métis expanded beyond its initial scope relative to recognizing the people of the Métis Nation as an Aboriginal people for the purpose of Aboriginal rights. Further to the issues at stake with the Powley decision, as the term Métis became conflated and more and more people adopted the term to simply refer to any form of Indigenous/non-Indigenous "mixed racedness," it moved further and further away from its constitutional significance. Even at the time of the Special Joint Committee meetings, as previously discussed with reference to the case of the (now) Nunatukavut, there were individuals and communities intent on identifying as Métis strictly for the purpose of inclusion in the Constitution—as an access point to protected rights in the absence of (for whatever reason) their own effort to establish their voice in the constitutional process.

As these events unfolded, 1982 ushered in the recognition of Métis as distinct communities of "aboriginal peoples," but the absence of an attached definition of Métis in the formal text of the Constitution has given rise to what critical race theorist Darryl Leroux refers to as "raceshifting." In his critical work Leroux traces the way that formerly white-identified (and in some cases white supremacist) people refashion themselves as Métis via identifying (sometimes erroneously) with a quite distant Indigenous ancestor; in the fervour over genealogy and DNA testing, people's identification of remote Indigenous ancestry leads them to understand their identities as "mixed race" and this—in efforts to read themselves into legitimacy within Canada's structure of recognition—in turn leads to self-identification as Métis. Such self-identification arises seemingly out of nowhere in areas lacking entrenched histories and experiences vis-à-vis the colonizing state *as* Métis.[91] Claims to Métis identity have in some cases been used to overcome roadblocks encountered by white settlers in an effort to gain access to (more) Indigenous land and to constitutionally protected Aboriginal rights such as hunting and harvesting. This is also reflected in the demographically improbable rise in Métis identification within census reporting, and by the proliferation of organizations from outside of the Métis Nation homeland, all geared towards claims to distinctive status relative to section 35 rights.[92] Métisness is then used as a troubling political strategy.

As anthropologist Joe Sawchuk recounts, at the 1984 Annual Assembly of the Métis Association of Alberta (MAA), after a process of consultation in Alberta and across the Métis homeland, a bylaw was passed to give greater clarity as to who the Métis are. The 1984 bylaw declared that "[a] Metis is an Aboriginal person who declares himself/herself to be a Metis person, and can produce satisfactory historical or acceptable legal proof that he/she is a Metis, or has traditionally held himself/herself to be a Metis, and is accepted by the Metis people as a Metis."[93] Inasmuch as this reflects that the organizations undertook the work they committed to in the Constitution—to devise a clearly structured process for identifying *who* Métis people are—it demonstrates the way organizations such as the MAA adopted the term Aboriginal to tether articulations of Métisness to constitutionally entrenched Aboriginal rights.

The problem it creates is that it also demonstrates a pathway for Aboriginal itself to be taken up as a form of personal identification, furthering the possibility that someone will come to see, and express, themselves *as* an "Aboriginal person." As I will discuss shortly, the failure to entrench a nation-based definition of Métis along with section 35 inclusion left room for literal interpretations of Métis as broadly referring to all peoples of Indigenous and Euro-descendent mixed ancestry. By extension, and through applications of the term as discussed above, individuals began to read themselves into Aboriginal—that one need only invoke an identity as Aboriginal to *be* Aboriginal. The consequences of this have been laid bare in recent years, demonstrated with the public concerns raised regarding Canadian filmmaker Michelle Latimer's shaky claims to Aboriginal, and now Indigenous, identity. The case of Joseph Boyden is another prime example of how self-identification as Aboriginal came to require very little evidence of actual Indigenous parentage and ancestry.[94] It is, I would argue, no coincidence that both began to find their footing in the "era of Aboriginality" under study in this book—generating social capital and financial gain based upon little else but self-identification, and with a term wiggled loose from its purpose and intent within the Constitution.

This shift is further reinforced at the pan-Indigenous organizational level, whereby, following the splitting of Métis and non-status Indian membership within the NCC, the remaining non-status members would gravitate towards using the word Aboriginal. The NCC restructured and renamed itself in 1993 as the Congress of Aboriginal Peoples (CAP).[95] It purchased a domain name— www.abo-peoples.org—and a number of its affiliates adopted the language of Aboriginal and placed it front and centre. In 2016 the then head of CAP changed its name to the Indigenous Peoples' Assembly of Canada (IPAC). Seven months later, it was changed back.[96] While many organizations have in recent years renamed themselves in light of the turn towards "Indigenous," others, like the Coalition of Aboriginal Peoples of Saskatchewan, the New Brunswick Aboriginal Peoples Council, and the Aboriginal Congress of Alberta Association, continue to use it.[97] It is unsurprising that as an organization with little other legal weaponry with which to leverage government action, CAP felt a reversion from IPAC to CAP, from Indigenous to Aboriginal, was necessary. It is also not surprising that Indigenous peoples would make use of the term given the recognition and protection of rights and title in Canada's Constitution and its legal embeddedness; it serves as a reminder to Canada of its responsibilities.

Embedding Aboriginal rights within Canada's Constitution is a powerful strategic move. The language of Aboriginal therefore had to be refracted back to the Canadian state to serve as a constant reminder of its frequent failures to meet its legally-binding, constitutional responsibilities towards First Nations, Métis, and Inuit.

From Indians and Others to Aboriginal People: Canadian Federal Discursive Change

For its part, the Canadian government gradually incorporated Aboriginal into its political lexicon. The state's deployment of the word Aboriginal is highly significant given that it sets the tone for other governmental and non-governmental entities and for public discourse. It appears within the context of the Canadian census and is then woven into four significant moments: (1) the creation of National Aboriginal Day; (2) the establishment of the Royal Commission on Aboriginal Peoples (RCAP); (3) the Statement of Reconciliation; and (4) the 2011 name change of the former Indian and Northern Affairs Canada (INAC). A brief examination of each tells us how the word is being used but also what kinds of relational dynamics it speaks to; ultimately, I argue, it represents a gradual attempt at the multiculturalization of Indigenous peoples through deference to an Aboriginality that would be increasingly untethered from constitutional rights.

THE CANADIAN CENSUS

Statistics Canada, a federal government agency, is responsible for the national census and other data collection that can be channelled into policymaking. While the government had been enumerating Indigenous peoples since 1871 through "the use of an ethnic 'ancestry' or 'origins' question, the same question long used to measure all socio-cultural variation in Canada," in 1986 Statistics Canada introduced two nodes of self-identification: Aboriginal ancestry and Aboriginal identity.[98] While Andersen notes that initial data was not released because of concerns about its validity, and in fact no data "of the Aboriginal 'identity' population" was released until the 1996 census data was collected, at the time of publication of Andersen's 2013 article, the focus on Aboriginal identity had overtaken ancestry for the purposes of policymaking. According to Andersen, the 1986 census introduced the question, "Do you consider yourself an aboriginal person or a native Indian of North America, that is, Inuit, North American Indian or Métis?"[99] In this moment, Aboriginal personhood was entrenched as something one could self-identify as, a clear term of identification in and of itself, separate and apart from the distinctive context of Aboriginal rights.

Of course, it follows that upon recognizing Aboriginal rights, the Canadian government would seek a fuller picture of whom those rights extended to, especially for the classes of Aboriginal people it did not thoroughly track and manage (such as Métis and non-status Indians). This is relevant to the discussion within this book because, as Andersen has pointed out elsewhere, census-taking is the backbone of policymaking.[100] But it is also relevant because it marks the first major export of the term Aboriginal, first as category, then as identity, beyond the Constitution. By separating it out from the discourse of rights, its use opened the floodgates for self-identification *as* Aboriginal. This gave rise to the kind of worrying overgeneralizations and misappropriations of the term discussed by Williams and others.

NATIONAL ABORIGINAL DAY

The incorporation of Aboriginal into governmental mechanisms was not confined to the census. It took on a distinctively culturalist tone via the development of National Aboriginal Day (NAD). At various points throughout the First Ministers' Conferences that would take place following the passage of the new Constitution, Indigenous organizations expressed interest in the creation of a national day of solidarity in which everyone—Indigenous and non-Indigenous—would come together in solidarity with Indigenous peoples in support of Aboriginal rights. In 1982 the NIB explicitly called for the establishment of "National Aboriginal Solidarity Day" as a day for the recognition of Aboriginal rights.[101] In 1995, at a gathering of Indigenous and non-Indigenous peoples known as the Sacred Assembly, Elijah Harper called on the federal government to inaugurate "National First Peoples Day," again as a day of recognition but also of a "coming together" for Indigenous and non-Indigenous peoples. This followed land defence actions at both Kanehsatà:ke (1990) and Ipperwash (1995). The difference between the call in 1982 and that in 1995 is stark. By 1995, in the wake of high-profile land reoccupations—which were met with police and militarized aggression—the word solidarity is notably absent. The language of solidarity would continue to be eschewed in favour of softer language. The Royal Commission on Aboriginal Peoples (RCAP) issued a recommendation in 1996 to establish a national holiday with the express purpose of generating "'awareness and understanding' between aboriginal and non-aboriginal peoples as part of the strategy of 'public education.'"[102] On 23 May 1996, then Governor General Roméo Leblanc announced the official creation of National Aboriginal Day. According to the federal government, Indigenous organizations provided input on both the day selected—21 June to coincide with the summer solstice—and the name.[103]

Given the activist slant associated with the word solidarity and the anxieties of the Canadian government at the time, on some level the exclusion of solidarity makes sense. But the exclusion of solidarity also primed it to become a depoliticized cultural expression, a pan-Aboriginal variant of Canadian multiculturalism. This is evident in National Aboriginal Day's inclusion in a series of nationally recognized days known as the "Celebrate Canada!" days. At least since 2013, the day has been marketed as a part of a suite of days, followed by St-Jean-Baptiste Day (24 June), Canadian Multiculturalism Day (27 June), and ending with Canada Day (1 July).[104] The gradual depoliticization of the day ultimately enabled Canada to draw it within its national narrative, contributing to the nation state's imagineering (again, to borrow from Werry) of its national identity as open, tolerant, and innately multicultural, and as a model of settler-Indigenous, post-colonial cohesion. Its embedding within Celebrate Canada days reinforces Canadian supremacy, positioning it as one of three pillars of Canadian identity—Québécois culture, multiculturalism, Aboriginalism—that make up Canada.

In many ways the heavy marketing of National Aboriginal Day (NAD) as a day focused on cultural distinctiveness (yet integration), cultural pride, and unifying cohesion with non-Indigenous peoples, rather than serving as a day of recognition of *rights* and of Canada's rights responsibilities, served as a stultifying discourse that in its powerful rhetorical function concealed the deep entrenchment of ongoing processes of settler-colonial genocide. The active disentanglement of Aboriginal from rights is precisely why NAD faced such ardent opposition and why a number of Indigenous communities organized protests to coincide with it.[105] Part of the rejection of NAD, however, was also motivated by dissatisfaction with the term Aboriginal, which Zhu writes was taken as a reference to and description of "various ethno-cultural groups as a whole."[106] On some level this reflects, I think, an awareness among the wider, non-political Indigenous public that the term Aboriginal was "out of place" outside of the Constitution. There was palpable unease with its extension into public life. This in turn highlights the extent to which Indigenous peoples express unease and a wariness of the multiculturalization, and indeed the culturalization, of what was intended only to be legal-political discourse.

ROYAL COMMISSION ON ABORIGINAL PEOPLES (RCAP)

Undoubtedly, RCAP had a significant impact on establishing the discourse around Aboriginal and Aboriginality. While it in some ways presented a logical expansion of the term Aboriginal in a manner that embraces the spirit and intent of Indigenous activists' attempts to holistically frame it, for Métis it in effect worked *against* the earlier efforts to gain recognition of the rights of the Métis Nation. The RCAP (1991–96) was commissioned by the federal government in the wake of the reoccupation at Kanehsatà:ke, or the Oka Crisis, as it was frequently referred to by government bodies and in the media. The commissioners included a number of high-profile legal specialists and had representation from the three main Constitutionally recognized groups—First Nations (both status and non-status), Métis, and Inuit, alongside a number of non-Indigenous legal experts. The commission carried a budget of roughly $60 million, and the commissioners visited ninety-six First Nation communities, holding 178 days of public hearings. Organizations could submit reports to RCAP as well. Its five-volume, 4,000-page final report was issued in 1996 and set out a twenty-year plan for addressing the situation of Indigenous peoples and the dynamics between Indigenous and non-Indigenous peoples and levels of government.[107]

Given the size, scope, and impact of RCAP, the definition it creates of Aboriginal in the context of referring to *Aboriginal people* is significant. It has, in fact, created a substantive widening of the meaning of Métis via its discussion. The commission reintroduced the word Indigenous, using it to define Aboriginal people as "the indigenous inhabitants of Canada," noting that "Aboriginal people" was the preferred term "when we want to refer in a general manner to Inuit and to First Nations and Métis people, without regard to their separate origins and identities."[108] This gives voice to the distinctions communicated by Indigenous organizations in their interactions with the Special Joint Committees, that while "Aboriginal people" is a generalizing term, there are, in fact, separate origins and identities in need of attending to. RCAP's commissioners further clarify that their use of *Aboriginal peoples* "refers to organic political and cultural entities that stem historically from the original peoples of North America, rather than collections of individuals united by so-called 'racial' characteristics. The term includes the Indian, Inuit, and Métis peoples of Canada (see section 35(2) of the *Constitution Act, 1982*)."[109] They make a significant clarification here, that "Aboriginal peoples" as a placeholder refers to distinct collectives, not to individuals who identify as such on the basis of perceptions of "racial characteristics."

When the commissioners elaborate on their definition of Métis, however, a contradiction arises. First, they reiterate that their use of the term Métis "is consistent with our conception of *Aboriginal peoples*."[110] But they soon muddy the waters by saying that when they use the term Métis they are referring broadly to "distinct Aboriginal peoples whose early ancestors were of mixed heritage (First Nations, or Inuit in the case of the Labrador Métis, and European) and who associate themselves with a culture that is distinctly Métis."[111] The problem here is immediately apparent in that they previously outlined that at the heart of their definition of Aboriginal peoples, racial characteristics are not the basis for such understanding. Yet when it comes to situating Métis as an Aboriginal people, appeals to racial characteristics coded in the language of "mixed heritage" is at the forefront. It is only *second* that collective self-determination is given footing whereby they clarify that they use the "more specific term *Métis Nation* . . . to refer to Métis people who identify themselves as a nation with historical roots in the Canadian west."[112] This is significant given that the former Labrador Métis, the Nunatukavut, have acknowledged that they are not, in fact, Métis at all. Further, it entrenches the notion that the Métis people's purported "mixedness" comes before their Indigenous nationhood. This presupposes, as Andersen has pointed out, that Métis are somehow "more mixed" than First Nations and that mixedness is the basis of Métis nationhood itself. The focus is thus on *identity* rather than *ways of living, being, and seeing*.

This is inconsistent with the more expansive definition of Métis brought forth in the Constitutional moment and tied to an explicitly *political* articulation of Métisness—one that was reified in the 1992 Métis Nation Accord. Had the Charlottetown Accord been ratified, the "constitutional place of the Métis

Nation within the Canadian federation" would have been addressed "for the first time since 1870."[113] It would have committed the federal government and the provinces "to enter into negotiations with the Métis Nation on self-government and land, and it provided a framework for the transition of Métis advocacy organizations into representative governments."[114] The defeat of the Charlottetown Accord and thus the Métis Nation Accord left room for the perpetuation of ambiguity, seen within the RCAP Final Report and the decentring of a definition of Métisness anchored in nationhood and political existence. The effect of this has been a rise in people reading themselves in RCAP's definition as Métis on the basis of mixedness and identification with Métis culture, even in the absence of affiliation with a Métis community.[115] This in turn has spread outward as people untethered from Indigenous communities self-identify as Aboriginal according to this loosened definition of Métis.

Still, RCAP's definition of Aboriginal peoples brings some much-needed clarity, as it does offer a more expansive definition than that which is included in the Constitution, and it fills in some of the gaps left by the First Ministers' Conferences. Teme-Augama Anishinaabe political philosopher Dale Turner posits that RCAP has done much more for advancing recognition of Indigenous peoples as "Aboriginal nations" than the Supreme Court has.[116] RCAP's inclusion of references to Aboriginal nationhood therefore encroaches on the gradual individualization of the term. While it can be said to have arisen from their consultations with Indigenous peoples, it is difficult to know to what extent terminology was the primary subject of conversation in RCAP gatherings. The other terminological challenge posed by RCAP's articulation of Aboriginal peoples is that in emphasizing a focus on Aboriginal *peoples* versus the Constitution's primary focus on Aboriginal *rights*, it continues to conflate the original intent of the term's use. This conflation is also demonstrated by RCAP's introduction of "culture" in relation to Aboriginal, generating a formal definition that makes repeated use of the word culture/cultural. The text directly reads, "*Aboriginal people* (in the singular) means the individuals belonging to the political and cultural entities known as 'Aboriginal peoples.'"[117] Culture, in this sense, is a nebulous thing. By invoking culture, RCAP unwittingly also tethers Aboriginality to Canada's multicultural paradigm because, as Andersen points out, in "a colonial country such as Canada, culture is pinned to indigeneity in the form of cultural difference."[118] With the appeal to culture in such a monumentally significant report, it offers legitimacy—although unintentionally, I would argue, based on its wording—to the notion that such concepts as "Aboriginal cultures" and thus "Aboriginal people" do exist as actual, discrete entities.

Aboriginal's role as a placeholder is disrupted by the perpetuation of a notion that culture can be Aboriginal—and that individuals can be Aboriginal. Further, in RCAP's platform, composed of four principles—recognition, respect, sharing, and responsibility—it also creates an *identity* for "non-Aboriginal Canadians"—as an antithesis of "Aboriginal Canadians." The construction of this binary misappropriates a very specific Constitutional term to prop up rhetoric around "peacemaking" and "bridge-building," depoliticizing and thus "de-threatening" expressions of Indigenous realities. In this way Indigenous peoples are rendered more palatable to anxious masses of "non-Aboriginal" Canadians deeply shaken by the reminders of Canada's precarity as identified by Indigenous land defenders. A massive undertaking such as RCAP, charged with issuing recommendations to restructure the relationship between Indigenous and non-Indigenous peoples—or Aboriginal and non-Aboriginal people—has had a profound impact on establishing a discursive terrain (one that is, as I will argue in further chapters, temporally bounded) through which people become far more invested in Aboriginal (and non-Aboriginal) identities than in the central tenets of Aboriginal and treaty rights, land repatriation, and redress for entrenched and ongoing colonial harm.

THE STATEMENT OF RECONCILIATION AND GATHERING STRENGTH —CANADA'S ABORIGINAL ACTION PLAN

The federal government devised a carefully constructed political response to RCAP's recommendations. On 7 January 1998, Jean Chrétien's Liberal government issued a Statement of Reconciliation, delivered by Jane Stewart, Minister of Indian Affairs and Northern Development, along with a document entitled *Gathering Strength—Canada's Aboriginal Action Plan*. The Preamble to the Statement draws from the RCAP's report and its assertion that the policy direction of the past 150 years has been fundamentally wrong.[119] It offers a minuscule summary of RCAP's findings: "The Commissioners identify four stages in relations between Aboriginal and non-Aboriginal people. First, separate worlds—prior to European arrival in Canada. Then, contact and cooperation—a time when settlers and Aboriginal people were co-dependent. Next, a deterioration to displacement and assimilation—the period from the early 1800s until about 30 years ago, a time when colonial governments imposed their ways on Aboriginal people. Finally, renewal—our chance now in this generation to correct past wrongs and move forward in cooperative relationships once again."[120] The claim made as to the fact that there existed an ideal moment of relationship to return to is contentious. First, the generalization of distinctive moments of encounter—and of conflict—places a positive gloss over colonialism's foundation on these lands and constructs a binary of equal positionalities (Aboriginal/non-Aboriginal). The framing of such encounters as giving rise to codependency infantilizes First Nations and Inuit who in fact did *not* need Europeans but were rather later forced into carefully crafted state dependency through policies aimed at assimilation and eradication. The statement ignores the repeated, calculated attempts at the destruction of Indigenous nations and centuries of abuse. It also completely ignores the devastating impacts of what Mi'kmaq scholar Bonita Lawrence refers to as mercantile colonialism, and the subsequent acts of resistance by First Nations and Inuit to colonial presence.[121]

At the same time, both the Preamble and the Statement further the establishment of Aboriginal/non-Aboriginal as distinctive identities. Through careful wordsmithing, the Statement acknowledges that distinct "Aboriginal nations" existed (coterminous with RCAP's definition) but falls short of acknowledging the influence of laws and governance structures. The Statement "culturalizes" Indigenous nations, suggesting that what was contributed to "newcomers" was quite simply "assistance and spiritual values."[122] Further to this, it frames the central problem at the heart of relations between Indigenous peoples and Canadians as plainly attributable to the existence of "attitudes of racial and cultural superiority [that] led to a suppression of Aboriginal culture and values."[123] The overemphasis on *culture* and *values* obscures the dispossession of Indigenous peoples of land, the misappropriation of resources, and the negation of Indigenous legal orders and governance structures. It implies that what has transpired is a simple lack of appreciation and recognition, not genocide; it implies that Indigenous peoples have been desirous of Canada's existence, not that it is a nation born in and through blood. It individualizes racism by positioning it as "attitudes" rather than thoroughly debated, tested, and applied policies. It refers to "erosion" rather than deliberate detachment. It obscures the violence through which Canada *becomes* a country. Lastly, it further contributes to the development of the idea that such a thing as "Aboriginal culture" (and values) exists, feeding into the swirling currents of constructing Aboriginality as a figment of multiculturalism.

While blithe references to Indigenous peoples' distinctiveness are made, along with references "to the political, economic, and social systems of Aboriginal people and nations," in essence the Statement further pulls Indigenous peoples into Canada's multicultural milieu. While the Statement delivers a vital acknowledgement of the violence of residential schooling, it seeds originary visions of reconciliation—a reconciliatory discourse contingent on the construction of "Aboriginal people" as willing participants in Canada:

> Reconciliation is an ongoing process. In renewing our partnership, we must ensure that the mistakes which marked our past relationship are not repeated. The Government of Canada recognizes that policies that sought to assimilate Aboriginal people, women and men, were not the way to build a strong country. We must instead continue to find ways in which Aboriginal people can participate fully in the economic, political, cultural and social life of Canada in a manner which preserves and enhances the collective identities of Aboriginal communities, and allows them to evolve and flourish in the future. Working together to achieve our shared goals will benefit all Canadians, Aboriginal and non-Aboriginal alike.[124]

Here Canadianness is clearly invoked, encompassing both Aboriginal and non-Aboriginal. To be Aboriginal, then, is to be unequivocally Canadian. It is also to be a multicultural subject who must be properly socialized into the (perhaps in order of importance) economic, political, cultural, and social life of Canada. In a near mirror of Canadian multiculturalism rhetoric, what must be preserved are, simply, collective identities.

While the Canadian government has expressed regret, it has laid out no expectations as to what non-Aboriginal Canadians must contribute to a purportedly shared vision of Canadianness. As John Borrows (Anishinaabe), Canada Research Chair in Indigenous Law, has argued, in the context of the legal system and judicial interpretations of Aboriginal rights, they must be reconciled *to* Canada and its claims to sovereignty.[125] This reconciling *to* Canada is precisely what the engine of Aboriginal Canadian is all about. It sets the discursive terrain for Indigenous peoples, remade as multicultural subjects in the form of Aboriginal people or Aboriginal Canadians, to be assimilated into a multicultural Canada and thus into Canada's core neoliberal brand identity. It is in fact the rhetoric of Aboriginality that serves as a salve for Canadian anxieties about Canada's genocidal policies and practices aimed at Indigenous peoples; as different actors adopt and expand it, moving it further away from its original purpose and intent, Aboriginality and the diffusion of the discourse of Aboriginal into all aspects of federal government policy conceal that this new wolf-in-sheep's-clothing era of Aboriginal policymaking is still, ultimately, subjugation.

This is evident in the Statement's frequent invocation of support for self-*government* versus what Indigenous organizations sought during constitutional activism as self-*determination*. As political and cultural anthropologist Stephanie Irlbacher-Fox clarifies, self-government denotes "the extent to which Canada is willing to recognize Indigenous peoples' authorities in a range of areas, from education to natural resource management"; it "refers to the various authorities available for negotiation as determined by the Canadian state, deriving from within the Canadian legal and constitutional framework."[126] Self-determination, by contrast, is far more expansive. Canada's fear of self-determination was most clearly reflected in 2007 when, along with the United States, Australia, and New Zealand, Canada rejected the United Nations Declaration on the Rights of Indigenous peoples (UNDRIP) because of the use of the word self-determination.[127] Canada, along with the other countries, "articulated their apprehension that the UNDRIP could be misrepresented as conferring a right of possible secession and minority groups . . . [who] could . . . exploit [it] to claim the right to self-determination, including exclusive control of their territorial resources" in spite of the fact the UNDRIP "plainly provides that it does not sanction secession."[128] Aboriginal self-government is therefore coded language for a form of delegated authority, granted by the Canadian government, that renders Indigenous peoples as subject to Canadian sovereignty. It is not self-determination. The discourse of Aboriginal in all its iterations beyond the constitutional placeholding from which it was born acts merely as a veneer over mechanisms and pathways for engineering the assimilation of Indigenous peoples. Insofar as actors change in the context of particular moments, the overriding, foundational ethos that structures relations, particularly on the part of the state, is neoliberal colonialism.

GOODBYE INAC . . . OR NOT?
In 2011, the Conservative federal government under Stephen Harper (and without substantive consultation of First Nations, Inuit, or Métis) quietly changed the *applied title* of the Department of Indian and Northern Affairs Canada (INAC) to Aboriginal Affairs and Northern Development Canada (AANDC).[129] While Indian Affairs was most commonly used as the administrative portfolio for government policy, in 1966, under the Government Organization Act, the Department of Indian Affairs and Northern Development (DIAND) was created. In 1985, the Department of Indian Affairs and Northern Development Act outlined a distinctive mandate and organizational structure for DIAND. Commonly referred to as Indian and Northern Affairs Canada (INAC), it dealt exclusively with Inuit peoples and status Indians (those registered under the Indian Act and thus recognized by the federal government as Indians). Non-status and Métis peoples, on the other hand, had (since 1985) been primarily dealt with through the branch titled the Federal Interlocutor for Métis and Non-Status Indians. Although the applied title change to AANDC signalled an inclusive restructuring of the department, it also, I argue, committed to a federal *rebranding* of the branch of federal government that has been the driving force behind the state's violence against Indigenous peoples.

This is evident in the fact that the applied title change was not a *legal* title change. With an applied title change the federal government, through its Federal Identity Program (FIP) policy, essentially gave a new face to what it refers to as its "corporate identity." The renaming through FIP is essentially "a management technique for communicating an organization's unique characteristics in a memorable manner" from a vantage point that understands that "corporate identity is based on the premise that key publics must perceive an organization clearly and accurately if management objectives are to be achieved."[130] Although the Harper government changed its applied title, the legal name for the department remained DIAND and the legislation charged with "administering" and "managing" First Nations peoples remained the Indian Act.

According to Andrew MacDougall, spokesperson for Harper, the applied title change arose from the state's desire to brand itself with a title that is "more up to date and inclusive, consistent with the government's focus on moving forward in our relationship with Aboriginal peoples."[131] FIP ensures the state brands itself in the most effective and efficient ways possible while affirming the state as a corporate entity. Taken in context with MacDougall's words, FIP and the INAC-applied title change are emblematic of the wider circulation of Aboriginal discourse that belies something more than a simple administrative name change.

As Canada has sought to distinguish itself in the global marketplace, it has incorporated a commodified form of Aboriginality (that which is intended to mark Aboriginal material and spiritual cultures and knowledges) into revenue-generating spaces. It has also made desirable the repackaging of the nation's image "for commercial consumption and nostalgic renarration purged of historical responsibility."[132] While a number of departments may have applied titles that differ from their legal titles, in this case the applied title change is a metaphor for the era of Aboriginal reconciliation, in which *appearing* to dismantle structures of oppression was far more important than the *actual* work of doing so.

Conclusion

The word Aboriginal has been on an eventful journey. While all of the word's political interpretations and transformations are significant, this book's focus is on the way that the word has spread even further outward into public life. It has found a home among non-profit organizations, for-profit companies, and charities, including the Canada Council for Aboriginal Business (CCAB, 1982), the National Aboriginal Achievement Foundation (NAAF, founded in 1985 and renamed as Indspire in 2012), the Aboriginal People's Television Network (APTN, 1992), the Aboriginal Financial Officers Association of Canada (AFOA, 1999), and the Aboriginal Curatorial Collective (2014). It has, indeed, left a lasting impact. For example, a search of Corporations Canada's registry of federal corporations yields 220 results for entities with the word Aboriginal in their names, including coffee distributors, resource consultancies, firefighters, IT companies, mining and construction companies, finance companies, for-profit and non-profit tourism outfits, arts organizations, educational organizations, environmental protection organizations, veteran relations businesses, journalism associations, health and wellness companies, and (perhaps unsurprisingly given all of this) for-profit genealogy companies.[133] Post-secondary institutions in Ontario, in particular, embraced the language of Aboriginal through the formation of Aboriginal Education Councils (AECs), in accordance with provincial guidelines. These councils had as their main objective working towards the enhancement of Indigenous student life on campus with a goal of increasing student enrolment. Relatedly, scholarships were created geared towards Aboriginal students, and jobs were allocated on the basis of Aboriginality. Indeed, my first academic job title, in addition to Assistant Professor, was that of "New Sun Visiting Aboriginal Scholar" (2012).

What I have not discussed to this point is that it is also important to be attentive to how capitalization does (or does not) appear within each use of Aboriginal. Within the Constitution all uses of "aboriginal" employ the lower case. By contrast, in section 35(2), Indian, Inuit, and Métis peoples are all capitalized. The lack of capitalization of Aboriginal marks the way in which the word functions as an adjective—a term that describes the state of being of Indian, Inuit, and Métis peoples in terms of the rights associated thereto. When the word is capitalized—as in National Aboriginal Day, the Royal Commission on Aboriginal Peoples, Canada's Aboriginal Action Plan, Aboriginal Affairs and Northern Development—it foments the idea that Aboriginal people/s are a noun; it gives credence to the idea that Aboriginality is itself (whether tethered to any of the Indigenous communities or identities discussed by Williams or not) a *real* identity. To borrow from Williams, then, the people of the Métis Nation, Inuit, Anishinaabek, Haudenosaunee, Mi'kmaq, Skwxwú7mesh, and many others have rights respective to their nations to which "aboriginal rights" is stuck as a constitutional placeholder. Aboriginal is not a community, nation, or an identity in and unto itself. But it is the wider circulation of the term and the disconnection of it from legal and political conceptualizations encapsulated within the constitutional moment that, at least for a time, enabled it to become something much more than it was ever intended to be.

Aboriginalized Multiculturalism™: Canada's Olympic National Brand

The Olympics provide a potent forum for the exportation of a nation's brand. Nations exercise their influence in the Olympics through a variety of means, from offering support for the actual Olympic bids, to supplying funding for venue building and advertising, to providing security support through the deployment of federally affiliated policing services. The Olympics are, as former Olympian and scholar of sports politics Jules Boykoff writes, an example of celebration capitalism. Celebration capitalism takes hold within a state of exception in which "normal rules of politics can be temporarily suspended," and in which state actors are deployed "as strategic partners, putting forth public-private partnerships."[1] Partnerships are innately lopsided, intended to serve the interests of the primary beneficiaries of capitalism, while the deleterious realities of celebration capitalism are "buoyed by feel-good claims of environmental and social sustainability."[2] The Olympics, as the most recognizable example of celebration capitalism, aggressively work to produce a festive and commercially appealing spectacle guaranteed to generate capital.[3]

As such the opening and closing spectacles of the Olympics allow for a state's return on investment by offering them a major forum to advertise their brand. With Canada's Olympic hosting engagements taking place within the last quarter of the twentieth century, and two of the three in the thick of neoliberal globalization, within the expanding reach of television communications, Canadian Olympic organizers have found themselves increasingly concerned with the "symbolic impact of the pageantry, ceremony, and message-making of the Games' televised opening and closing moments."[4] As the event most widely broadcast (estimates for the 2010 Vancouver Olympics pegged global spectatorship at over three billion people), Olympic ceremonies provide cities and their nations with the opportunity to market a version of themselves, essentially putting on display a highly crafted narrative of the nation that they believe will enhance their public image.[5] In this light, Olympic ceremonies might best be understood as a form of what Joseph S. Nye Jr., former dean of Harvard's Kennedy School of Government, refers to as "soft power." Soft power "is the ability to affect others to obtain the outcomes one wants through attraction rather than coercion or payment. A country's soft power rests on its resources of culture, values, and policies."[6] Soft power in this instance is reflected in how, during the three Canadian-hosted Olympic Games, Indigenous desires for self-representation collided with the Canadian government's desire to leverage Indigenous peoples as part of its "cultural resources" in order to enhance its national brand identity. Through different discursive formations, Indigenous peoples were brought into local and national narratives crafted for export to wider Olympic audiences—all with the end goal of painting Canada as a multicultural haven. This, in turn, would contribute to the work of enhancing Canada's national brand on the international stage.

Indigenous peoples have been involved in each of the three Canadian-hosted Olympics to varying degrees. In the 1976 Montreal Summer Olympic closing ceremony, the 1988 Calgary Winter Olympic opening ceremony, and the 2010 Winter Olympic opening ceremony in Vancouver. Each Olympic organizing committee recruited Indigenous peoples to take part, in one way or another, in expressions of regional, provincial, and Canadian national identity on the Olympic stage; each organizing committee put forth a distinctive narrative about Indigenous peoples relative to these identities. Let me emphasize, before I proceed further into this chapter, that I greatly respect those who opted to participate in the Indigenous Youth Gathering (IYG), the 2010 opening ceremony, and in the previous Olympics. The freedom to make decisions for oneself, to be self-determining in both individual and communal senses, is one of the things First Nations, Inuit, and Métis have been fighting for. As such I do not see Indigenous involvement in any of the Games and their associated events as instances of outright victimization. The broader narrative productions in which Indigenous peoples were called on to take part were predetermined for them by production managers, choreographers, and other Canadian Olympic officials, but that does not mean that the participants subscribed to those narratives. Nor should we presume that participants were unable to exercise any kind of agency or to challenge the narratives by working from within them. Indeed, it is through the concerted efforts of those participating in the Games as performers that we have come to see a shift in the discursive representation channelled into visual form.

An exhaustive discussion of the various motives for Indigenous peoples' participation is, however, outside the scope of this chapter. I am less focused, at this precise time, on people's motives for participation, as I understand these as far-reaching; rather, I am concerned here with the discursive effects of that participation—asking what grander narratives the Canadian government was able to mobilize to the aid of its national brand via the production of Aboriginality. I am also concerned with what these representations tell us about how Canada has depicted its relationship to Indigenous peoples at various points through a very public, global platform. It is important to critically explore the evolution of the way Indigenous inclusion/involvement has been managed and framed to highlight the ways that Canada has sought to capitalize on Indigenous participation via expressions of Indianness, Nativeness, and Aboriginality. There are several central questions that animate this chapter: Why is it that organizing committees view Indigenous peoples as central to Olympic narratives when Indigenous peoples are only minimally present as athletes in the Games?[7] What are local host committees and the Canadian government trying to say about themselves by insisting on Indigenous presence within the Olympic ceremonies when in so many other spaces in Canadian society Indigenous peoples are purposefully invisibilized? How does the change in discursive framing of Indigenous participation reflect the gradual entrenchment of Indigenous peoples in Canada's multicultural brand?

Organizers for the 1976 Montreal closing ceremony recruited a select number of First Nations peoples to "play Indian" in accordance with visions that organizers had for their involvement. While appearing to be more inclusive of First Nations involvement in the planning stages of the Games and their ceremonies, organizers of the 1988 Calgary opening ceremony drew on steadfastly racist tropes about Cowboys, Natives, and Mounties. The organizers for the 2010 Vancouver opening ceremony, on the other hand, invoked a pan-cultural Aboriginal fantasyland, one in which the racism had been spun through multiple cycles of multiculturalism rhetoric. To effectively sell multiculturalism, Olympic organizers carved out their own vision of Aboriginality, incorporating Indigenous peoples into the cultural rhetoric and national fabric of the nation. Advancing a vision of Aboriginality allowed the state to market Indigenous peoples as symbols of Canada's uniqueness and diversity (key themes of multiculturalism), an ambition amplified in a climate of growing global market competitiveness. This is, sadly, nothing new, as demonstrated by the shifting narrative through successive Olympic Games; Canada has actively sought to repackage the nation's image. The Vancouver opening ceremony imagineered Canada's brand through Aboriginality, by figuring Indigenous peoples as a symbol of Canada's supposed diversity and thus tolerance and inclusiveness.

This chapter is thus concerned with examining the discursive formations arising within the planning and execution of each of the Olympic Games held in Canada. The goal of the early part of the chapter is to elucidate, as in Chapter 1, discursive shifts over time, critically analyzing how and *why* the Olympics "keep pace" with terminological changes pertaining to Indigenous peoples and how diverse actors working under the auspices of the Olympics are directly implicated in further widening the discourse of Aboriginality. In building on the analysis of leading scholars on Indigenous representation in the Olympics, such as Janice Forsyth (Cree) and Christine M. O'Bonsawin (Abenaki), the chapter addresses the role of Indigenous inclusion/participation in the Olympics in solidifying Canada's national brand identity. As I discuss in the latter pages of the chapter, however, this was not a seamless process. Olympic organizers frequently saw their plans for tokenistic inclusion waylaid as Indigenous peoples worked as potent advocates for their own interests. This led to, I argue, a splitting of discursive constructions: Indigenous peoples who assented to lending visual credence to Canada's Aboriginal multiculturalized brand were cast as "good" Aboriginal people; conversely, those who refused were, figuratively and literally, cast out of the national narrative.

Montreal 1976

Many nations, like Canada, have used the Games' ceremonies as a form of nation-branding, an opportunity to "represent versions of their national history, as well as their current social, political, and economic trajectories, to the rest of the World."[8] In the summer of 1976, Montreal, Quebec, a city that is home to Canada's largest francophone population, became the first city in Canada to host the Olympics. With the Quiet Revolution of the 1960s and the FLQ/October Crisis of 1970 still fresh in the minds of many Canadians, Olympic organizers strove to extol the virtues of Quebec and its partnership with English Canada within a national Canadian identity. The 1976 Olympics, then, provided the first large-scale opportunity for the Canadian government to begin developing and exporting multiculturalism as the foundation of its national identity *and* its national brand, a trend that would continue through all three of its Olympic Games.

As many critics have noted, one of the many problems with Canada's vision of itself as a multicultural nation is that it anchors this identity in an English-French duality.[9] Otto Schantz, a specialist in the area of physical cultural studies, writes that the ceremonies of 1976 emphasized the dual character of Canada's identity: "This was the first time ever that two people had simultaneously lit the Olympic flame in the stadium. One was Sandra Henderson from Toronto and the other Stéphane Préfontaine from Montreal. Together, in the coordinated run, they represented the two founding peoples of Canada, the two cultures living side by side in the Canadian State."[10] While the Montreal Olympic ceremonies emphasized Canada's duality, "the mass participation of American Indians in Montreal during the Closing Ceremony was intended to be a symbol of their emancipation and integration."[11] Indigenous peoples were not positioned as a pillar/pillars of Canadian nationhood in spite of successful efforts to resist their minoritization, a resistance reflected on in my introductory chapter. Their inclusion, however, principally foregrounded the depiction of the state (and its citizens) as innately open, accepting, and tolerant towards difference: their image was cast as exemplary of the success of Canadian multiculturalism.

To coordinate the closing ceremony, the Olympic organizing committee hired Québécois choreographers Michael Cartier and Hugo de Pot; Cartier and de Pot then arranged for 250 non-Indigenous amateur and professional Montreal-based dancers to teach a select number of Indigenous participants "how to move through their own ceremony."[12] Recorded numbers of Indigenous participants vary across sources with some suggesting 500, some 250, and others pegging the number at 75.[13] The Montreal dancers, with faces painted and dressed in caricaturized buckskin costumes replete with fringe and feathers, led the Indigenous participants, similarly dressed, into the arena. In the background the Olympic orchestra played a processional piece inspired by André Mathieu's *Danse sauvage*. *Danse sauvage*, which sounds like an orchestral companion to Dante's *Inferno*, features a series of long trumpet notes and shorter, staccato, trumpeted quarter notes. Just past the one-minute mark in the ceremony, a chorus of male voices, "whose rhythms evoke the chants of the American Indians," bellowed "ahhhhhhey-heeey-ey-heyahhhhhh-hey-heyah-ha-hey-hey."[14] The Olympic orchestra played "the March of the Athletes, a symphonic suite performed on traditional instruments augmented by Amerindian folk instruments such as tom-toms, rattles, and small bells. To the strains of this march, whose rhythms evoke the chants of the American Indians, a group of seventy five Amerindians in full dress enter the stadium by the marathon gate, under the glare of spotlights sweeping across the field."[15] The "Indian actors" marched through the stadium in a choreographed arrowhead formation and then entered five rings formed in the shape and colours of the Olympic logo. Standing in the centre of the rings, in the heart of the arena, the participants erected five large teepees, colour-coordinated with the rings.

Four local chiefs, Andrew T. Delisle, Mike McKenzie, Aurélien Gill, and Max Gros-Louis, who, according to the organizing committee's Official Report, were wearing "full tribal dress . . . escorted" Lord Killanin, then president of the International Olympic Committee (IOC), to his seat in the royal box (reserved for heads of state and royal families).[16] As the ceremony began to wind down the performers broke from their circular formation and handed out feathered headbands and beaded necklaces to athletes, officials, and spectators. Once Killanin finished his speech the final dance of the closing began and the "athletes, dancers, Indians, and COJO [Comité Organisateur de Jeux Olympiques] hostesses formed a friendship chain and left the stadium in oddly shaped, curving lines."[17] The Official Report erroneously identifies the final dance as "a simple Indian dance," although the choreographers actually based the dance on a French-Canadian farandole.

Newspaper accounts published the morning following the ceremony declared the ceremony a resounding success, suggesting that Olympic organizers had accomplished a remarkable feat. The *Ottawa Citizen* described the show as a "dazzling celebration of unity" and "innocent exuberance" that was unmatched in Olympic history.[18] The Official Report claims that news media were dazzled and that the parade created "remarkable, iridescent effects, with its Amerindian costumes, its plumes and feathered flags, and its drums and colored wigwams, all surrounding the athletes."[19] Yet in spite of the accolades, for a ceremony said to hold Indigenous peoples in such high regard, the Indigenous performers/participants were not thanked in the closing ceremony words of gratitude. COJO's celebration of Indigenous peoples was instead delivered through its facilitation of a visual narrative founded on assumptions of Indigenous peoples' sameness, something demonstrated through the featuring of Plains-style clothing and the use of teepees. That these elements bear little relevance for First Nations local to the Montreal area, or to First Nations peoples in general, appeared to matter extraordinarily little. Further, the Indianness of the "Indian" appeared to be based on stereotypes of Indigenous peoples as "Hollywood Indians" or "Imaginary Indians"— replete with stilted, and stifling, characterizations.

Yugoslavian-born Artur Takac, the technical director for the 1976 Olympics, asserts that he was responsible for having "North American Indians" in the closing ceremony. The original plan for the ceremony was to have young European Canadian women form five circles in the Olympic colours in the centre of the arena. The athletes would carry coloured cards directing them to their assigned circle. Other organizing committee members raised concerns about the "dignity of the young women," feeling that having women placed in such exposed circles might indeed invite "horseplay, which would go beyond the line of fun and offend."[20] To respond to these concerns Takac states that he proposed using Indigenous participants to form circles around the young women to protect them. Killanin hesitated, fearing that were Indigenous peoples to be included, they would use the international attention on the Games to highlight what he called "their dissatisfaction with historical and more recent treatment" by the government.[21] Takac countered that if the organizing committee were to invite two Indigenous chiefs to stand in the royal box as ceremonial guards to Queen Elizabeth II, their presence would prevent any impropriety by their people on the ground. Takac recounts, "I knew that if the chiefs were in that position they would ensure the best possible behavior and dignity of the young men of their tribes."[22]

Takac's plan to use Indigenous peoples to "protect" non-Indigenous women directly plays into romanticized notions of the noble savage—strong and heroic warriors who view themselves as servants/subservient and who would gladly protect non-Indigenous peoples. What is interesting about this exchange, however, is that while Takac, perhaps because he was from a country with no history of direct colonization of Indigenous peoples, felt Indigenous peoples might conform to such a stereotype. Killanin, on the other hand, as an Irish-English person, was well aware of both Indigenous peoples' mistreatment and their frustration with the Canadian government. Rather than lean into the stereotype, Killanin suggested avoidance of the possibility of disruption altogether. Through this detached exchange, it becomes clear

Indigenous involvement in the ceremony was initially conceptualized in a manner that reinforced stereotypes of Indigenous peoples, and in a way that would reify ideas about the subjugated relationship of Indigenous peoples to the French, to Canada, and to the Crown. Takac's own position and origins, as a (then) Yugoslavian, give credence to the extent in which ideas about Indians and Indianness circulated to areas outside of the "colony" and the "colonial metropoles"—the stereotypes did not end at the borders of either, but rather were globally circulated.

The way that Canada's 1976 Montreal Olympic Organizing Committee envisioned Canada-Indigenous unity, multiculturalism, and appreciation for Indigenous peoples was by *not* consulting "with the populations who[m] they professed to respect in the construction of the program. From start to finish, the celebration was designed by Olympic organizers for Aboriginal peoples."[23] In order to promote Canadianness the organizing committee sought "to release evidence of . . . the uniqueness of the host nation's Indigenous peoples" as a marketing ploy, crafting and executing an Indian theme that played up and traded in Eurocentric ideas of the noble savage.[24] This is evident in the language used: the chiefs were chosen to *escort* Killanin to the royal box rather than *accompany* him. In most colloquial uses the term escort implies aspects of labour and of inferior status; they were not his *guests* or *companions*, they were there to serve as aides. They were not there as dignitaries, they were there, quite plainly, as figureheads, to stand for the successful integration of Indigenous peoples into Canada.

They were not there as equal partners; they were there to "protect" Killanin from other Indigenous peoples, to protect non-Indigenous peoples from Indigenous peoples or, rather, they were utilized to protect non-Indigenous peoples from a threat that non-Indigenous organizers *imagined*. A closer examination of this moment, and of the role that, on the surface, appeared to signal a modicum of respect towards/for Indigenous peoples, reveals that Indigenous peoples were conceived by non-Indigenous organizers as little more than props. According to Janice Forsyth and Kevin Wamsley (an expert on the Olympics and Olympic history) the closing ceremony was promoted as a tribute to Indigenous peoples of *Canada*; that ultimately "The official intent . . . was to convey the idea of multiculturalism with its emphasis on the 'emancipation and integration'" of Indigenous peoples.[25] The organizing committee saw the inclusion of Indigenous participants as an avenue to advance their own, very specific, vision of multiculturalism—one that masks the atrocities of Indigenous dispossession while promoting the supposedly successful integration of Indigenous peoples via assimilatory policy agendas.

While Olympic organizers viewed the nearby reserves of Kahnawá:ke and Kanesatake as fertile ground for finding Indians for the closing ceremony, many Onkwehón:we declined to participate because of concerns over racist, stereotypical, and contrived representations.[26] Others who elected to participate saw it as a chance to exercise agency, insisting on their presence rather than erasure.[27] Olympic organizers were able to find people willing to participate because some Kanien'kehá:ka from the communities felt that it was imperative that they take charge of the images represented as best they could. In fact, just a few years prior to the 1976 Olympics, the National Indian Council (NIC), a political organization advocating for First Nations and Métis rights, lobbied for inclusion in Expo 67, held in Montreal. As part of a circuit of international exhibitions, Expo 67 allowed Canada to advertise itself on a global stage. Yet Indigenous participants wanted to use the limited inclusion granted to develop an exhibit that would "exhibit present distinctively indigenous perspectives regarding the historic oppression and ongoing mistreatment of First Nations people in Canada."[28] In the end, Indigenous participants effectively challenged Canada's positive presentation of its "century-long policy of assimilation" by using the exhibit to tell truths about the horrors of the residential school system and by highlighting the enduring beauty of Indigenous arts and cultures.[29]

Those who chose to take part in the 1976 Olympics likewise worked within images that were constructed for them and that were "culturally demeaning and fraught with serious ideological implications"[30] with the intent of reclaiming and challenging the narratives to be presented. As with Expo 67, the media attention garnered by the Olympics did ultimately provide an opportunity for a different kind of self-representation, for the chance to disseminate fair and accurate representations of, in particular, local Kanien'kehá:ka. Kahnawákeró:non proposed an Indian Days celebration to be hosted by their community; it would be a seventeen-day cultural display and event coordinated to run alongside the Olympics. Olympic organizers were concerned that, should they back the event, Kanien'keha:ka would use it as a "public forum to make explicit statements about their social, political, and economic situations."[31] When the Indians of Quebec Association (IQA) submitted a request to host the event as a formal part of the Olympic Arts and Culture Program for the

Games, the organizing committee immediately rejected the proposal because they feared what they referred to as a "'a feather show,' referring to the possibility of Indian demonstrations."[32] Frustrated but undeterred, Kanien'keha:ka persisted and committed to hosting the events in their community southwest of Montreal, and invited Olympic athletes, support staff, and spectators to see and experience how Mohawk people really lived.

The community also used it as an opportunity to sell arts and crafts to tourists.[33] Indian Days was planned to counterbalance the consumption of racist Indian imagery at the Olympics and to provide people with the opportunity to interact with local Indigenous peoples on their own terms. As Janice Forsyth (Fisher River Cree Nation, and an expert in Indigenous involvement in Olympic Games) explains, "At the same time the Mohawks were attempting to work within the limits of Canadian understandings of Indians and Indianness, they sought to overcome them by utilizing the audience and mass media at the Games to forward their own images and ideas about who they were as contemporary Aboriginal peoples through their Indian Days celebration."[34] It effectively worked to counter a multitude of stereotypical, negative, and harmful images at the foreground of the Olympic closing ceremony—images which Indigenous peoples tried to reclaim by participating within the limited scope available to them.

Whether Indigenous peoples participated or not, Olympic organizers appeared to have no problem in using large numbers of non-Indigenous peoples, dressed as they imagined Indians would be, to pay tribute to Indigenous peoples because, as Métis scholar Howard Adams writes in the context of the Calgary Stampede, the public would not pay to see Indigenous peoples in any other way.[35] Any expressed desire on the part of local Indigenous peoples to appear in their own traditional regalia and to represent their own nations was ignored. Olympic organizers were not looking to work meaningfully with and alongside Indigenous peoples. They feared giving unfettered access to a global platform that could be used to shed light on Indigenous realities; they also feared that it would be used to shame Canada and damage its multicultural brand. Through this they only wanted to then manifest a highly managed, imagined Indianness that represented something distinctive about Canada and which they knew held broad market appeal. The ultimate goal was to highlight the assimilation of Indigenous peoples as *part* of Canada's multicultural framework. This differs from articulations of Aboriginality in relation to Canada's multicultural brand that would come to the fore with the Vancouver Olympics. Yet the seeds were planted with the Montreal Olympics, with a distinction between "good" Indians, who participate within the national pro-assimilation narrative, and "bad" Indians, who were seen as threatening to upend the narrative entirely. It would, in fact, be through the planning and organizing of the Calgary Olympics and the oppositions to the Calgary Games where this juxtaposition would further take root; the focus on assimilating Indigenous peoples would remain, but it would come to be framed both strategically and rhetorically in a much different way.

Calgary 1988

By the time the 1988 Winter Olympics in Calgary began, the relationship between Indigenous peoples and Canada had shifted significantly. Indigenous activists had effectively ushered in a new era in Indigenous-Canada relations through the entrenchment of section 35 of the Constitution. While this ultimately had limited effect in transforming the overarching trajectory of regional and national representation within Calgary's ceremonies, there was greater acknowledgement of the need for some kind of inclusion of local Indigenous peoples in decision-making processes. Sykes Powderface of the Chiniki Band was chosen in 1986 as the Native Liaison Coordinator and a full board member of the Calgary organizing committee, Olympiques Calgary Olympics '88 (OCO'88). He was tasked with building a relationship with local Treaty 7 peoples and in ensuring their willing participation in the Games. Yet Powderface was the lone First Nations board member and was not directly involved in the design and choreographic planning of the opening ceremony, thus the images constructed for the event ultimately reveal the limits of engagement with one of the most powerful sights of meaning-making within the Olympics themselves.

The inclusion of Indigenous peoples in the 1988 Winter Olympics was motivated, in part, by the Calgary bid committee's desire to promote "Calgary's unique western heritage."[36] The bid committee argued that Calgary's western heritage translated to a pervasive "warm, western hospitality" that the city could share with people "from around the world."[37] In order to demonstrate this the bid committee drew on three figures that they felt embodied Canada's western history and that would be both recognizable and memorable on the international Olympic stage: the Mountie, the Cowboy, and the Native. The bid committee reasoned that these three figures have been the backbone of the city's identity, as evidenced by their centrality to the city's long-running and widely known Calgary Stampede.[38] Perhaps given the lengthy involvement of local First Nations in the Calgary Stampede, organizers thought, rather erroneously, that they could simply tap Indigenous peoples to play the role of "Native" and to round out additional Olympic cultural programming. OCO'88 had taken stock of criticisms that had emerged in the aftermath of the 1976 ceremonies about the lack of Indigenous presence in the closing ceremony and sought to localize participation in the opening ceremony of the 1988 Games to avoid questions about the performance's authenticity. The inclusion of Treaty 7 "Native" representatives provided a pathway through which OCO'88 could claim the accuracy and authenticity of the visual narratives produced for the Games.

This was evident from as early as the bid for the Olympics themselves. The bid committee felt that the three figures were so central to Calgary's identity and to the identity of western Canada that they brought flapjack breakfasts, traditionally served at the Calgary Stampede, and "mounted police, Native dancers, and cowboy hats" on the trip to Baden-Baden, Germany, for the IOC's announcement of the site of the 1988 Games.[39] Of the IOC reception to Calgary's display, Frank King, chairperson of OCO'88, recalls, "Our Mounties were a big hit. They gave out thousands of autographed photos. And when Chief Fox and his wife danced to the beat of Native tomtoms, people crowded into our area, leaving the other bid displays virtually empty. We learned that our unique western heritage is interesting to people from other parts of the world."[40] The images of the Mountie, Cowboy, and Native provided so great a foundation for both the Olympic bid and the opening ceremony of the Games that the head of the Calgary Stampede Board, serving as a member of OCO'88's board, suggested that "an 'Indian attack and wagon-burning' be a part of the Opening Ceremony," an idea that was ultimately rejected.[41] Speaking to a journalist from *Windspeaker* in 1987, Calgary mayor Ralph Klein called proposals by OCO'88 members to incorporate war dances and the torching of wagons into the Games "unfortunate."[42] Klein noted that "we have all got to become more sensitive to these kinds of issues. They can really hurt relations between Indian people and non-Indian people."[43] While the language used by OCO'88 oscillates between Native and Indian, what we see clearly here is on some level a shift in cognition that marks the rise of a "new era" of discourse and of Indigenous representation.

War dances, wagon burning, and "Indian attacks" were not, ultimately, part of the opening ceremony. Members of local First Nations representing Treaty 7 (an 1877 treaty involving the Siksika, Tsuu T'ina, Stoney, Piikani, and Kainai and the British Crown representatives of Canada) were invited to participate and were directed to rush into the stadium arena on horseback. Paddy Sampson, the executive director of the ceremony, approved the participants' apparel, with outfits consisting of feathered headdresses, buckskin clothing, and face paint. Treaty 7 peoples on horseback, in keeping with oco'88's vision for "Natives," were juxtaposed against the Cowboys, who entered on horseback and on chuck wagons while showing off their lasso skills. The Mounties, in a performance of the RCMP Musical Ride, paved the way for Governor General Jeanne Sauvé's entrance to the anthems "God Save the Queen" and "O Canada." The Musical Ride performers executed a number of cavalry drills and formations before making way for the procession of athletes. Between the Cowboy and Mountie performances, a group of people entered the arena wearing folkloric outfits and carrying banners displaying country names such as "Russia," "Austria," and "Japan." Their inclusion was intended to signal waves of multiethnic/multinational immigration to the Prairies and to the city of Calgary.

First Nations performers captivated the crowd, singing and playing big drums, as they waited for the Olympic torch to be brought into the stadium; the musical performance continued through the Olympic cauldron torch-lighting. First Nations musicians provided the musical backdrop as a series of blue and indigo, yellow, red, green, and white steel beams rose up around the cauldron in visual reference to the Hudson's Bay Company's point blanket colours and to symbolize the poles of a teepee (Figure 2). Later on in the ceremony, Daniel Tlen from Burwash Landing, Yukon, sang a translated version of "O Canada" in his Southern Tutchone language, before the singing of the English/French version of the national anthem. The apposition of the image of *real* Native people against Cowboys and Mounties, along with the invocation of fur trade colours, was planned in order to visually depict the core western mythology of "how the West was won."

As Canada has long based its national image on the myth of peaceful frontier settlement, First Nations participation was needed to shore up the marketing of Calgary's, and thus Canada's, western hospitality. Cowboys are positioned as representing positive values, like "love of freedom, fairness, individualism, toughness, enterprise, forward looking attitude, and whiteness"; by contrast

Figure 2. The Snowbirds fly over the Olympic Flag during the opening ceremonies of the 1988 Calgary Winter Olympic Games. Also visible are the colours of the Hudson's Bay Company, painted on metal poles intended to look like a teepee structure. Source: xv Olympic Winter Games, Olympic Photograph Collection fonds, City of Calgary Archives, CalA 55-19 MR56#22A.

"Indians . . . have remained the savage, primitive, losing, dark-skinned, evil, antagonistic enemy."[44] With the incorporation of the Mountie, the dichotomy of Cowboy-Indian is softened.[45] The figure of the Mountie has long been one of an "unassuming, patient, impartial, self-disciplined, sober, and completely incorruptible" figure, embodying Canada's/Canadians' sense of itself/themselves as a civilized society.[46] The Mountie's job in the nation-building was to ensure that "a new [European] society replaced the old [Indigenous peoples] with as little upset as possible."[47] As previously discussed, Mounties were central to the work of "clearing the plains" (as Daschuk terms it), to further the ultimate goal of dispossession of Indigenous peoples. The Mountie is characterized as making the "West safe for settlement," which, according to Canadian historian Daniel Francis, "is one of our basic cultural myths."[48] The Mountie is thus figured as the gentler hand of civilization, one that allows for the exaltation, glorification, and indeed romanticization of Canada's approach to westward colonial expansion.

The iconization and promotion of the Hudson's Bay Company colours in the ceremony ignored a brutal history of economic and mercantilist colonialism and displacement. In a moment that effectively sums up the image oco'88 was hoping to convey, Peter Jennings, in ABC's coverage of the opening ceremony, opined, "Canada is particularly proud of having dealt with its Indians. No Indian wars in Western Canada in the 1800s of any significance . . . There are actually more Indians now in North America than there were at the time of Christopher Columbus."[49] Statements like these, which reflect triumphalist attitudes about the genocide of Indigenous peoples in both Canada and the United States, are precisely why Mandan, Hidatsa, and Arikara scholar Michael Yellow Bird argues that the tropes of the Cowboy and the Indian are indeed the "nation's most passionate, embedded form of hate talk."[50] Ceremonial displays such as Calgary's really only serve as a veneer covering the ongoing legacies of colonization and assimilation. They also downplay the extent to which Indigenous peoples stand in active opposition to these accounts of history. This was reflected in both the criticism of oco'88's approach to inclusion and the response from oco'88 to the criticism.

oco'88 faced strong criticism for what many argued was a largely tokenistic approach to Indigenous involvement in the opening ceremony and the Games overall. oco'88 was criticized, in particular, for allocating $250,000 towards the establishment of what was called the Native Participation Program (NPP). The NPP was established in the middle of 1987 and would result in the organization of a national Native youth conference, a Native fashion show, proposed funding for two Native powwows, and a Native trade exhibition; these were to be taken as evidence of the wider commitment to inclusion. OCO'88 head Frank King argued that "this project has been developed by Native people. It is important we have a Native element, not a token. That old statement, 'let's do something for Indians,' really bothers me, it is tokenism. This exhibition is not."[51] In spite of King's platitudes, however, the nature of Indigenous involvement in the Games was in constant question and plagued with controversy. Some Indigenous representatives, such as Chief Leo Youngman of the Olympic powwow committee, and Bruce Starlight, an organizer for the trade exhibition, withdrew from involvement because of the prohibitively slow pace with which OCO'88 approved and funded the development of programs. Indigenous scholars such as Forsyth and O'Bonsawin have since separately argued that these initiatives were undertaken to draw attention away from Indigenous resistance movements, and to, as O'Bonsawin writes, "ensure that the Calgary Olympics maintained its apolitical veneer."[52]

Part of this apolitical gloss was applied with terminology. The choices made with respect to terminology tell us a great deal about the intent and purpose of inclusion. Within the formal planning documents of the Games, Indigenous peoples are ubiquitously referred to as Native. This is a shift from the use of the term Indian in the 1976 Games. The language reflects the gradual shift towards all-encompassing "pan" terminology, but it also reflects the relationship between politically mobilized Indigenous peoples and Canadian society; the linguistic terrain shifted as Indigenous peoples collaboratively worked to reject the racism encapsulated by the word Indian and called for more respectful terminology.

In spite of this terminological shift, however, the images constructed through the opening ceremony were founded on persistent visions of Indianness held by board members, the majority of whom were settler Canadian. The use of the term Native in the context of the Games does not then reflect a significant shift in ideology but rather a show of political correctness. Despite the flaunting of multiculturalism in policy circles, strongly racist discourses continued to circulate in such moments. We can see this insofar as the figures of the Cowboy and the Native are positioned in relation to one another; ultimately, as Yellow Bird writes, "they are symbolic of the white colonizer's claim of superiority and Indigenous peoples' inferiority."[53] The absence of the word Indian did not change the visual discourse—the ceremony marketed a western heritage built on the backs of subjugated Indigenous peoples, thus showcasing an image of a "western Canada" multiculturalism propped up by pillars of assimilation.

OCO'88's vision for the opening ceremony was a celebration of Calgary's and Canada's western hospitality. This hospitality did not appear, on the surface, to have a direct connection to discourses of multiculturalism. However, as ethnic peoples were drawn into the triangular Native-Cowboy-Mountie core of western hospitality, we see the refinement of Canadian multiculturalism; it appears as a beacon of Canadian national identity, one that is rooted in the assimilation of Indigenous peoples. The inclusion of people in clothing representative of distinct and ethnicized cultural heritages in the ceremony reveals the growing strength of multiculturalism as an important aspect of Canadian identity—but also of a growing awareness of the value of such distinctiveness as a national *resource*. The addition of this fourth prong, really, to the Native-Cowby-Mountie triad allowed Calgary (and by extension Canada) to play up the "welcoming nature" of the Prairies. Taken together, the figures present depicted a coming together of the nation, in which the settling of the West paves the way for the influx of immigrants to the Prairies. In the 1976 ceremony, Indians were imagined as frozen (much like Aboriginal rights would become fixed via the courts) and then absorbed by and integrated into anglophone and francophone societies; with the 1988 ceremony Natives are positioned as part of the foundation of the nation, as exemplary of Canada's originary diversity, whose pacification and restrained inclusion allow for the flourishing of contemporary multiculturalism. Spectators are drawn into this, a storying of Canada's past that refashions the colonization of Prairie Indigenous peoples.

This is echoed in the opening ceremony of the 1988 Games, notably in OCO'88's rejection of the "Indian attack" and "wagon-burning" display. While we could read OCO'88's rejection of these performances as emblematic of a shift away from imagined Indianness and born of greater self-awareness and respect for Indigenous peoples, there may be something else going on. In a climate in which western hospitality and thus multiculturalism were increasingly fashioned as important foundations of Canadian identity, a display wherein "Indians" actively rejected settlement through outright aggression would be less than desirable. To show "Indians" in such a manner, as rejecting the "peaceful hand of assimilation," would in fact highlight those things that the juxtaposition of the Native-Cowboy-Mountie had sought to conceal: the brutal realities of colonization, displacement, and dispossession, as well as, and most critically, First Nations and Métis resistance to Canadianizing the Prairies. Further, the lens through which viewers would interpret "Indian attack" could no longer be guaranteed as positive, as Indigenous peoples had become increasingly (and effectively) politically organized across regional and community lines. Rather than reading such a depiction as a quaint, old-timey narrative of the "wild Canadian West," there was a realistic possibility that people would interpret "Indian attacks" (again, however racist this construction already would be) as acts of resistance to settler encroachment and aggression.

For all its efforts to avoid confronting the realities of Indigenous dissent, the 1988 Olympics and its attending narratives did not go without being challenged. For example, Chief Leo Youngman questioned the lack of meaningful consultation with First Nations. In late May 1987, in a handwritten memo, Powderface refers to Youngman as irritated and as asking for a report on all Olympic projects and activities involving Treaty 7 peoples. Frustrated himself, Powderface mentions in the memo to King and other OCO'88 board members that OCO'88 should have brought the Treaty 7 Chiefs together prior to developing the NPP.[54] Further, and most notably, OCO'88 faced strong criticism in the run-up to the Games for its "beads and feathers" approach from people such as Lubicon Lake Cree leader Bernard Ominayak. This approach to Indigenous inclusion was, he contended, symbolic. In Calgary tensions arose with regard to the contradictions inherent in the sponsorship of certain Games events by big oil companies. Companies such as Shell and Petro-Canada, while sponsoring Indigenous involvement in the Games, are responsible for ecological genocide. Both companies play significant roles in damaging the traditional and contemporary territories of Indigenous peoples through the extraction of oil, specifically in the traditional territory of the Lubicon Nêhiyawak peoples, living approximately four hundred kilometres from Calgary.

In 1986 the Lubicon started a boycott of a museum exhibit, put on to coincide with the Olympics, titled *The Spirit Sings: Artistic Traditions of Canada's First Peoples* (originally titled *Forget Not My World*—changed in response to protest by local Indigenous communities). *The Spirit Sings* was the flagship of the visual arts part of the Olympic Arts Festival and was the "most ambitious and complex museum project ever undertaken in Canada," opening its doors on 14 January 1988 and running until 1 May 1988.[55] The exhibit was installed the following Canada Day, 1 July, in Ottawa for a five-month display. The exhibit itself would accentuate Canada's liberal inclusion of Native peoples and enhance the overall focus on promoting Canadian identity. The popular exhibition cost over $2.5 million; its promoters boasted that it involved "627 rare Indian and Inuit art objects on loan from 82 lenders in 16 countries" and that more than "two-thirds of the objects had never been seen in Canada before."[56] Yet while OCO'88 and various media outlets considered the exhibit to be a resounding success, one major controversy plagued the exhibition.

According to Julia Harrison, the Glenbow coordinating curator for the exhibit, the exhibit was intended to act as "an important vehicle to educate the Canadian people about the native heritage of their country and to bring the wealth of Canadian native materials held in foreign museums to light."[57] Yet, as with the ceremonies themselves, the Lubicon were concerned that such an exhibit—in addition to positioning Indigenous peoples as a *past* presence—in essence made a mockery of the ongoing genocide against their people. The reality of contemporary life for the Lubicon involves the legacy of damage caused by the federal government's persistent denial of a land claim settlement/treaty agreement and the expansion of oil sands development on their land. The exhibit therefore lacked "contemporary Native voice and presence" and as such the Lubicon contended that "the museum needed to promote, rather than deny, the relationship between the historical pieces and the realities of contemporary Native life."[58] As a result, the Lubicon asked museums from around the world, those from whom artifacts were requested, not to transfer any artifacts to the exhibition.

Shell Canada had since the 1950s been drilling for oil in the lands that the Lubicon identified as their traditional territory—"unlike most of the other Aboriginal groups in Alberta, [the Lubicon] was not a party to any treaty, and therefore was without the settlement rights and reserve land provided under these agreements."[59] The drilling posed a significant threat to the ecosystem of the Lubicon's traditional territory under claim and by extension posed significant threat to the survival of the people who engaged in hunting and trapping. Shell Canada, as a part of what OCO'88 affectionately referred to as "Team Petroleum'88," co-sponsored *The Spirit Sings* with the federal government.[60] While OCO'88 felt it had to allow equal participation to major oil corporations who served as both Olympic sponsors and as the backbone of Calgary's economy (and by extension its identity as a city), the Lubicon deemed it highly problematic that Shell should sponsor *The Spirit Sings* while directly "engaged in destroying the traditional economy and way of life of the Lubicon Lake Cree."[61] As Olympic scholars Kevin Wamsley and Michael Heine write, "The exhibition itself gradually became the focus of the boycott since its very existence was assured only as the result of a substantial grant from Shell Oil Canada Ltd."[62]

According to Chief Ominayak, "The irony of using a display of North American Indian artefacts to attract people to the Winter Olympics being organized by interests who are still actively seeking to destroy Indian people, seems obvious."[63] Representatives from Glenbow met with the Lubicon, who reportedly (according to curator Harrison) had "no objection to the content of the exhibition but only to its sponsorship and association with the Calgary Olympics."[64] Harrison responded to the objections by offering that "Museums, like Universities, are expected by the[ir] constitutions, to remain non-partisan."[65] The Lubicon retorted that by accepting Shell's sponsorship the museum was anything but non-partisan—it had already taken a political stand, to which Harrison countered that there is no "evidence that the public confuses corporate support for corporate policy."[66] Yet for an exhibit which claimed to be about respecting and honouring Indigenous peoples to accept sponsorship monies from a corporation directly contributing to the environmental genocide of Indigenous peoples was, for the Lubicon, a decidedly politicized (and personal) act—regardless of public perceptions of that act. This exchange highlights the significant tension between shifting discourses with respect to Indigenous peoples and the contradictions at the heart of efforts to incorporate Indigenous peoples within an Olympic paradigm and within sites of local and national image-making. The Lubicon Lake resistance to the Games pokes holes in the seamless entrenchment of Calgary's western hospitality myth and Canada's attempt to mobilize Indigenous peoples as multicultural resources for the nation's public image.

The shift in language from "Indian" in 1976 to "Native" in 1988 is undoubtedly a reflection of the fact that Indigenous peoples shifted the discursive terrain of Olympic meaning-making. It could also be said that OCO'88 saw this as an opportunity to appear politically correct while remaking Nativeness via its own visions for enhancing Canada's national identity; given the development of globalization and the rise of neoliberalism, this willingness to adopt new terminology also marks a gradual shift towards Indigenous peoples as a vital resource for Canada's nation-branding project. The Calgary Games laid the groundwork for the organizing committee of the 2010 Vancouver Olympics to cultivate a predetermined vision of Aboriginality, intended to signal a turning point in Canada's relationship to/with Indigenous peoples. Yet such inclusion functions as a discursive, yet also economic, counterpart to political/judicial attempts at the very same thing—to do the bare minimum in order to pacify Indigenous dissent while rhetorically splitting Indigenous peoples into "good" and "bad." Ultimately nothing is done to destabilize the power that the state continues to try to exercise over Indigenous peoples and lands.

Vancouver 2010: *Aboriginality*

The bid committee for what would become the Vancouver Games identified two major faults of past Games: OCO'88's failure to account for Indigenous resistance and Indigenous peoples' efforts to use the global spotlight to amplify their voices, and the lack of authenticity in the 1976 closing ceremony alongside the exclusion of Indigenous artistic programming from the Games. In response, two competing narratives have appeared regarding the origins of Indigenous involvement with the Vancouver Olympics. One narrative suggests that the bid committee opted to engage in inclusive planning by consulting with the Skwxwú7mesh (Squamish) and Lil'Wat, whose traditional territories overlapped in the Whistler area to be used for the bulk of the Games. By 2001, bid organizers began working with the provincial government and sought to acquire the support and endorsement of the Skwxwú7mesh and Lil'Wat throughout the bidding process.[67] The other narrative asserts that the Vancouver/Whistler 2010 Bid Society (hereafter referred to as Bid Society) did not permit the formal participation of either the Skwxwú7mesh or Lil'Wat Nations and that it was the Indian Act–elected band council chiefs from both First Nations who, as early as 1998, approached the Bid Society, asserting that since the Games would take place on their lands and within their traditional territories they must be involved.[68]

While they were not ultimately accorded any formal inclusion at this early stage, the Skwxwú7mesh Nation wrote a letter of support and the Bid Society "recognized the value of incorporating Aboriginal participation in the planning and hosting of the 2010 Games, through its referencing of Aboriginal participation throughout its domestic bid submission."[69] In 1999, tours of prospective host cities were curtailed, following a scandal with respect to the Salt Lake City bid. By the time Vancouver was preparing its bid, bid books had come to be widely used in cities' Olympic pitches. IOC selection committee members were expected to analyze books and videos and focus primarily on city features and technical aspects. With the aforementioned concerns in mind, the Bid Society, by then transformed into a formal bid committee, created rich, visually evocative books that proudly proclaimed that Vancouver's "embrace of multiculturalism uniquely position[s] Vancouver to host the world. Canada brings together the cultures of the world, as well as an ancient and rich First Nations culture, in one harmonious society."[70] The bid books further suggested that Canada "is a living mosaic of peoples and cultures from around the world. Virtually every nation has joined Canada's First Nations, making us a truly multicultural society."[71] Almost immediately, then, the bid committee drew on an as-yet undefined relationship with the Skwxwú7mesh and Lil'Wat in order to highlight the city's "natural multiculturalism" and, in particular, the nation's "historical predisposition" towards social and cultural equality and harmony.[72] This rhetoric was accompanied with colourful visual renderings of west coast First Nations art.

The newly formed Vancouver/Whistler 2010 Winter Olympic and Paralympic Games Bid Corporation (hereafter referred to as Bid Corporation) took a two-pronged approach towards putting this concept of inclusive planning in practice. First, they attempted to generate broader support from Indigenous peoples "outside of the Nations involved" through the "development of an Aboriginal Participation Strategy" guided by a non-Indigenous employee seconded from BC Hydro, and the creation of the position title "Director of Community and Aboriginal Relations."[73] Second, First Nations were offered financial incentives, directly linked to commercial values in terms of the Games.[74] Janice Forsyth, a leading scholar of Indigenous peoples' involvement with the Olympics, notes the Musqueam and Tsleil-Waututh were two other First Nations engaged in early negotiations, but given that "no new venues were planned for development" on their lands, they held considerably less negotiating power than the Skwxwú7mesh and Lil'Wat.[75] At least initially, then, a number of separate financial agreements were made, primarily with the Skwxwú7mesh and Lil'Wat First Nations and the Bid Corporation (and later, the official organizing committee for the Vancouver Olympics).

Most of these financial agreements, named "financial legacies," involved the exchange or promise of money and/or economic development opportunities; in return the Skwxwú7mesh and Lil'Wat would offer support of future/timely building projects for the Games. In November 2002, the Bid Corporation and the Province of British Columbia collaborated on a financial agreement (often referred to as the "Shared Legacies Agreement") with the Sḵwx̱wú7mesh and Lil'Wat First Nations. In this agreement, the most notable of outcomes was the Sḵwx̱wú7mesh's and Lil'Wat's consent to future development of the Callaghan Valley Nordic Competition Venue for ski jumping and other related events.[76] This agreement was made on a bed of feel-good claims to environmentalism—claims that indicated that construction and development would proceed in a way that was respectful of the people and of the environment.

In another agreement, the provincial government granted what it deemed three hundred acres of Crown land (in fact unceded land), "the value of which is provided for within the Province's $600 million Games funding commitment . . . for the Sḵwx̱wú7mesh and Lil'wat First Nations to pursue economic development opportunities within their shared territories."[77] The province's funding commitment would also extend to the creation of an "Olympic Housing Legacy," by which "the Bid Corporation agreed to allocate a portion of the planned Whistler Athletes' Village, valued at $6.5 million, as a post-Games housing legacy for the Sḵwx̱wú7mesh and Lil'wat First Nations."[78] For the 2003–2004 fiscal year, the province further agreed to commit $3 million "to the Aboriginal Sports Legacy Fund, which is managed by the 2010 Legacies Now Society and the Sḵwx̱wú7mesh and Lil'wat Nations."[79] These financial legacies intensified in the wake of Vancouver's successful bid when, on 2 July 2003, Vancouver was selected to host the 2010 Winter Olympics. In the 2006–2007 fiscal year, the province agreed to transfer three hundred acres of fee simple lands (back) to the Sḵwx̱wú7mesh and Lil'Wat, at a value of approximately $13 million.

As is typical within celebration capitalism's state of exception, the agreement sidestepped legal, collective land claims processes, while dedicating acquired private ownership lands for the purposes of economic development. This transfer was contingent on the Sḵwx̱wú7mesh and Lil'Wat agreeing to find ways to use the lands for economic development. The Vancouver Organizing Committee (VANOC) prepared its own recommendations as to how the Sḵwx̱wú7mesh and Lil'Wat should use the land, most notably championing tourism-oriented initiatives such as the construction of a public golf course, a Nordic lodge, and either a recreational campground or housing.[80] The way that land was purportedly returned, with a myriad of strings attached, reflects the core of Aboriginal recognition processes vis-à-vis the Canadian state. Such requirements reflect the bounded and limited way Indigenous self-determination is seen in the era of Aboriginality/Aboriginalism. It is illusory in its promise of autonomy while deeply embedded in colonial power structures.

Nevertheless, as discussed with respect to previous Games, Indigenous peoples (particularly those located in Olympic host regions) have always advocated for their own interests. In this case, while the Skwx̱wú7mesh and Lil'Wat received the majority of financial incentives for their involvement with the Games, all four First Nations mentioned did nevertheless come together in the wake of the successful bid for the Games in 2004, forming a non-profit corporation called the Four Host First Nations Society (FHFN). The FHFN signed a separate formal Protocol Agreement with VANOC in November of that same year. Unlike earlier agreements with the Skwx̱wú7mesh and Lil'Wat, the Protocol Agreement was largely promissory, offering a verbal commitment to the development of future opportunities in exchange for the FHFN's support (verbal, visual, and otherwise) of VANOC. On the surface it would appear that the Agreement, in fact, arose from FHFN's straightforward, good-natured endorsement and promotion of "harmony, sharing, education, fairness and partnership" before and during the Games.[81] Yet the entire so-called relationship, as seen in earlier agreements made with the Skwx̱wú7mesh and Lil'Wat, was founded on the furthering of capitalist interests. On both sides, be it the financial interests of First Nations or the financial interests of VANOC (linked to those of the City of Vancouver, the province, and Canada), this agreement-making was not simply a desire to demonstrate amicable relations; it was principally about maximizing the accumulation of wealth for selected parties.

If it were about more than this, then, as Forsyth shows, the Musqueam and Tsleil-Waututh would have been treated on par with the Skwx̱wú7mesh and Lil'Wat in the relationship. The only time this occurred was with respect to the branding of the Games. The FHFN's formal logo demonstrates the way in which VANOC sought to incorporate visions of Aboriginality into the spectacle of the Games—Games that were more inclusive than the financial agreements that underpinned them. Jody Broomfield of the Skwx̱wú7mesh Nation designed the FHFN logo, which "features four faces representing each of the Four Host First Nations encased in a rim representative of the Creator and their ancestors."[82] The logo also features "four feathers in the centre [that] point to the cardinal directions and can also be seen as open, out-stretched arms, welcoming and inviting athletes and people from around the world to the 2010 Winter Olympic Games in Vancouver and Whistler."[83] With no acknowledgement of the imbalances between the agreements made with the various First Nations, the logo portrays the symbolic equality of each. All four First Nations accorded VANOC a touchpoint signalling Indigenous peoples' approval of the Games. Fiscal partnerships converged with the cultural branding and marketing of the FHFN in such a way as to mask the consumptive sickness at the heart of the Games. The 2010 Vancouver Olympics were heavily invested in consuming Indigenous peoples, lands, and resources, while working to portray this consumption as rooted in a partnership by mutual agreement and for mutual benefit.

Branding Aboriginality

While many positive initiatives grew out of the FHFN and VANOC partnership, a critical assessment is necessary of "the employment of politically persuasive visual imagery that has been outside, and at times in opposition to, the FHFN Protocol Agreement" for the precise reasons laid out above.[84] Instead of generating recognition for the independence of First Nations (and Indigenous peoples more broadly), the VANOC-FHFN partnership was often used to lend symbolic legitimacy to the nation's core ideas about its multicultural identity. In part buoyed by the constitutionalizing of "aboriginal peoples" in 1982 and the rise of political activism among First Nations, Inuit, and Métis, by the time the bid and planning of the 2010 Vancouver Winter Olympics took place, the term Aboriginal as a noun was widely used as shorthand to refer to the three broad groups the term constitutionally encapsulates. With the force of the FHFN behind it, VANOC promoted Aboriginality as one of the defining narratives of the Games. Both the Bid Corporation and VANOC used the relationships with local First Nations as a platform for crafting a Canadian Olympic narrative of Canadianized Aboriginality, a story about a nation living in harmony with nature and with its Aboriginal peoples.

According to VANOC CEO John Furlong[85] in his Olympic memoir *Patriot Hearts*, Opening Coordinator David Atkins came up with the idea of foregrounding this story by having representatives from "Canada's First Nations . . . welcome the athletes of the world to their country"; this would help show, he rationalized, the *truth* of Canada's relationship to "its" Indigenous population, and that VANOC could "use the moment to give the world a real insight into Canada's view of the Aboriginal community."[86] The committee decided it would dress Indigenous youth in what Furlong referred to as *"modernized versions of their tribal regalia to create the colour and pageantry for which we were striving."*[87] Wanting to keep their plans for the opening under wraps, Furlong writes that the dancers for the ceremony were Indigenous youth whom VANOC had invited to Vancouver under the auspices of participating in an "Indigenous Youth Gathering" in the two weeks leading up to the opening of the Games. On the day after the opening the youth would be sent home. Once the youth arrived in Vancouver, organizers would launch a guerrilla-style surprise on the youth, revealing to them their participation in the "big show" of the opening ceremony. Furlong recalls, "We had to get between 300 and 400 young people to Vancouver and keep them quiet about what they were here for once they arrived. We decided to invite them to Vancouver for a Native youth forum and added the confidential piece about the ceremonies *when we had them locked in a hall in Squamish*, a week or so before the Games."[88]

At the outset of the opening ceremony, as the chiefs of the FHFN took their seats as temporary Olympic heads of state, members of the FHFN nations, dressed in "traditional" regalia, stepped into the Olympic arena. Pillars constructed to resemble icy totem poles rose from the floor to face the four directions of north, east, south, and west (Figure 3). The FHFN logo illuminated the ground as each of the Four Host First Nations offered Indigenous-language and English-language greetings, raising their arms in a sign of welcome. The participants then moved to the centre of the floor and began to play a big drum that rose from the ground in front of them. The announcers proceeded to welcome "the Aboriginal peoples of Canada," as group-by-group, Indigenous youth from "the North," "the Métis Nation," "the Inuit," "the First Nations of the Prairies," and "the First Nations of the East" danced their way into the arena.

The Olympic announcer wrapped up this opening Aboriginal segment as the Indigenous youth finished entering the arena, announcing that, "on behalf of all Canadians, the Aboriginal peoples of Canada welcome the athletes of the 21st winter games."[89] The athletes entered the stadium while the Indigenous youth hung back, and the presentation gradually and methodically became less Aboriginal-focused. Bryan Adams and Nelly Furtado sang atop the giant drum; athletes and Indigenous peoples made their way from the staging area; the drum and the totems sank back into the floor (soon followed by Adams and Furtado).

Figure 3. A scene from the 2010 Vancouver Winter Olympics Opening Ceremony. Photo by Sue Curtis and Martin Curtis, https://commons.wikimedia.org/wiki/File:Vancouver_2010_opening_ceremony.jpg.

Obvious markers of Aboriginality and Aboriginal distinctiveness disappeared and were replaced by simulations that referenced a pan-Canadian landscape.

As the scene transitioned to the main cultural section, "Landscape of a Dream," totem poles were replaced by a simulated frozen tundra with a whitish floor and glittering "snowflakes." Donald Sutherland, the narrator of the segment, began to share a story of an Indigenous-to-Canadian transition—of immigration and diverse peoples coming together on shared land. As Sutherland spoke, a figure cloaked in fur and carrying a large stick led other shrouded, cold-looking people, donning all-white pseudo-hide winterwear, braids, and headdresses, onto the simulated tundra. Once the lead figure began banging his staff into the ground, digitized waves moved out across the tundra, and the people stood in awe as a glittery illuminated wolf, eagle, buffalo, and bear in turn materialized above them. The ground shifted, and a spirit bear (also known as a "kermode bear" among some First Nations) rose from the base of the stage. The tundra began to "melt," and the people drifted away from one another on faux floes as flashing whales ushered out the spirit bear.

The display transitioned towards the "Sacred Grove" segment, where projections of totem poles (in a nod to Euro-Canadian painter Emily Carr) rose from the ground and transformed into a grouping of Douglas fir trees. The people who shed their nomadic winter wear re-emerged on the scene wearing "contemporary clothes" and broke into a ballet-inspired dance. The ceremony continued with images connected to various regions of Canada and expressions of Canadianness—minus Aboriginality. Visual references to Aboriginality and Indigenous participants were all but absent as the ceremony moved through the regions of Canada. Although VANOC declared that the "Landscape" segment was intended to signify the diverse regions of Canada, it might be more accurately described as the "Bering Strait Theory on Olympic (Fake) Ice." While Aboriginality dominated the beginning of the narrative, Aboriginality is gradually phased out and the end of the segment leaves spectators with the "modern" Canadians who live side-by-side in harmony.

I recall feeling apprehensive while watching the entire opening ceremony. I wanted so much to like the display and to allow myself to sink into an Aboriginalized settler nationalist bliss. But the juxtaposition of narratives—locally specific, broadly Aboriginal, all used as a touchpoint for reinforcing Canada's multicultural brand—led to a great deal of confusion. The confusion, I felt, is perhaps best echoed by Cherokee scholar-blogger Adrienne Keene of the

Native Appropriations blog. Keene writes, "I have very mixed feelings about the opening ceremonies—on one hand, it was fantastic to see the extensive Native presence (when has the US ever done anything like this?) and a lot of it was culturally sensitive and true portrayals."[90] On the other hand, she notes, there were "cringe worthy moments" like the icy tundra scene that "just felt a little stereotyped—mystical Native guy tied to nature brings magic to the 'normal' community—oh look, his magic created the constellations in the night sky!"[91]

Lisa Charleyboy of the *Urban Native Girl* blog also expresses a sense of disillusionment, writing that while she felt "proud that Native peoples were being included and celebrated" and recognized as partners by the IOC, she "can't help feeling like it's a little token."[92] She identifies the many reasons Canada would not want to offer a national narrative that was a little more honest, writing of "its long legacy of genocide toward the Native people of this country . . . We have so many health, poverty, education, social issues which have many people living in third world conditions right here in Canada, in our backyards."[93] Ryan McMahon (better known in his comedic form Clarence Two Toes) writes on his website, "Who doesn't like [among other things]: CG'd Whales; Modern Dance; canned music performances; [and] Ashley MacIsaac holding it down on the fiddle."[94] He also acknowledges, however, that as soon as discussions began about the Games, so too did discussions about "how the host city would hide its 'problems' . . . Vancouver's lower East side is known to be as rough as it gets, and while some money was spent on 'programs and services' for these folks, displacing them seems to be the answer VANOC, the city of Vancouver, and moreover—Canada, seemed to go with."[95]

McMahon's assessment is spot on. In the years leading up to the bid and to the Games, the City of Vancouver, the Province of British Columbia, and Canada faced a "public relations nightmare" with regard to reports in American news media which chastised Vancouver for its "questionable" street population, citing the danger the people of the Downtown Eastside (DTES) posed to tourists. For example, in July 2006, *The Economist* offered up an unflattering review of Vancouver as Olympic host city: "the once-pleasant downtown . . . causes [the] most alarm. Homeless panhandlers yell at theatre-goers, while young addicts deal drugs on street corners. They spill out from the Downtown East Side, an area of decrepit boarding houses, sleazy bars, and boarded-up shops infamous for the country's highest rates of poverty and drug addiction."[96] A couple of months later, the *Vancouver Sun* indicated that *The Economist* had fallen out of love with Vancouver and was "holding its editorial nose at the human detritus stinking up our downtown core."[97] While *The Economist* does not make specific reference to Indigenous peoples, who make up a disproportionately high number of DTES residents (estimates range from 40 to 70 per cent), as John O'Neil of Simon Fraser University stated, "In some people's minds, it's [DTES is] the largest reserve in Canada."[98] Sex work, panhandling, homelessness, and visible poverty are endemic in the DTES. In the case of the Indigenous residents, many of these issues are attributable to the continuing effects of colonial policy, the Indian Act, residential schooling, and the reserve system, as are the disappearances of Indigenous women—a large number at the hands of serial killer Robert Pickton (arrested in 2002). The homeless, poor, sex workers, and drug-addicted were figured as problems to the city's image and subjected to excessive legislation, anti-panhandling, anti-prostitution, and anti-homelessness laws in the form of the provincial Safe Streets Act (2004) and Vancouver's Project Civil City (2006) initiative in the run-up to the Games.

Project Civil City came in the wake of Vancouver's attempts at introducing bylaws to regulate panhandling (1999) and British Columbia's reluctant commitment to Ontario-style methods through the introduction of its own Safe Streets Act. The concern in Vancouver was that panhandling had become more *aggressive* since the city's recession in the 1990s, a trend Prashan Ranasinghe maps through an analysis of local print-media portrayals of panhandling encounters.[99] In response to an increasingly vocal collective of business owners and local politicians disillusioned by the Safe Streets Act, the City of Vancouver launched Project Civil City to reclaim and ensure "civility on our streets."[100] Project Civil City was hailed as an effort to "restore the public's sense of personal safety, promote civic pride, and encourage personal responsibility through incremental change."[101] Beyond the hype, however, it had a dark side.

The Safe Streets Act was not repealed, however, and worked in tandem with Project Civil City, the latter centred on sweeping promises to substantially reduce homelessness, the open drug market, and aggressive panhandling, and to increase public satisfaction with "the City's handling of public nuisance and annoyance complaints" by 2010. While not directly attributed to the impending Olympics within initiative documents or by Ranasinghe, 2010 was set as the benchmark date for improvements through Project Civil City. Karla Fetrow links Project Civil City to Vancouver's efforts to "present itself as affluent and thriving" in the "tradition of most cities that have sponsored the Olympics."

The result of such efforts is that they criminalized the poor: "As part of Project Civil City, new laws have passed to make begging for money and sleeping outdoors criminal acts, new garbage cans make it difficult to dig through, and new outside benches make it impossible to lie down."[102] While Project Civil City is cloaked in the language of civility, its fundamental position is that the ways that Vancouver's poor residents live are inherently criminal.

Why is a discussion of Vancouver's street-cleaning initiatives relevant in a discussion of Indigenous participation in the 2010 Olympics? Even though, as previously mentioned, Indigenous people live in the DTES in high numbers, nowhere in the particulars of Project Civil City or in Ranasinghe's analysis is there mention of their overrepresentation. Most importantly, there is no mention of the serious systemic issues at work in the social construction of the DTES, namely the intergenerational effects of Canada's colonial projects and the enduring systemic racism within the nation. There is a cruel irony in that at the same time Indigenous peoples were unfairly targeted and disappeared by both the Safe Streets Act and Project Civil City, they were sought after as featured performers in the ceremonies as a display of regionalism and nationalism. Civil city and safe streets acts are themselves hallmarks of the neoliberal era (as seen with the Mike Harris Ontario government's Safe Streets Act of 1999);[103] for Indigenous peoples they are calling cards of neoliberal colonialism—the ongoing dispossession and displacement of Indigenous peoples, but this time under the banner of doing what is right for the market. Thus, the narrative produced during the Olympics is one that split Indigenous peoples into "good" Aboriginal peoples who fell in line with Canada's new "Aboriginalized settler nationalism," and those that needed to be hidden so as not to counter-narrate Canada's Olympic identity.

To reflect on the city's unwillingness to account for the effects of colonialism and racism in victimizing Indigenous peoples is to hold to account the way *racial neoliberalism* operates at municipal levels but also more broadly within the nation. The mistreatment, marginalization, and criminalization of Indigenous peoples living on the streets in Vancouver, in juxtaposition to the selection and exhibition of Indigenous peoples for official Olympic participation, reveals the way Olympic representations of national identity are deeply tied to racist representations. Indigenous peoples who could not (and perhaps would not) conform to the representations desired by Olympic organizers, by virtue of their socio-economic status or problems with drug addiction (those who failed to meet the vision that VANOC had for its "Aboriginal" component of the Games), were systematically removed from the sightlines of Vancouver's streets.

From this position, then, the FHFN agreement served as a politics of public distraction that the Canadian state, the province, the city, and VANOC drew on to deflect attention and criticism. Fetrow writes that VANOC's relationship with the FHFN was enacted to portray relations between Indigenous peoples and the Canadian government as peaceable and harmonious. This was visually reinforced with chiefs from the FHFN being positioned as temporary Olympic heads of state in the 2010 opening ceremony, with the centring of members of the FHFN in the early portion of the opening, with the FHFN's traditional language greetings, and with the FHFN logo on the ground of BC Place Stadium. The spectacle of the Games made it appear as though VANOC's effort to develop a relationship with local Indigenous peoples was both positive and generative—and that Aboriginal relations were based on inclusion, multiculturalism, equality, agreement, consent. Through its partnership with FHFN, VANOC apparently assumed that in exchange for economic compromises, nearly every cultural site of the 2010 Olympic Games could involve an uncontested representation of Aboriginal peoples that they could claim had been explicitly approved (and implicitly authenticated) by local First Nations.[104]

Fetrow argues that while the agreements made with the FHFN may have positively impacted the economic status of "between five and six thousand members" of the FHFN, most of the Indigenous population of Vancouver, representing a much wider array of Indigenous nations, consisting of "approximately 60,000 people" in total, were negatively impacted by the Olympics.[105] This is in part why a larger resistance movement sprung up under the banner "No Olympics on Stolen Native Land" (Figure 4). In addition to furthering the criminalization of Indigenous peoples, as editor of No2010.com Gord Hill argued, the Olympics were having "huge social and environmental impacts, including ecological destruction along the Sea-to-Sky Highway, [through] the venues constructed in Whistler, [and from] the massive amounts of concrete used in all related construction work."[106] The No Olympics on Stolen Native Land movement also addressed the issues of unresolved land claims in BC First Nations territories, and inadequate housing for Indigenous peoples on the streets of Vancouver.

The resistance movements arose because people were aware Indigenous involvement was little more than symbolic posturing intended to prevent

Figure 4. The wall of a building depicting the anti-Olympic movement Non aux Olympiques sur des Terres Volées—No Olympics on Stolen Native Land. The artwork of Gord Hill featured prominently within anti-Olympic movements and this image became synonymous with Indigenous peoples' and non-Indigenous peoples' opposition to the Olympics. Photo by Ambiguous Furry Rocking Thing, https://commons.wikimedia.org/wiki/File:Non_aux_Olympiques_sur_des_Terres_Volées_-_No_Olympics_on_Stolen_Native_Land.jpg.

demonstrations and protest regarding land usage and unresolved land claims: "VANOC has made considerable efforts to ensure indigenous visibility and economic support in the organizing and hosting of the Games. Large sums of Olympic dollars are being directed at indigenous programming and economic projects within communities; however, a troubling reality looms overhead: the Vancouver 2010 Olympic Winter Games are being hosted on unceded and nonsurrendered indigenous lands."[107] Internal documents from the Vancouver Bid Corporation drafted prior to the establishment of the Skwxwú7mesh and Lil'Wat partnership indicate that they foresaw Indigenous resistance and articulated the need for drumming up some proactive (yet symbolic) First Nations support: "If the First Nations perceive that their rights are not being acknowledged and accommodated by British Columbia, they may go to the media, take direct action, or initiate litigation. This would have a negative impact on the bid."[108] VANOC's inclusive posture, rather than growing from a genuine ethic of care and respect, arose from a desire to pre-emptively pacify dissent.

An additional benefit VANOC derived from its formal partnership with the FHFN was using it as a forum to publicly address the opposition voiced by Indigenous peoples. The FHFN took up a defensive posture in relationship to the partnership, one that included publicly condemning anti-Olympic protests that challenged, among other things, the ecological destruction caused by the Games. Those resisting the Games were "playing into the politics of appropriation that put us into this situation in the first place."[109] FHFN CEO Tewanee Joseph painted anti-Olympics protesters as "non-Aboriginal naysayers . . . [who] want us to remain forever the Dime Store Indian . . . We fought to participate in the Games. As full partners . . . That is why few Aboriginal people are likely to be swayed by salvoes of warmed-over, anti-corporate rhetoric. That is yesterday's news for the Aboriginal people of this country."[110] The FHFN aggressively defended themselves in media releases claiming that protestors of the Games were "a tiny group of self-described 'anti-racism' demonstrators who claim to be acting on behalf of Indigenous peoples in British Columbia" and who were attempting to "steal the voice" of the FHFN.[111] Yet by its own admission, the Bid Corporation, and by extension VANOC, saw the involvement of the respective host nations as a largely symbolic gesture.

Perhaps the most problematic part of the symbolic power held by the VANOC-FHFN partnership is that it conceals the fact that the relationship was predicated on a corporate partnership, a non-profit-to-non-profit partnership, whereby, as the FHFN writes on their website, they are "incorporated [as] a non-profit society."[112] That FHFN elected to incorporate themselves is not at issue, but under current federal regulation any group that wishes to receive funding support in any form requires a business number and registration, in accordance with regulations governing Canadian businesses, as a corporation. This reveals that FHFN is subject, like any other organization, to the laws and regulations of Canada; the FHFN (all illusions aside) does not enter into the partnership on equal terms and with equal footing. This is one of the central problems with the way the 2010 Olympics were presented—they offered an illusion of Aboriginal equality, partnership, and freedom, while reinforcing the power Canada tries so desperately to wield over Indigenous peoples.

Conclusion

At a superficial level, the narratives produced within each of the ceremonies represent noble gestures—the incorporation of Indigenous peoples into the multiculturalism fabric of Canadian national identity. As mentioned at the outset, in this project I am not preoccupied with questions of why people choose to participate in Olympic narratives produced for them. The reasons for participation are complex and I respect them; some people see the ceremonies as a break from their everyday lives, as a chance to be on television, to meet athletes, to reclaim images produced; others become involved as a continuation of a long tradition of acting as "'show Indians' in the entertainment industry."[113] Some, such as the FHFN, appear to be motivated by significant financial concessions and incentives that promise to revitalize their communities. Some participants view the Olympics, even in their problematic state, as a possible site for awareness-raising, truth-telling, and resistance. All of these positions need to be respected given the detrimental effects of colonization—specifically the insistence that Indigenous peoples behave in uniform fashion.

This insistence that Indigenous peoples speak with one voice is a longstanding problem; although outside the scope of this project, it nevertheless needs to be acknowledged. This is why it is important to listen carefully to voices of resistance, for they reveal to us, as Forsyth and Wamsley state, Canada's attempts to use multiculturalism's supposed good intent to conceal the extent of the colonial relationship and its resonances in the present. In 1976 French-Canadian dancers led Indigenous peoples through a multicultural tribute that was a contrived performance of Plains-style Indianness, a performance that left many spectators frustrated by the use of so many French Canadians in place of more "real" Indians. In 1988 there were no Euro-Canadians "playing Indian," as Indigenous peoples were presented as one of three core figures (Native-Cowboy-Mountie) at the heart of Calgary's regional identity. Janice Forsyth and Kevin Wamsley write that while OCO'88 counted on the draw of "Aboriginal imagery" to attract tourists to Calgary, they ultimately "ignored issues of concern to the Aboriginal peoples around them."[114] Yet OCO'88 did not draw on "Aboriginal imagery," instead putting forth an image of Nativeness that was still explicitly tied to fantasies of Indianness, propping up narratives that would more accurately be understood as glorifying Canada's westward expansion and colonial nation-building project.

By 2010, however, Olympic organizers offered a narrative that repressed histories of colonial oppression and genocidal nation-building through the presentation of an inclusive, "Aboriginalized" Canadian national brand identity. The 2010 ceremonies were the first Games to bring together First Nations, Métis, and Inuit, those broader classifications of Indigenous peoples recognized by Canada's 1982 Constitution Act as populations of "Aboriginal peoples." They were presented as the core of Canadian diversity, naturally assimilated via innocent processes of immigration, and ultimately a willing partner in the establishment of the nation. The narrative VANOC promoted derided histories of colonial oppression and genocidal nation-building in order to present an inclusive, "Aboriginalized" Canadian national identity. Aboriginal rights receive no mention in framing this relationship; it is one oriented purely towards economic exchange, couched in the language of multicultural inclusion and partnership. Aboriginal is thus put to work as a harbinger of Canada's liberal multiculturalism.

But more than that, Aboriginalism, as seen here, and Indigenous peoples' willingness to take on the discourse of Aboriginality, provide Canadians with a foundation to split Indigenous peoples. Good Aboriginal people accept corporate partnerships in lieu of true self-determination and with little complaint; by contrast, bad Aboriginal people are positioned as failures, unable to properly assimilate—not because they bear the deep wounds of systemic illness, pain, and grief arising from colonial violence, but because they, individually, have failed to put themselves on a path of "economic betterment." Those who oppose the Games are cast outside of good Aboriginality. This opposition is akin to, as Kanien'kehá:ka political anthropologist Audra Simpson writes, a politics of refusal. In the context of her home community of Kahnawà:ke, Simpson asks, "What happens when we refuse what all (presumably) 'sensible' people perceive as good things?"[115] When Indigenous peoples refuse to give up "being Indigenous" (as Alfred and Corntassel put it) by engaging in neoliberal colonialism, inhabiting the category of Aboriginality in exchange for limited financial gain, they are positioned, to build on Simpson's work, as somehow outside a "natural" order of reason. But Simpson also crucially points out that if we meaningfully consider Indigenous peoples in the projection of the "good" and what is perceived to be "good," the very conceptualization of good finds itself on shaky ground. As Simpson writes, "from this perspective, we see that a good is not a good for everyone."[116] To this end, the voices of dissent, then, lend an important counterbalance to the Olympic narratives produced. They also provide a fundamental challenge not only to the material consequences of the Games, but also to their symbolic intent and meaning, blowing apart the dark heart of Canada's Aboriginalized multiculturalism.

Overall we see a gradual shift in Olympic narratives towards reimagining Canada as a "culturally tolerant cosmopolitan," which in effect "facilitat[es] a more fashionable and politically acceptable form of white supremacy, which has had greater currency within a neo-colonial, neo-liberal global order."[117] As it has continuously been adapted, from 1976 to 1988 to 2010, multicultural discourse around the Olympics conceals the basis of state-Olympic-Indigenous relationships that are still "built on racism and colonial exploitation" and effectively "foment[s] a wider confusion about Indigenous peoples as an ethnic minority within Canada's multicultural milieu."[118] Aboriginality is the latest in a series of attempts at generating a pacifying national discourse, the effect of which is that as it celebrates diversity it obliterates histories of difference and insists that all peoples now, regardless of cultural difference, are equally Canadian.

By rendering Indigenous peoples as a part of the multicultural milieu, Olympic narratives minimize the significant histories of colonization and racist marginalization while at the same time assuaging white settler guilt and anxiety. They encourage a public act of forgetting, inducing an historical amnesia in order to make easy work of the repackaging, rebranding, and selling of the national narrative. The production of positive narratives and the use of Indigenous symbols have sought to conceal that race and racism towards Indigenous peoples are not merely "intrinsic parts of the discourse of the nation";[119] they, in fact, have provided the very foundation of the nation, which is why the state has consistently put forth nostalgic recollections of pasts filled with harmonious relationships to Indigenous peoples, and of a present based on mutual partnership and respect—despite evidence to the contrary. The confusion caused by these narratives has served to effectively obscure the fact that, in contemporary society, Aboriginalized multiculturalism has been mobilized for the purpose of branding national identities, and in the context of an increasingly corporatized national interest.

Selling Aboriginal Experiences and Authenticity: Canadian and Aboriginal Tourism

One evening, my partner alerted me to a breaking news report about tourists to the Andaman Islands who bribed local police in order to "view" Indigenous Jarawa peoples.[1] Video footage leaked to the media shows tourists and tour leaders throwing bananas and biscuits to the people while demanding that they dance and eat the strewn food. As partially nude women and children sing and dance, one particularly insistent guide demands that a woman refusing to move should dance for the food that has just been thrown at her feet, with the promise of more to come as a reward for her dancing.[2] The spectacle is gut-wrenchingly callous and dehumanizing. I recalled Canadian historian Daniel Francis's reference in *The Imaginary Indian* to English traveller Edward Roper, who on a journey through the Plains in the late nineteenth century, was disappointed by the lack of "authentic Indians" he saw. Upon realizing that all he would see were dirty and hungry-looking "Indians," Roper decided to entertain himself by throwing coins and oranges from the back of the train "to watch young Native[s] scramble in the dust for them."[3] Although a century apart, what the juxtaposition of these two incidents reveals is the continuity of tourist fascination with "primitives."

While the the Jarawa incident and Roper's experience reflect a dark side of tourism in both a contemporary and historical context, in recent decades some Indigenous peoples have embraced (with varying degrees of enthusiasm) a reworked form of tourism as a means of economic development. Some have posited tourism as a pathway for a reclaimed self-determination and resurgence of their people, and as such there are many instances now in which Indigenous peoples design, construct, manage, and actively participate in selling particular visions of Indigeneity. While Indianness and the Imaginary Indian (to borrow from Francis) have been defining discourses of nineteenth- and twentieth-century tourism, in the latter decades of the twentieth century the representational landscape had shifted and was dominated by the rhetoric of Aboriginality. Under Aboriginality everything is anchored to market language and focused on shifting the moral and fiscal responsibility of the state towards Indigenous peoples, who are in turn expected to "fix themselves" via marketization and economic development. Thus, while the "Indian" is a figure positioned as ancillary to the state, the "Aboriginal" is inside of it, ready and willing to partner and "develop." As in so many other sites since the passage of the Constitution Act, 1982, Aboriginal had become institutionalized through other means—in the case of this chapter, within Canadian tourism discourse as a strong, eminently profitable, *corporate* brand.

Aboriginal tourism (as it was called in the wake of the Constitution and up until a few years ago when it was revised to Indigenous tourism) became one of the fastest-growing branches of the tourism industry in Canada. Revenue generated by what was then commonly referred to as the Aboriginal cultural tourism industry had grown substantially—from $20 million in 2006, to roughly $42 million in 2011.[4] This chapter engages with the following questions: What is the relationship between the industrialization of imagined Aboriginality (referring to a broader field of image, culture, and spirituality framed as Aboriginal), discourses of Canadianness, and how the nation imagined and marketed itself through Aboriginality? What insights may be gleaned from these intersections with the ways Indigenous peoples envisioned this relationship? Had Indigenous peoples engaged in tourism over the past three decades simply been "playing Aboriginal," a performance related to, but somewhat different from, "playing Indian"? What nuances or complexities do these performances introduce to Aboriginal/Aboriginality as a discursive formation?

To answer these questions, I begin with a brief overview of the historical relationship between Indigenous peoples and Canadian tourism. I then turn to an examination of the marketing of Aboriginality across two sites: the Canadian Tourism Commission (CTC) website, circa 2009–2012, and the site of the Aboriginal Tourism Association of British Columbia (ATBC), circa 2009–2012 (now renamed the Indigenous Tourism Association of British Columbia). The appeal to Aboriginality in tourism, I argue, is directly linked to the state's emphasis on and interest in the web-based marketing of Canada's identity as an Aboriginalized nation that in effect seeks "through Aboriginality, to create for itself a more secure and legitimate national identity that can be shared by all the diverse groups that make up the ... nation."[5] It is yet another iteration of the induction of Indigenous peoples to Canada's multicultural brand via appeals to/

framings of Aboriginality. Despite projecting the illusion that Indigenous spiritual and cultural practices matter, when cloaked in the language of Aboriginality, tourism performances of culture are appropriated and manipulated into being "a touchstone for the formation of new ethnic adaptations of a dispossessed and decultured 'Aboriginal Canadian' identity."[6] Whereas Indianness was previously marketed as the antithesis of Canadianness—something to be marvelled at on a temporary basis before being obliterated through assimilatory measures— Aboriginality can remain insofar as it is a shell of what Indianness was. Aboriginality, as a marker of assimilation into the neoliberal colonial state, keeps enough cultural distinction to be a positive Aboriginal add-on to multiculturalism, but without the threat that the difference of Indianness posed to the "civil order" of white supremacy. Under neoliberal colonialism a de-indigenized Aboriginality is a highly desirable, and profitable, brand.

Aboriginal then emerges as a brand identity but also as a substantial economic brand, as outlined in the previous chapter. With VANOC financial legacies and governmental funding tying First Nations to tourist development projects, the economic dimensions of Aboriginality situate tourism as a long-standing, rather than transitory, mechanism for revenue generation that enables Canada to off-load its fiscal obligations to First Nations directly onto tourists—domestic and international. Whereas Aboriginality as an economic brand is lucrative for Canada, for Indigenous peoples the appeal of Aboriginality is linked to a desire to capitalize on non-Indigenous peoples' seemingly endless fascination with representations of Aboriginality in order to find sustainable ways to adapt to changing economic conditions.[7] Colonialism has supplanted many Indigenous peoples' traditional forms of livelihood with a capitalist order that places value on the extreme polar opposite of what sits at the core of Indigenous existence. The manner in which the earth's non-human inhabitants have been transformed into products through the capitalist ethos betrays Indigenous peoples' responsibilities to respect and protect non-human relatives. As such, Aboriginal tourism, with its emphasis on sustainability and as a form of ecotourism, has enabled Indigenous peoples to bridge these seemingly irreconcilable worlds of the human and the non-human. In order to do so, and as I will discuss directly, this has required Indigenous peoples to craft an explicit notion of "authentic Aboriginality," a reconceptualization that in turn extends Aboriginal far beyond what it was ever initially intended to do.

The Colonial Roots of Tourism's Relationship to First Nations, Inuit, and Métis

Humans have long engaged in temporary travel outside of their own locations of habitation, with access to wealth mediating the terms, distance, and content of such travel. With the rise of what many European theorists refer to as modernity in Western Europe, tourism organized around notions of leisure became a key revenue source for many European-colonized territories in the late eighteenth and nineteenth centuries. Romanticist literature and painting were vitalized by colonial contact; Indigenous homelands were figured as *terra nullius*, a land empty of inhabitants, a barren landscape, and a vast wilderness. Romanticist-driven tourism, then, enabled Europeans to "experienc[e] bodily what was already known imaginatively through literature and art."[8] The "New World" promised Europeans an escape from their complicated urban lives.[9]

While the notion of tourism has deep origins, it was refined by imaginative worlds born of colonization. A desire to visit "wild places," as figured through European literature and art, was so widespread that "Middle-class Europeans, Americans, and Canadians . . . became convinced of the restorative value of a wilderness holiday, embracing the idea that 'brain workers,' in particular, required 'the tonic of wildness,' in measured doses, to combat physical and nervous disorders."[10] The purported wildness of scarcely inhabited lands and naturalized landscape was touted as a remedy for societal ills arising from industrialization and the deepening of class inequality arising from capitalism. This desire for nature was figured as a reversion to a primitive state, and a change to take (albeit temporary) refuge from the rigours of urban intensification and English (white) civility.[11]

This genesis of tourism is also tied directly to colonization and Canadian nation-building. As historian Patricia Jasen argues, the tourism industry in the Canadian colonies "preceded—or accompanied—immigration and resource exploitation, and the tourist industry made its own contribution to a distorted representation of Native cultures and the transformation of their economies."[12] Tourism to New England and Upper and Lower Canada became increasingly popular, eventually bringing thousands (and in the present, millions) of travellers to the Niagara region and in and through Indigenous communities like the Tuscarora village near Lewiston, New York.[13] As they became increasingly disillusioned with pressure-filled urban life, Euro-tourists "flocked from the enervating city to the exhilarating wilderness, hoping to cast themselves under the care of Mother Nature and to rediscover the power of the primitive within themselves."[14] In doing so, tourists saw Indigenous communities as providing "a sort of laboratory where visitors might observe the people's way of life and speculate upon their capacity for survival or improvement."[15] Viewing European conquest as both inevitable and necessary, Europeans engaged in a tourist-organized pastime of "lamenting the destruction of the primeval forest and savouring the tragedy of [Indigenous] peoples' expected demise."[16]

While tourists could visit colonial settlements in the East, mass travel to the Northwest was forbidding owing to the rocky terrain and a widespread fear of large and powerful Indigenous nations that had yet to be dominated by Canada's colonial hand. For the better part of the 1800s, while much of the Northwest had long been claimed by the Hudson's Bay Company (HBC), the company was relatively powerless to impede the lives of Indigenous people on the Prairies. Without suppressing both First Nations and Métis on the Prairies, the Canadian colonies could not extend themselves westward and head off potential annexation of the West by US imperialist expansionism. As part of the dream of westward expansion born in the wake of Canada's assertion of itself as a nation in 1867, Canada's first prime minister, John A. Macdonald, promised citizens that he would realize his government's goal of building a railway that would link the newly formed province of British Columbia (1871) to the eastern provinces, and prevent American incursion into the areas the Canadian government sought for itself. Following both small- and large-scale military and police aggressions against First Nations and Métis on the Prairies through the 1870s and 1880s, the expansion of treaty-making to Indigenous nations on the Prairies, and the institution of oppressive policies intended to (in theory) assimilate Indigenous people as Canadian citizens, Canada had been able to successfully extend the Canadian Pacific Railway (CPR). With Indigenous people confined to reserves (or "prisons of grass," as Howard Adams has called them in a book of the same name), Canada expanded its railway through to the Pacific coast.

This is significant to the discussion here because, as cultural historian Daniel Francis highlights in his work, the extension of the railway was a key turning point in early Canadian tourism. The government came to see the extension of tours through the Plains and into the mountains, capitalizing on the beauty and "wildness" of the landscape, as a viable option for funding the railway and keeping it afloat.[17] As discussed in the Introduction, boosterism was central to this activity, and Indigenous peoples soon were drawn into this work. Many small towns and cities in British Columbia used the expansion of the railway and the growing invasion of tourists into the province to boost their municipal profiles.[18] Those employed as boosters sought to market the land they claimed in such a way as to attract settlers and investors rather than tourists. But the practice of boosterism as a form of strategic marketing worked in tandem with Romanticist ideologies to fuel the growth of the tourist industry.

Efforts by the state and by tourism promoters to draw tourists to the land, for temporary and, especially, permanent settlement, relied on the existence of racist discourses about Indigenous peoples and Indigenous land ownership and tenure. The idea that the lands were uninhabited by *real* human beings meant that, in the eyes of Europeans, Indigenous peoples had no legitimate claim to their own territories. Indigenous peoples were not regarded as such. While treaties were negotiated for certain parcels of land, the Canadian government and visiting Americans and Europeans operated under racist assumptions that did not recognize Indigenous people's humanity, assumptions driven by Romanticist rhetoric and colonial rationalizations that lands could only be classed as occupied if the people residing on them met rigid (yet often shifting) requirements of English land ownership. If Indigenous peoples were not white, anglophone, Christian, agricultural, and Eurocentrically commercial (which no Indigenous people *could* be in racialized, colonialist terms), the land was deemed empty and "free for the taking."

While Indigenous people were seen as the legitimate and rightful owners of the land, they were seen/used as props in aid of the intertwined destinies of tourism and settler colonialism. The early Ontario tourism industry capitalized on the racist stereotype that Indigenous people would inevitably "die out," as "noble savages" were destined to do, with increased settlement by British colonists.[19] Whereas these beliefs about Indigenous peoples carried weight in the tourism industry in the East, Indianness was not an early marketing ploy for tourism promoters in British Columbia. Indigenous peoples were not initially engaged in the tourism industry (except in the role of guides for individual explorers) due to the persistence of scientific racism, which posited that Indigenous peoples were "unproductive and backward."[20] Eventually, however, the government and the CPR "realized that the Indians were a surefire tourist attraction" and from the late 1800s and early 1900s the CPR sold and orchestrated train tours through the Prairies for non-Indigenous tourists to view "wild Indians in their natural setting from the safety and convenience of a railcar."[21] "Seeing Indians" became such a popular tourist draw that in 1894, when floods wiped out CPR tracks, the company invited Indigenous peoples from the Stoney reserve at Morley to entertain travellers marooned in Banff. The Indigenous people who elected to participate (inasmuch as they were free to make such decisions in the face of colonization) performed modified traditional dances while dressed in buckskin, in accordance with tourist fantasies of Indians, and competed in rodeo events "for prizes put up by the railway company."[22]

Like the tourists in Ontario, tourists on the Prairies wanted mementoes of their adventures. The developing ties between Indigenous peoples and the tourist industry had inspired new forms of Indigenous economic engagement as Indigenous peoples came to work in tourism in multiple capacities as "picturesque figures, as wilderness guides, and as makers of keepsakes."[23] Indigenous people engaged in the industry in part due to coercion, but they also engaged proactively; in fact, "cash income earned in this manner became an important element of the Native economy."[24] Tourism promoters in Ontario, as an extension of colonial authority, actively sought Indigenous engagement and thought that an "authentic Aboriginal culture" could be captured in representations and marketed to potential tourists.[25]

In response to market demand in the latter part of the 1800s, photographers began selling images of Indigenous people going about their daily lives to tourists wanting souvenirs of their journeys. The government and tourism promoters also started selling packages for travel on the newly built Canadian National Railway (CNR) on the Pacific coast and marketed "the scenic wilderness of western Canada through images of 'wild Indians' and 'totem poles.'"[26] Indians, as imagined by these tourism promoters became, to borrow from Jasen, one of tourism's most powerful "saleable commodities." Train tours to see "wild" landscapes and "Indians in their natural habitat" were so successful that by 1913, 15.5 million passengers rode the "Indian express" train in British Columbia.[27] Renewed fears of American imperialism spurred by the First World War appear to have sustained the tourist industry, with train tours reaching their peak through the 1920s, but as various droughts and the Great Depression took hold in the years preceding the Second World War, tourism numbers declined. By the 1920s Canada had solidified its colonial nation-building project through the negotiation of treaties (some forced) and the extension of the reserve system. Canada extended from the East to the BC coasts.

The impacts of assimilatory legislation, residential schooling, and the pressures of settler colonialism led to Indigenous people adapting under duress and with their purported modernizing, tourists found that fewer and fewer Indigenous people resembled the Indian of their imagination. Indianness thus began falling out of favour as the CPR's go-to marketing ploy. The tourism industry witnessed a decline in tourists interested in viewing Indigenous peoples. Tourists were less interested in seeing Indigenous peoples who had adapted to modernity and who were not (contrary to popular colonial mythology) dying out. Into the mid-twentieth century, however, some peoples, such as Cree from Mistissini, continued to find ways to work within the tourism industry; they continued a centuries-old practice of working as tour guides for European and Euro-Canadian tourists.[28] Overwhelmingly, though, the "modernization of Indians" meant that tourists were less attracted to tours through Indigenous communities and in observing Indigenous people as props of the tourism experience.

Whereas tourists had become disillusioned with so-called modernized Indians and thus with Indigenous *people* as objects, *material* objects that evoked Indianness still remained "a fascination among travelers."[29] Perhaps the most exoticized, aggressively promoted, and most noticeable symbol of Indianness is the totem pole.[30] The first totem pole erected in Stanley Park in Vancouver in 1903 quickly became a symbol associated with a romantic Indianness entrenched within a regionally specific Canadian identity. Although tourism had declined during the Depression, the totem poles in Stanley Park continued to draw tourists and provided a boost to Canada's economy well into the mid-twentieth century (and, some would argue, into the twenty-first). The totem poles served as "visible markers of Otherness [that] were a necessary reminder to tourists and travelers that while Canada no longer had an 'Indian problem' it did indeed have an 'ancient past,'" ones that provided an exotic and romantic spectacle for the leisure/pleasure-seeking tourist.[31] At the same time the totem poles were used to serve as a form of homage to Canada's imperial might. In the absence of Indians, markers of Indianness underscored Canada's own insistent indigenized existence. While Indigenous peoples became less popular, symbols of Indianness retained a powerful hold over tourist imaginations.

Tourism as a central feature of the modern period is unquestionably interlaced with Canadian nation-building and the colonization of Indigenous lands and peoples; perhaps most importantly it provided a different kind of financial base for the realization of nation-building. At the same, however, it was also cemented as a form of nationalist pedagogy aimed at educating the nation's occupants and its visitors, furthering the notion that westward expansion (or the "westward march of European civilization") and the disappearance of the "original habitants" of the land was inevitable.[32] Colonial discourse is therefore inextricably linked with tourism, as both have "strategically functioned to produce geopolitical myths about destinations."[33] Tourism provided a stage on which the colonial national story, a story long foretold in European writings, could be embodied. Tourism cloaked the visual spectacle of colonization in romantic narratives, allowing (predominantly) Anglo-European people to visit places they had only read and dreamt about. Tourists and tourism promoters, as extensions of colonial processes, "reconstructed images of the Indian to suit their own immediate needs and purposes, including their need to affirm their own culture's notion of progress, racial superiority, and rights to this 'new' land."[34]

Experiential Tourism

While the Depression had a negative net impact on tourism overall, in the postwar era tourism rebounded on a tide of economic growth. In their field-defining works, scholars John Urry (*The Tourist Gaze*), a sociologist of travel and tourism, and cultural anthropologist Dean MacCannell (*The Tourist*) document the consolidation and industrialization of tourism and its growth throughout the twentieth century into mass tourism, noting that, on the wings of an expanding world order and the availability of lower-priced, standardized tourist options, tourism came to outpace other economic sectors. Tourism became one of the world's leading economic forces.[35] Following the Depression, the field became dominated by small companies and growing corporations, and a bona fide tourist industry emerged.

The 1950s and 1960s saw the development of standardized, packaged tours and vacations with "low levels of personal involvement" in the planning and organization.[36] The tourist industry grew so much so that in 1963 the United Nations (UN) held its first conference on tourism and international travel; at the conference the UN agreed with the International Union of Official Travel Organizations (IUOTO) that it was time to consider defining a field of tourism and terms for travellers such as "visitor," "tourist," and "excursionist."[37] These terms would continue to be refined through the 1970s and in the 1980s. Tourism was transformed in the 1980s; no longer confined to an economic elite class, an identifiable form of mass tourism emerged that hinged on the packaging of affordable, resort-based pleasure vacations available in a range of prices. Mass tourism grew as governments, hotels, tour companies, and travel agents made travel more accessible for middle-income earners, with resort vacations becoming the preferred tourist mode.

Tours, such as those the CPR had historically marketed to white tourists, were elaborated as comprehensive travel packages (including such things as travel, accommodation, meals, and entertainment). In Canada's case the exoticization and marketing of difference continued to focus on Indigenous peoples' distinctiveness from Anglo-European Canadianness. Tourism packages carried on the earlier ideological project of portraying the legitimacy of colonial regimes through the depiction of tourism as a non-invasive modernizing force that, while promoting standards of progress and civility, did not "threaten the primitiveness of Indigenous peoples."[38]

In the 1990s standardized tourism was gradually displaced in favour of experiential tourism. Tourism scholar Richard Prentice writes, "Resort-based mass tourism progressively eroded the immediate cultural experiences" of earlier tourism.[39] Tourists bored by aspects of mass tourism began to seek more authentic and personal experiences, a phenomenon reflected in the wider (non-tourism) market. The Minister's Roundtable on Parks Canada defined experiential tourism as "an outgrowth of a global movement toward experiential learning, whereby people create meaning through direct experience."[40] Experiential tourism sits in contrast to mass tourism in that it moves the tourist experience from passive to active. It allows tourists to, quite literally, experience for themselves. The experience "shows rather than describes" and "encourages visitors to actively participate in the experience," and it includes "the people one meets, the places they visit, the accommodations where they stay, activities participated in, and the memories created."[41] Experience-based tourism is tied to characteristics of neoliberal economies whereby everything becomes marketable and everything is a market. By extension there develops an emphasis on customization—that each and every person has their own market personality, and eventually, that each and every person is themselves a brand. According to the Roundtable, "In this sense it is very personal and individual. Essentially, experiential tourists seek memorable experiences."[42]

The language used to frame these experiences is what Prentice refers to as the "New Romanticism of Evoked Authenticity." The new romanticism is tied to a sense among tourists that "self-realisation is not completely attainable by Western populations without travel away from home" (or, in the Canadian context, travel away to a nostalgic past).[43] Experiential tourism is intimately tied to notions of personal growth and reflection and to feelings of personal accomplishment. Tourists seek to "connect with unique and cultural heritage" through experiences that are customized to their interests, arising from a desire to feel as though they have somehow developed elements of their personality and/or character.[44] Companies and the industry at large have responded to this change in demand by shifting their focus towards offering and promoting experience-based travel activities that draw people "into cultures, communities, and the outdoors."[45] Tourism marketing shifted towards personalizing the tourist experience in the mid-late 1990s, inviting prospective consumers to "'explore' and to 'discover' for themselves: personally to find surprises or 'hidden' worlds, to seek adventure, to admire grandeur, to share secrets, to sample flavours, and to uncover mysteries or solve enigmas."[46]

The movement towards experiential tourism is linked to a preoccupation with culture (specifically "authentic culture"), in that tourists began to seek to "experience the cultural attractions and the cultural distinctiveness of the area they visit."[47] Cultural tourism is epitomized, for anthropologist Robert Kelly, by the "consumption of cultural experiences (and objects) by individuals who are away from their normal place of habitation."[48] This transition has led to tourism marketing that stresses that a traveller's worth is tied up in "the consumption of cultural experiences," with tourism materials emphasizing "a country's or a region's art, craft and heritage forms; its museums, art galleries, and historic sites; its culturally different populations; and the different 'sense of place' that tourists can experience."[49]

The changing nature of tourism, towards a preoccupation with authenticity and experience, fuels the international competitiveness between market-driven nations. Thus the industry must continue to attract travellers seeking out authentic, meaningful tourism experiences. The state meanwhile is driven by its desire for economic dominance to compete with other nations for "its share of world tourism receipts.[50] The investments are large and the world tourism receipts are indeed vast; in 1992 tourism had grown to be the leading economic sector the world over.[51] Invigorated by the turn towards experience-focused tourism, tourism provided 10 percent of the world's gross domestic product in 2001. Bringing in US$10.8 billion annually that same year, Canada ranked eighth among the world's top earners in tourism and was ranked the ninth most popular tourist destination.[52] These changes in the desires and attitudes of tourists would also have monumental impact on the global tourism economy and on the nature of the Imaginary Indian as a saleable commodity.

"Start the Adventure, Discover Aboriginal Canada": The Canadian Tourism Commission and Marketing the Aboriginal

In the competition for tourism revenue, states around the world find ways to objectify and monetize their national identities. The Canadian Tourism Commission (CTC) was formed in 1995 as a federal Crown corporation.[53] As the federal branch of the Canadian government's tourism profile, it has responded to the turn towards experiential tourism by defining Canada's brand identity as an experience-based brand. In the window of time under study in this chapter, from roughly 2009 to 2012, the CTC defined Canada's tourism brand as "the imagination and emotion a country inspires in visitors. [It is a] set of beliefs and associations they hold about a place. A tourism brand is a promise of what to expect when you visit."[54]

The move towards experiential tourism in Canada came on the heels of studies of international tourists that found that many felt Canada was a country big on landscape and filled with friendly people, but that it lacked the draw of historical sites (as found in Europe) or lots of sunshine and beaches (as found in the Caribbean). In terms of economic global competitiveness, the CTC feared "that other countries are better known as destinations with impressive cultural attractions" such as "the spectacular historic sites of Europe" and the "'peasant peoples of Third World countries.'"[55] The CTC addressed this fear on its website: "In 2004, we set out to change this outdated idea of Canada. Going back to this country's roots, we put our stake in the ground. We aren't a specialty destination for sun-worshippers who wanted to lie on the beach for a week. We're a country built by—and for—explorers. We attract travellers who want the freedom to express themselves through travel. If Canada is an adventure story, our hero is the curious traveller who thrives on surprising, unexpected and out-of-the-ordinary experiences."[56] The reaction to the nation's sense of its own destination deficiency and its desire to go back to its "roots" resulted in the CTC configuring Canadian tourism through the language of frontier mythology; its tourism branding was replete with words like "adventure," "discovery," and "exploration." The CTC's official tourism brand tagline in particular, "Canada. Keep exploring," constructed an image of Canada as a playground for experiential tourists, calling to them with promises of unbridled adventure.

To paint this vision for tourists and to promote Canada as a site for adventure, discovery, and exploration, the CTC devised what it termed its five unique selling propositions for the industry: "Vibrant cities on the edge of nature ... Personal journeys by land, water and air . . . Active adventure among awe-inspiring wonders . . . Award-winning Canadian local cuisine . . . [and] Connecting with Canadians."[57] The first of these speaks to the idea that Canada's landscape, its nature, is more than a backdrop to cities: it is "a symbol of freedom—the freedom to explore and be yourself."[58] The second selling proposition is about "discovery, surprise, landscapes, and waterways of unimaginable beauty, about a journey that brings you back to yourself. After all, Canada is a land built for explorers."[59] On the land built for explorers you can "drive Newfoundland's wind-raked Viking Trail to reach the earliest-known European settlement in the New World."[60] With the fourth set of experiences tourists are told they can be the "hero of [their] own adventure story," a framing directly tied to tropes about the land as historically wild and foreboding, but in the present day made accessible (presumably by settlement and modernity): "Once upon a time, Canada was considered a vast, remote, even forbidding wilderness. To get out and be active in our wondrous nature, you had to suffer the elements or sacrifice comfort. But that was around the 18th century. Today, you're the hero of your own adventure story in Canada. And the story couldn't be more inspiring."[61]

As an example of the kinds of experiences available to those seeking to be active while surrounded by awe-inspiring wonders, the CTC offers that tourists can "sit mesmerized by the aurora borealis (Northern Lights) from the comfort of a hot tub."[62] The fourth proposition simply refers to sampling the "flavor of a place" through the consumption of "unique, locally sourced ingredients, a taste of ethnic fusion, a return to national freshness, and sharing the bounty of low-intensity farming."[63] With the final proposition the CTC alludes to Indigenous-related experiences by suggesting that tourists interested in connecting with Canadians who are "witty, fun, approachable, authentic" take in the Yukon International Storytelling Festival and "share stories," or alternatively head to Alberta to "learn the traditional life of the Great Plains people at Alberta's famous buffalo jump."[64]

Continuing to play up Canada's suitability as an experiential tourist destination, the CTC coaxes tourists by appealing to their need to feel special and spiritually fulfilled by their travel with statements like these: "What matters is that you're unique and that you value the power of an experience. A product is what people buy. An experience is what they remember . . . Visitors who fully engage their senses, make a strong emotional connection to their travel experience and feel as if they've enjoyed a personal exploration are more likely to be satisfied and inspired. This is precisely how extraordinary memories are made."[65] To ensure that tourists feel they have a hand in making travel memories and that their travel experiences are sufficiently personalized, the CTC developed an online quiz/online marketing tool called the "Explorer Quotient," which helped prospective tourists figure out which sort of adventure they would be best suited for. The quiz then placed people into one of nine categories of Explorer Types as Authentic Experiencer, Cultural Explorer, Cultural History Buff, Personal History Explorer, Free Spirit, Gentle Explorer, No Hassle Traveller, Rejuvenator, and Virtual Traveller, offering each customized list of travel suggestions based on their personality.[66]

Each of the personality types and list of experiences perpetuate CTC's overall tourism brand and are replete with references to travel that allow tourists to engage in discovery and exploration, and experience the country's roots. These discursive frames, however, are deeply problematic as they are intimately tied to the displacement and colonization of Indigenous peoples. Discovery, an important frame for experiential tourism, is tied to the longstanding misrecognition of the colonial relationship as one of Europeans "finding" Indigenous peoples and the "New World." The CTC eschews acknowledging the colonization of Indigenous peoples and lands and the subsequent intergenerational impacts of such a horrific project by romanticizing discovery and reinscribing it through tourism's brand as the core of Canadian national identity. The desire of settler-colonists for "speedy indigenization" is thus reflected across the CTC's branding strategy. As a branch of the Canadian government, the CTC works to reconcile the state's *anxiety of belatedness* through positivist tourism narratives that are perhaps more accurately described as a contemporary reimagining of frontier mythology.

The concern over destination deficiency I identified earlier is reflected here as settler anxiety and a psychopathological condition of belatedness, referring to the tension arising from Euro-Canadians position as "the bearer of the civilizing mission" while at the same time suffering from a "paranoia [over] colonial civility's legitimacy."[67] Drawing on Homi Bhabha, Daniel Coleman highlights that the anxiety of belatedness is tied to the settler-colonist's internalization of "imperialism's temporal gap," wherein the settler-colonist feels "caught in the time-space delay between the metropolitan place where civility is made and legislated and the colonial place where it is enacted and enforced."[68] Indigenous peoples' survival of colonialism and insistence on reclaiming land and identity challenge Canada's attempts to shore up its legitimacy and identity. The effect of these anxieties is that the settler-colonist "must construct, by a double process of speedy indigenization and accelerated self-civilization, his priority and superiority to latecomers; that is, by representing himself as already indigenous the settler claims priority over newer immigrants and, by representing himself as already civilized, he claims superiority to Aboriginals and other non-Whites."[69]

Insofar as settler-colonists desire their own indigenization they experience an anxiety that feeds and yet is also fed by what cultural anthropologist Renato Rosaldo refers to as "imperialist nostalgia." Imperialist or colonialist nostalgia appears in two stages: "The first is a nostalgia for colonialism itself, a desire to re-create and recover the world of late Victorian and Edwardian colonialism as a culture of extraordinary confidence and conspicuous opulence . . . The second moment is more oblique. It involves the recovery not only of *fin-de-siècle* claims to power but also its claims to knowledge."[70] Canada romanticizes a history of conquest and colonization through the perpetuation of Aboriginality—to assure itself that all is right with the nation and to reconcile its anxieties. Linguistics scholar Bob Hodge and cultural theorist Vijay Mishra write that this is why Indigenous peoples are not made absent from public life: "There is another reason why Aborigines cannot be completely effaced from the record. They still have a crucial role to play in the process of the foundation myth: to confer legitimacy on those who raped, pillaged, poisoned and dispossessed them. So they cannot be silenced: or more precisely, a voice that is labeled as theirs must have a place, legitimated as theirs yet not disrupting the fine balance of contradictions in the foundation myth."[71] While early Canadian tourism sought to market "authentic Indians," contemporary tourism trades in representations of a multitude of First Nations, Inuit, and Métis under the umbrella of "Aboriginal tourism" and "authentic Aboriginals" because it so desperately seeks ways to legitimate Canadian national identity.

Canada's tourism industry imports and then exports the image of the Aboriginal in an effort to portray the nation as a multicultural utopia founded on its innate diversity (a diverse "Aboriginal population"), civility, compassion, generosity, and humanitarian superiority, claiming to highlight "the nation's distinctive cultural forms" and pacify its own sense of unease.[72] Political theorist Peter Van Ham asserts that Canada transforms its national narrative "to present distinctive images in order to attract foreign investment and skilled labour."[73] CTC's efforts to "brand Canada," then, effectively proposes actualizing the selling of diversity to transform the national narrative.[74] Specifically, the CTC endeavours to "capitalize on its strength in this market" in terms of its "rich native and multicultural heritage."[75] The interest in capitalizing on and marketing native and multicultural heritage as a core feature of Canadian diversity corresponds with the push among economically dominant nations in the 1980s towards "selling diversity."[76] Thus the increasingly corporatized state views Indigenous peoples and multicultural Others as saleable commodities for the purposes of marketing a Canadian identity. Canadian studies scholar Richard Nimijean explicates that "Canadian diversity has become a key element of the transformed Canadian narrative" and ultimately a "selling point" for the restructuring of society along neoliberal lines.[77] Indigenous peoples are drawn into the transformation of Canada's national narrative as Aboriginal and are positioned as signifiers of Canada's originary diversity, a diversity that the nation professes it has possessed since its inception. It also positions Indigenous histories as part of a *Canadian* prehistory. In most instances the return to the country's roots involves an active claiming of Indigenous peoples, cultures, and identities as a part of Canada's pre-Canada Canadianness.

The appropriation of Indigenous cultures is an attempt not only to define the nation's brand but to cater to tourist desires for uniqueness, individuality, meaningful experiences, and authenticity. In a 1996 survey of tourists from the United Kingdom, Germany, and France a sizeable number of tourists identified Indigenous peoples as a site/source of tourist attraction when visiting Canada.[78] While the research conducted does show that interest in "Aboriginal culture" is not what generally motivates tourists to come to Canada in the first place, once here tourists view experiences that involve Indigenous peoples as value-added. While images of Indigenous peoples as symbols of Canadian culture and Indigenous-made material culture have been visually consumed and sold as souvenirs to tourists interested in "seeing Indians" since the early days of Canadian tourism, the market changes in the broader tourism industry have generated demands for Indigenous-related cultural experiences and the accumulation of Indigenous traditional, environmental, and spiritual knowledges. In recent decades tourists have expressed an interest in directly *experiencing* Indigenous peoples' cultures (with a special emphasis on ecological knowledge and spirituality), meaning that, instead of passively viewing Indigenous performances, they would prefer to actively participate in the expression of culture and the making of arts and crafts.

Of all of the Traveller Types designated by the CTC, those who meet the profile of the Cultural Explorer are provided with the most recommendations for Aboriginal-related experiences. The Cultural Explorer is said (among other things) to enjoy "ancient history and modern culture" and to want to "experience the culture as genuinely as possible," alluding to the existence of "ancient" and "authentic" Aboriginal cultures. The image used to entice the Cultural Explorer is that of an Indigenous man with long braids next to a campfire. He appears to be telling a story to a European man, woman, and two young children, while a teepee, picnic table, and the rolling hills of the Plains are laid out in the background. Tourists are told that they, too, can participate in these sorts of "ancient" practices. They can

> paddle a dugout canoe, mush sled dogs, stomp to a beat at a Pow Wow, nibble caribou jerky, sleep in a tipi. Dance a jig to a Métis fiddle tune. Savour wild salmon grilled on a fragrant cedar plank. Paddle a canoe down a river wilderness. Toss aside your shyness and launch into throat-singing. Hike through ancient towering rainforest and touch damp moss. Smell sweet grass smolder in a purifying ritual. Cheer on a walrus using his tusks to haul himself onto an ice floe. Weave a basket. Aboriginal folks are proud to share their culture, so join them at a traditional feast or walk through the woods as native healers do. They can teach you how to carve a totem pole or feel the freedom of riding horses across the prairie. Visit cultural centres shaped like longhouses. Party at Pow Wows where elaborate dresses, masks and feathers whirl in a blur of colour. Or watch an Inuit carver calmly unleashing a polar bear from a chunk of soapstone. Dine gourmet on the wild, the original organic. Grilled elk, caribou stew, muskox sausages, caramelized sky apples. Drop a fishing line into a remote lake or sink into a sauna bathed in the glow of the midnight sun. Then, turn in to your tipi or your stylish Aboriginal lodge to awaken in the morning to the aroma of freshly baked bannock bread.[79]

These are some of the many things that tourists are told they can expect to become involved in should they embark on a journey to see "Canada, Aboriginal-style."

Other options are advertised to tourists on the CTC website through formal profiles and reports: these include visiting "the Riel Rebellion's heartland," the chance to "go Inuit for a weekend," and the opportunity to "dance at Ahbee

Festival." Going "Inuit for a weekend" refers to "signing up for a home stay with a local family and getting an insider's look at the workings of a typical Nunavut hamlet" and "learning to navigate the Inuit's quirky sense of humour."[80] The recommendation to "dance at Ahbee Festival" encourages tourists to visit the Manitoba powwow at Whiteshell Provincial Park, "where First Nations people traditionally gathered to share teachings and wisdom." Tourists are invited to "stroll through the Indigenous Marketplace and Trade Show, [to] decid[e] whether to buy a carving, sweet-grass braids or a hand drum" at the Manito Ahbee powwow. When the intertribal dance "is called out" they are encouraged to find themselves "on the dance floor, too, twirling and stepping to the driving drum beat and the intoxicating rhythm of the songs."[81] Manito Ahbee is marketed by the CTC as a pan-Aboriginal festival that bridges the old and the new through the music of the "soulful chants of the elders" and "everything from hip hop to country" and as a playground for the non-Indigenous tourist.[82] Contrasting the Inuit and First Nations experiences, which are organized around "culture," the Métis profile beckons tourists to see the "battlefields that shaped Canada and began the long struggle for Aboriginal rights": "Meet the people of Batoche. Hear and learn their stories, as well as the story of the Métis people and the struggle for Aboriginal rights in Canada."[83] Claimed as a National Historic Site of Canada by Heritage Canada, Batoche is marketed by the CTC as a pan-Aboriginal site of "the Northwest Rebellion, Canada's greatest insurrection."[84]

The marketing of these experiences reflects the state's investment in representing and reducing a diversity of Indigenous peoples/cultures as a palatable, depoliticized Aboriginal brand. While there are other experiences depicted as Aboriginal on the CTC's website, these examples are notable for the breadth of the CTC's marketing of the Aboriginal across First Nations, Inuit, and Métis lines. This marketing of Indigenous peoples facilitates the inherently reductive and essentialist frame of "aboriginalism" to which Alfred refers. He argues that via the deployment (and I would suggest the adaptation) of colonial myths, aboriginalism manipulates Indigenous peoples "into a submissive position."[85] The coded language of aboriginalism misleads people by concealing the embedded colonialism inherent within marketed Aboriginal experiences.

The CTC's branding of Inuit through the lens of "going native" is one such manipulation; although its exact origins are unknown, the phrase is an expression that has been in use since the early stages of colonialism and refers to colonizer's fears of assimilating into "uncivilized" Indigenous societies.

"Going native" reflects a "widespread ambivalence about modernity as well as anxieties about the terrible violence marking the nation's origins."[86] Ethnic studies scholar Shari Huhndorf (Yup'ik) argues that the twentieth-century deployment of "going native" has served as a means for "constructing white identities, naturalizing the conquest, and reinscribing various power relations within American culture."[87] In addition to the problematic reference to "going native," the CTC's branding of the Inuit "Aboriginal experience" relies on racist representations of Inuit peoples as happy and smiling simpletons. Religion scholar Christopher Trott cites an image caption in the *Anglican Churchman* from March 1960 that refers to Inuit people as the "Eskimos," claiming that they are "a happy people and they love to sing and dance . . . Eskimo babies join the dance. They bounce around on the mothers' backs and enjoy the fun."[88] Inuit are depicted as even happier in the face of "terrible ecological adversity."[89] Mid-twentieth-century writings about Inuit people reflected similar views and "portrayed them as rather happy and simple, a view reinforced by the staged photographs of smiling Inuit made available by missionaries."[90]

Tourists are also encouraged to "go native" at Manito Ahbee through the buying of traditional medicines (sweetgrass, the purchase of which is not in accordance with protocols regarding traditional medicines); they are invited to see themselves as intertribal through taking part in the intertribal dance. Taking part in powwow dancing and envisioning oneself as intertribal are other aspects of the "going native" trope, because as "real Indians were destined to disappear, European Americans are the proper heirs of 'Indianness' as well as of the land and resources [and cultures] of the conquered Natives."[91] Further, the description of Manito Ahbee paints a problematic picture of Whiteshell Provincial Park being a place open to Indigenous peoples who can gather freely (as has *traditionally* been done) to share "teachings and wisdom." In fact, in Manitoba Indigenous "free" use of the park is mediated by the Manitoba provincial government, who in 2010 rebuked the Brokenhead First Nation's efforts to obtain sections of the park as legitimate compensation under the Treaty Land Entitlement Process. The Brokenhead in return threatened to block public access to the park in hopes of compelling the government to resolve "the issue of co-management of sacred aboriginal land in the Whiteshell."[92]

In a move aimed at the heart of Métis pride, the CTC portrays the Métis resistance against the Canadian state as an "insurrection" and abject failure in the face of a superior force. The CTC's Aboriginal rhetoric ignores altogether the stories the people themselves would tell, namely that the resistance movement at both

Red River and Batoche were never struggles for *Aboriginal* rights. They were a resistance to colonialism launched by a distinctive Métis Nation in the face of the brutality and racism of the Canadian state. As the Métis Nation continues to struggle as a largely landless people (with the exception of a small number of provincially designated Métis settlements in Alberta) who in the present are denied recognition of their rights and their inherent nationhood, the state endeavours to sell romanticized and mythologized Canadian frontier rebelliousness with reference to Métis leader Louis Riel. It also forments a myth that Aboriginal rights are something readily embraced, acknowledged, and respected within Canada.

Aboriginal, when used in this way, displaces "authentic indigenous identities, beliefs, and behaviours."[93] It also firmly locates Indigenous peoples in the past, with constant historicizing of Indigenous cultural practices and experiences. This is what Alfred refers to as the "genocidal function of aboriginalism," the "prettied-up face of neo-colonialism that is . . . the attempt to destroy authentic existences and replace them with ways of life and self-definitions that best serve Euroamerican wants, needs, and beliefs."[94] The discourse of Aboriginal in the CTC's promotion of Canadian tourism puts in place Eurocentric views of Indigenous peoples, histories, and futures that "are nothing more than the self-justifying myths and fantasies of the Settler."[95]

The state's marketing of the everyday lives (Inuit), spiritual/cultural practices and materials (First Nations), and histories (Métis) of Indigenous peoples under the umbrella of "Canada, Aboriginal-style" reflects the totalizing reach of Canada's attempts to imagineer itself. In the case of the CTC, the culture agents are working from within the field of tourism to engineer a nationalism (the national brand) that insists on its own ability to cut across, to borrow Werry's phrasing, "deep (racial or ethnic) disparities in power or entitlement."[96] The Aboriginal or Aboriginalism in tourism is deployed to aid in the performance of state identity, to imagineer it, and to give the nation the "appearance of solidarity"; however, it is perhaps best understood as a device of the ongoing colonial project that in fact serves as an "essential means of defining and regenerating racial whiteness and a racially inflected vision of [Canadian]ness."[97]

Our Story, Your Experience: Niche-Marketing Aboriginal Tourism and the Case of ATBC

When Aboriginality is constructed, as it has been by the CTC, it "fashions 'the people' as a symbol and concept constructed on, and totally amenable to, colonialism."[98] It is assimilationist in its efforts to reimagine Indigenous peoples as integrated into, and thus enabling, a supposedly superior Euro-Canadian way. Indigenous peoples are used as touchpoints for Canada's "innate" multiculturalism. Indigenous participation within Canadian tourism has increased, though, spurring the emergence of an Indigenously driven and definable "Aboriginal tourism" niche market as a part of the broader tourism industry. The CTC's depictions position Indigenous peoples as Aboriginal objects of the tourist industry, but there are other spaces in which Indigenous peoples are active agents in facilitating an Aboriginal tourism industry. Is it the case that Indigenous involvement in such productions of Aboriginality/Aboriginalism is always, necessarily, as Alfred has argued, a sign of being "amenable to colonialism"?

Aside from the CTC's representations, the consolidation and materialization of "Aboriginal tourism" or "Aboriginal cultural tourism" as its own entity is a significant effect of the mid-1980s shift towards experiential cultural tourism. The marketing of the "authentic" and "non-staged" sites and spaces that allow this sort of unprecedented tourist experience has, over the past thirty years, come to be framed as a distinct field of "Aboriginal tourism" or "Aboriginal cultural tourism," with the emergence of many Indigenous-run (Aboriginally labelled) tourism organizations.[99] Aboriginal tourism is now the single largest cultural tourism draw for Canadian tourism, surpassing "nature tourism, resource-based tourism, adventure tourism, eco-tourism, transformational travel, heritage tourism and other niche areas."[100] In 1996 a collective of Indigenous and non-Indigenous business and government representatives formed an organization called Aboriginal Tourism Team Canada (ATTC). ATTC proceeded to define Aboriginal tourism as "any tourism business that is owned or managed by Indians, Inuit or Métis people. It comprises the full spectrum of tourism products and services, be it traditional or contemporary. This includes accommodation, food and beverages, transportation, attractions, travel trade, events and conferences, adventure tourism, recreation, and arts and crafts."[101] In that same year, the Aboriginal Tourism Association of British Columbia (ATBC) was formed by a volunteer group of Indigenous peoples working in the tourism sector. ATBC, later renamed Indigenous Tourism

Association of British Columbia (ITBC), aimed to explore the possibilities of increasing Aboriginal tourism entrepreneurship in British Columbia. ATBC defines Aboriginal cultural tourism as comprising a mix of traditional and non-traditional experiences, such as "canoe journeys and interpretive jet boat tours to Aboriginal-owned museums, heritage villages, cultural centres, golf resorts, and wineries."[102] ATBC also takes a stab at defining the parameters of "experience" in experiential tourism, claiming that "put simply, more and more visitors are looking for experiences that immerse them in a foreign culture and allow them to experience customs and traditions firsthand."[103]

In 2005, researcher Michael E. Kelly, in "Atiik Askii: Land of the Caribou," a case study in community-based tourism development for Indian and Northern Affairs Canada (INAC), Canadian Heritage, Manitoba Culture, Heritage and Tourism, and Manitoba Aboriginal and Northern Affairs, defined Aboriginal tourism by first deferring to a nine-year-old (presumably) Indigenous girl from Brochet in northwestern Manitoba. The young girl, Sherilynn Thomas, reportedly drew a picture that expressed what she feels Aboriginal tourism means: "caribou hunting, camping and fishing."[104] Kelly elaborates Thomas's drawn definition, adding that while Aboriginal tourism may mean "something different for Aboriginal communities across Canada" it generally refers to "arts and crafts, pow wows, story-telling, and foods such as venison, bannock, and wild rice. It also means outdoor activities such as canoeing, dog-sledding, or staying in a tee pee or lodge."[105] These definitions echo the ATTC and CTC's joint publication, "Aboriginal Cultural Tourism: Checklist for Success," which identifies First Nations, Inuit, and Métis-owned *or* operated businesses as ones that "incorporat[e] an Aboriginal cultural experience in a manner that is appropriate, respectful, and true to the Aboriginal culture being represented" and are generally thematically based on authenticity and environmental, cultural, and economic sustainability.[106]

Encompassing all of these definitions, culturally specific tourism has come to mean big business for Indigenous peoples and the Canadian nation-state. In 1998 industry estimates pegged the revenue generated by "Aboriginal cultural attractions, eco-tourism and wilderness tours" at $270 million annually, with projected possible growth reaching $1 billion.[107] By 2008 revenue attributed to Aboriginal tourism-related businesses alone was determined as contributing approximately $35 million to BC's economy.[108] ATBC's five-year plan projected that tourists would spend roughly $320 million between 2012 and 2017.[109] While some studies, such as the 2003 National Study on Aboriginal Tourism in Canada, had suggested that, despite the fact that demand for Aboriginal tourism typically overrides the availability of Aboriginal tourism "products" and that the market is challenged by a lack of consumer confidence in the capacity of Aboriginal cultural tourism suppliers, the industry nevertheless has continued to grow.[110]

ATBC has thus far represented the most successful consolidated effort of Indigenous peoples working in the tourism industry, spurred in part by the boost to the BC Aboriginal tourism economy brought by Vancouver's hosting of the 2010 Winter Olympics. As a provincial organization driven by Indigenous peoples and representing a wide range of Indigenous tourism companies, ATBC came to serve as a mentor/role model for local Indigenous community interests in terms of economic development. It is an organization funded in partnership with non-Indigenous entities such as the Canadian government (at its founding, through Aboriginal Affairs and through Western Economic Diversification Canada) and by Tourism British Columbia. In its present iteration is also receives financial support from such large corporations as Coast Hotels & Resorts.

At the period under study in this chapter, ATBC's internet profile was divided into a corporate and a travel site. The travel site offered prospective tourists insight into the types of experiences available to them in British Columbia. The tourist site (www.aboriginalbc.com) was set up in a manner that echoed CTC's marketing of Aboriginal experiences. While there are some notable similarities, there are vast differences in the language used to describe the tourist profiles and the recommended forms of travel. Such options splashed across the main page: "Art & Culture Connoisseur," "Aboriginal Experience Seeker," and "Nature & Beauty with a Twist." The first of these, "Art & Culture," offers a picture of a man carving what could reasonably be assumed to be an upright totem pole. The "Art & Culture Connoisseur" is described as having "a keen interest to learn about the First peoples of this land [and] a great appreciation for Aboriginal Cultural expression and Cultural treasures."[111] ATBC makes sure that the tourist knows that culture is a living and breathing thing, that the cultural experiences being made available are rooted in "our living culture [that] has been passed down through the millennia from our ancestors," and in a direct challenge perhaps to pseudo-scientific or Darwinian theories of Indigenous evolution and migration, states that tourists can "discover artifacts that pre-date the pyramids; and learn about sacred transformer stones."[112] ATBC neither conceals nor expressly advertises the colonialism which has foregrounded Indigenous-state relations, but they do suggest that tourists can "view repatriated potlatch treasures," a nod to the violent expropriation of coastal Indigenous cultural materials.

The second profile shows a Plains-style First Nations person replete with feathers and the markers of powwow dress. The "Aboriginal Experience Seeker" is someone uninterested in sightseeing bus tours but is instead someone who wants "the real thing; to feel the pull of the paddle, hear the rushing water, view the timeless mists and ancient rainforests, and smell of the campfire." This tourist is told, "You want a full experience and perceive your world from a new angle,"[113] and is offered "Aboriginal guides [who] will show you a different way of discovering our land, [and] waters and embark on adventures as you have never experienced before. View killer whales spy hopping in the ocean, and be awed by the site of grizzly bears feasting on the spawning salmon. Paddle a traditional dugout canoe, take a jet boat tour on one of our great rivers, hike along mountain trails and hike our amazing rainforests. Whichever adventure you choose, we will teach you our way of seeing and experiencing our land."[114] The focus shifts here towards igniting tourist desires for wilderness sold to them as a part of *their* world but is also *our* (Aboriginal) land.

The third image, "Nature & Beauty," figures a young, light-skinned Indigenous woman. She offers a broad smile as she sits in a canoe, paddling. Accompanying her image are tourists who are told: "Revitalize and connect with yourself and the wonders of nature. Be exhilarated and inspired with tranquility and lush landscapes, new friendships and memories of a lifetime. Live your dream and experience the pure enjoyment of life."[115] Those with an interest in "Nature & Beauty" are also offered "a vacation of discovery with a cultural twist."[116] The cultural twist is that tourists can engage with "local Aboriginal people" (as symbols of the past) while enjoying the luxuries of Aboriginal-owned resorts and lodges, golf courses, spa treatments, and casinos. Tourists are told that they can "sample traditional foods and award-winning wines, [while] view[ing] traditional and contemporary art work."[117]

ATBC tries to maintain the integrity of the tourism initiatives it supports through its recently developed Aboriginal Cultural Tourism Authenticity Program. That is, ATBC provides its own seal of approval for those tourism companies it deems *legitimately, authentically* Aboriginal. The seal is a modified version of ATBC's logo, "a version of ATBC's hands motif fused with a feather and drum symbolizing the strength and celebration of Aboriginal cultures," along with the words "Authentic Aboriginal."[118] For consideration under the program, ATBC requires the completion of a lengthy application that can verify that a minimum 51 per cent of the business is owned by Aboriginal people or by "majority owned Aboriginal companies, OR if the business is owned by a society . . . at least 51% of the members [must be] Aboriginal."[119]

ATBC claims that its program "goes beyond evaluating the cultural component of a tourism business and assesses other criteria, including Aboriginal ownership/control, adherence to Aboriginal protocols, market and export readiness and operating and safety standards."[120] All Euro-economic marketing language ("market and export readiness") aside, the success of an application hinges on the board of directors determining that a company's application meets a floating standard of "Aboriginal protocols" and the determination that the services/experiences the applicant company provides are sufficiently cultural. The cultural activities (or cultural content) being shared with visitors are "approved by the 'Keepers of the Culture.'" Applicants whose nations do not have "a system in place to grant cultural approval" can have "the original Nation complete a declaration . . . granting that approval."[121] The program requires that companies present a minimum number of "cultural elements" in order to "be defined as a cultural experience" and that these cultural elements, regardless of their approval by Keepers of the Culture, must "engage the senses and heighten the visitor's experience and enjoyment."[122]

ATBC implies an interpretation of authenticity, a pre-existing understanding of what constitutes an authentic Aboriginal culture and experience—yet in terms of an actual definition, ATBC provides a glossary to its applicants in which authentic reads as something directly out of the Oxford English Dictionary; it is defined as "not a reproduction, copied or complying to fact, being worthy of trust, reliance, or belief; having a claimed and verifiable origin or authorship, not counterfeit or copied."[123] The difficulty with such a formulaic definition is that it is impossible for an Aboriginal experience to *not* be copied—the tourist industry (despite the shift towards personalized and experiential tourism) requires the replication of experiences. Given that ATBC's actual definition of authenticity is of little use (beyond establishing that it must have a connection to some sort of community-approved cultural content), it would be worthwhile to consider another perspective on the definition of tourism authenticity.

It would be reasonable to assume that the definition of authenticity is to an extent mediated by tourist interests. The Department of Tourism and Culture for the Yukon Territory posts on their website a report prepared by Michèle

Laliberté of the Tourism Intelligence Network of the ESG-UQAM Chair in Tourism at the Université du Québec à Montréal, titled "Authenticity—What Do They (Tourists) Really Want?" Laliberté connects authenticity with the growing interest in sustainable tourism, noting that "the notion of authenticity is open to many interpretations."[124] Laliberté does offer a framework for understanding authenticity in the context of ecotourism, writing that "urban tourists from industrial countries . . . [are] seeking something outside their daily lives, something innovative and different, as escape" in the quest of "new things and they enjoy the sensation of being where things are real and original."[125] Tourists, she suggests, want to be at the site of the authentic. Although people can purchase Paris-made clothing in Tokyo, people want to travel to Paris, where the clothing comes from—the site of the *original* and the *authentic*; tourists want to be able to say, "I was there." Laliberté defines authenticity as referring to "an original experience that is true to reality. Its meaning becomes clearer when one thinks of its opposites: falseness and imitation."[126]

She adds that authenticity in tourism refers to (among other things) "wanting to experience a different way of life," wanting "a window onto its culture, heritage, history, and identity [that differs from one's own]," and wanting the "opposite of globalization and its resulting standardization." Perhaps most importantly, tourists of today want the "discovery of places in a country that remain untouched by modernism and still maintain traditional methods and ways of life."[127] This latter tourist aspiration is revealing for interrogations into the workings of authenticity. In the early colonial period authenticity referred to the notion that Indigenous peoples were fixed in a "primitive past" and were destined to vanish from the earth forever. Those who adapted in any way were aligned with "modern"; those who assimilated to European cultures were no longer considered "authentic."[128] "By this logic," Raibmon writes, "modern Indians were not Indians at all, they were assimilated. Others were all too Indian; they belonged to a noble and tragic past but had no role in the future. Only the vanishing had legitimate claims to land and sovereignty; surviving modernity disqualified one from these claims."[129]

In contrast to what is suggested by ATBC's Cultural Authenticity Program, and by Laliberté's analysis of tourist desires, Raibmon counters that there is no such thing as authenticity, and that the word authenticity could best be understood as "shorthand for . . . historically specific notions of authenticity . . . authenticity is not a stable yardstick against which to measure 'the real thing.' It is a powerful and shifting set of ideas that worked in a variety of ways toward a variety of ends."[130] Authenticity has meant very different things at different times with regard to Indigenous peoples. The ideas of Laliberté as outlined above, and ATBC's development of the Cultural Authenticity Program, reflect the powerful and shifting set of ideas that inform understandings of authenticity in relation to tourism. In order to fully realize the authenticity of Aboriginal peoples, tourists demand practical engagement with Aboriginal cultures by knowledgeable (authentic) Aboriginal peoples; as such, Indigenous peoples have at times been "collaborators—albeit unequally—in authenticity . . . utiliz[ing] those same definitions to access the social, political, and economic means necessary for survival under colonialism." As was the case in the time and place under study in Raibmon's book, the same regions that ATBC's membership covers, authenticity has long served as a key element of "a colonial cosmology."[131]

Conclusion

Although there is no such thing as an authentic Aboriginal or an authentically Aboriginal tourism company, for the very low price of becoming a stakeholder in ATBC, the organization was willing to sell companies a logo saying they are authentically Aboriginal. While CTC's marketing of Aboriginality hinges on racist and colonial notions of Indigenous peoples and lands, ATBC's picturing of Aboriginality is rooted in references to diversified land-based and localized experiences. At the same time, ATBC trades in the notion that there is such a thing as authentic Aboriginality. This has the dual effect of capitalizing on non-Indigenous peoples' desire for authenticity while also working to limit the extent to which non-Indigenous peoples might appropriate the discourse of Aboriginality for their *own* tourism businesses.

ATBC as well makes another interesting intervention by referencing "non-traditional" experiences such as golf courses, wineries, spas, and casinos. By noting that certain communities offer such amenities, ATBC employs a broader vision of what constitutes authenticity in the context of Aboriginality. It diverges, most notably, from judicial interpretations of Aboriginality; in particular, the *Van der Peet* decision, which, as previously discussed, fixed Aboriginal rights to a pre-contact moment. Whereas one might be tempted to read such moves towards economic development as plain evidence of such communities' hearty embrace of and thus willing assimilation into neoliberalism, it bears mentioning here (as outlined in the introductory chapter) that Indigenous peoples *cannot*—and especially in the time period under study in this chapter—be the free subjects that neoliberal markets rely on. This is not to deny any particular person or community agency; rather, it is to account for how the overarching grip of colonialism remains vitalized in and through mechanisms such as the Indian Act, which has both the power to grant permission to Indigenous peoples to engage in forms of economic development such as casinos, and the power to deny them.

In some ways this is in keeping with the challenge arising in court cases as to whether casinos are an appropriate form of economic development. Courts have long intervened in denying/granting Indigenous peoples' participation in particular forms of economic practice. Most notably, as seen in *R. v. Pamajewon* (1996), when the communities of Shawanaga and Eagle Lake asked the Supreme Court "to rule that Aboriginal rights to self-government include high-stakes gambling," the Court relied on the Van der Peet Test and thus froze the rights of the communities in the pre-contact past.[132] While the communities sought affirmation of the their right to *self-government*, the Court could and would only consider whether high-stakes gaming could be seen within the scope of an appropriate economy for the people. Yet some communities, such as the Osoyoos Indian Band, have been able to subvert such constraints and engage in "non-traditional" economic development.

The Osoyoos Indian Band has been held up as a model of the ability of neoliberalism to solve the problem of poverty for Indigenous communities. Running over thirteen businesses, including a popular winery, spa, and golf course, the Osoyoos Indian Band also administers a number of lease agreements to non-Indigenous corporations, and operates the Nk'mip Desert Cultural Centre, an interpretative centre that offer insights into the lands and culture of the Okanagan people.[133] Osoyoos Chief Clarence Louie is well known for espousing neoliberal ideology. As he extols the benefits of capitalism and economic development as the solution to poverty, he also positions those who do not engage in such economic practices as lazy, arising from their dependency on the state. Louie's uncritical embrace of a capitalist work ethic and his adoption of neoliberal ideology of wealth generation conflates "an historical Indigenous work ethic with participation in the modern wage economy."[134] Clifford Atleo Jr., a Tsimshian (Kitsumkalum/Kitselas) and Nuu-chah-nulth (Ahousaht) scholar in the areas of Indigenous governance, political economy, and resource management, argues that Louie is playing to racial stereotypes of Indigenous peoples by not accounting for how, "Indigenous and Settler values . . . have previously inhibited Indigenous participation in the mainstream economy."[135] Atleo Jr. makes a critical intervention here, calling for recognition of the way that settlers and the state have actively worked to constrain the economic development of Indigenous peoples.

There are many examples of such constraint. For instance, in 1886, after the events of the Northwest Resistance wherein First Nations and Métis defied Canadian domination on the Prairies, Edgar Dewdney, then Indian Commissioner, coordinated a policy, referred to as "Reward and Punishment," by which First Nations bands "deemed 'loyal' were provided with livestock and other forms of assistance for good conduct . . . 'rebel' bands were punished: their [treaty] annuities were withheld, and horses and firearms were confiscated."[136] In some cases, food rations were withheld, contributing to widespread conflict. In a period of mass starvation and genocide on the Prairies, any form of so-called economic development was impossible for many, as agents of the Canadian government forced anyone classed as Indian to look to the colonizer for relief. In this instance "clearing the plains," as Canadian historian James Daschuk calls it, took precedence over the well-being of Indigenous peoples. Whereas First Nations bands were able to generate some modest return on their efforts, such as in the case of farming instituted on reserves via the Department of Indian Affairs, the federal government scaled back food rations; this would happen even when bands were not yet fully economically self-sustaining.[137] Further to that, such initiatives were chronically undersupported. Economic development was encouraged but never to a level that would enable Indigenous peoples to pose a market threat to settler economies.

Initiatives like those with which Osoyoos Indian Band and other First Nations have been able to leverage their position to engage in a form of economic development that is acceptable and compatible with Canadian economic interests are not ubiquitous. This is true particularly for those burdened by the legacies of starvation on the Prairies, and who do not have scenic views and capacity to market destination in addition to culture. Given these legacies, it is less clear how neoliberalism might provide a solution for all. The overemphasis on Osoyoos as a model of capitalist success elides other, tougher, questions about the legacies and ongoing impacts of economic development. Settler colonials never historically pictured the Indigenous peoples of the present *as* Indigenous.

Even if they imagined Indigenous peoples in a future state of existence, it was always as an emptied-out shell devoid of any vestiges of Indigeneity.[138] Osoyoos and other ATBC affiliates were able to upend colonizer expectations by playing to fantasies of Aboriginality while advancing their own agendas.

ATBC's Aboriginality is still marketed through allusions to "timeless mists" and "ancient rainforests," buzzwords of the colonizer's vision of Indigenous peoples, cultures, and ties to nature. As Alfred has highlighted, the Aboriginal, Aboriginalism, and Aboriginality are falsehoods. However tightly ATBC may spin the narrative about Aboriginal tourism and the authenticity of the businesses it represents, the Aboriginal is a construction of the state that bears little connection beyond the state to *actual* Indigenous peoples. While the state is concerned with drawing on Aboriginality to market itself, so, too, are Indigenous peoples implicated in the promotion and sale of the image of the Aboriginal through the marketing of Aboriginality and authenticity.

The language of ATBC's tourist profiles, however, varies from CTC's in that it focuses on localized histories, stories, and cultures in contexts separated from discourses of Canadian nationalism. While CTC based its understanding of "Canada, Aboriginal-style" on racist and colonial logic that props up the state's fantasies of its relationship with Indigenous peoples, ATBC has tried to reclaim an Indigenous-centred Aboriginal tourism that, on the surface, appears to move the focus away from the state's interests. While ATBC also consistently draws on language that can be read as relegating Indigenous peoples to a nostalgic past existence, like CTC does, ATBC still manages to assert the contemporary presence of Indigenous peoples by drawing tourist attention to the adaptation of Indigenous economic modes—through resorts, wine, spas, art, and casinos.

In the early years of building Aboriginal tourism, Indigenous peoples were fashioned as an identifiable tourism brand that hinged on marketing familiar to settler society and tourists. Alfred argues, "accommodations with colonialism are sought. Indigenous peoples who embrace aboriginalism become cultural mirrors of the mainstream society, and because they aspire to elevate their status inside settler society, they are afforded opportunities to usurp the voice and privileges of legitimate representatives of First Nations. Governments promote, and the general society accepts, the aboriginalist voice in politics and the arts, scholarship, media, and other public forums because it is the voice of accommodation and acceptance of the situation and allows settler society the hubris of its mistaken notion that indigenous dysfunction is responsible for

First Nations dependency and suffering."[139] This latter point speaks to the ease with which tourism has been taken up as a solution for Indigenous poverty and so-called dependency. Yet the fact that Indigenous peoples need this recognition in order to attract tourists, and thus capital, resonates with Alfred's analysis that an emerging Indigenous middle class has become "dependent financially and for their personal status on that [colonial] order."[140] Rather than ameliorating dependency it has altered the terrain of dependency. For this Alfred takes to task "aboriginalists" (politicians, economic elites, and moderate intellectuals) who employ a passive language of compromise and negotiation in dealing with colonial authorities in order to "prevent the activation of a political or cultural resurgence against the colonial order."[141]

Hawaiian scholar Haunani-Kay Trask, on the other hand, complicates such simplistic analysis, questioning whether Indigenous peoples are "complicitous" in the "co-optation of indigenous ways."[142] Trask insists that the state pulls Indigenous peoples into "cultural prostitution" by compelling them to take up roles "waiting on tourists, cleaning their rooms, selling them artifacts, and smiling for a living."[143] Trask writes, "Some of our people are bought, some are crushed between impossible demands, others are squeezed until they become but images of their former selves. Those who resist often find the price too high . . . Native resistance no longer results in death or imprisonment, as it once did, but now brings chronic unemployment or threats of lawsuits or constant hounding and public ridicule that threatens our sanity. For the sake of our loved ones, our families, our elders, and our relatives, we participate in the wage system because we feel that there is no other way."[144] It may be the case that working towards identifying and developing a new economic base from which to support and rebuild Indigenous nations necessitate the kinds of strategic decisions made by different Indigenous peoples and communities. Yet at the same time such decisions are hampered by a constantly transforming colonizing machine chomping at the bit to see Indigenous nations fold entirely.

Aboriginal tourism provided many rewarding economic opportunities for local communities and, as ATBC claims, it also served (and continues to serve, albeit in renarrated form) the revitalization efforts of local First Nations. ATBC credits cultural tourism with a "revival of culture."[145] These attestations reflect Raibmon's assessment that by "participating in the manufacture of authenticity" Indigenous peoples could "bring economic, cultural, and political gains" and in many cases playing Aboriginal continues to "provid[e] much-needed income."[146]

As we have seen, images that align with "dominant society's expectations" are images that sell.[147] What sort of work was done in this temporal moment by the term Aboriginal?[148] It is important that we recognize that contemporary tourism, even in its most aboriginalized of forms, did, as sociologist Mimi Sheller underscores, emerge out of romantic imperialism.[149] In light of this, Aboriginal tourism is rife with the "remnants of the earlier representational practices" of romanticist tourism.[150] It requires that those sites, spaces, and *people* perpetuate an entirely fabricated image of uninterrupted, continuous, and pristine Aboriginality that affirms, even as it attempts to negate, a neoliberalized form of colonial power.

Corporations like CTC and ATBC mobilized Aboriginality as a new market brand that would sell to tourists exactly what they were looking for—a modern and less contrived take on real Indianness. At the same time, such corporations aided the crystallization of Canada's national identity as inherently and innately multicultural. Further, the discursive formation of authentic Aboriginality as culturally salient, free from political complexity, and no longer shaped by the nasty vestiges of colonial domination, proved to be a valuable corporate brand. In turn it also functioned as a valuable *national* brand as far as it worked to export a particular image of the relationship between Indigenous peoples and the Canadian nation-state—as a relationship emblematic of *culturally* reconciled relations and congruent *economic* interests.

Marketing Aboriginality and the Branding of Place: The Case of Vancouver International Airport

While exiting the international terminal at the Denver International Airport, you enter a hallway where Native flute music wafts and the walls are adorned with Edward Curtis sepia-type pictures or other artwork dominantly displaying Native Americans of time past. The exhibit is called "'Spirit of the People." This appetite for the idealized Indian infiltrates and reinforces the incompatible understanding or belief of contemporary Native peoples.[1] – DOREEN E. MARTINEZ

Airports are potent sites for conveying meaning. In a matter of seconds and minutes information is taken in, absorbed, and digested, with little time to question the veracity of terminal displays and/or images. As the bookends to our journeys, telling us where we begin and where we end, the airport terminal is what *is*; it is the orienting point for dislocated travellers. There is thus something at once comforting and affirmative in those images being located in that space, for however little time we may acknowledge them. Writing of the early design stages for the Toronto Pearson International Airport terminal, architect Bernard Flaman reflects on this, noting that designers incorporated large murals to serve as "powerful orientation devices for travelers finding their way through the new jetports."[2] We are therefore oriented in moments of encounter, such as the one described by sociologist Doreen E. Martinez (Mescalero, Apache) above; signs and symbols, by their very existence in a space of orientation, appear to be authoritative.

While it may be that the inherent transience of airport terminals leads us to give them little regard, it is vital that we take their functions and meanings seriously. By approaching both the trajectory of Canadian aviation and the construction of airport terminals through an Indigenous-centred lens—reading for Indigenous presences and absences—it becomes clear that images, like those

Martinez reflects on, are not neutral. Air travel is as intimately wedded to Canadian colonization as anything else. Vancouver International Airport (YVR), for instance, was built on the land of the xʷməθkʷəy̓əm and is subject to a comprehensive land claim that was first filed in 1984. This land claim situation is not unique to YVR. The Macdonald-Cartier International Airport/Ottawa International Airport is built on the land of the Omàmiwininiwak, with whom no treaty agreement was ever made to cede the lands from their ownership to either the British Crown or to Canada. Because the lands on which some major Canadian airports have been constructed are subject to ongoing land claims, the airports themselves are therefore part of the landscape of colonization. In addition, the development of air travel in the early 1900s gave Canada easier access to remote areas, leading to the intensification of settlement and colonization in areas previously accessible only by land or water. Aviation has therefore intensified the pace of colonization as a whole—meanwhile creating new articulations of place. What does it mean when terminals, as anchor points for the aviation industry but also as a form of infrastructure linked to objectives of Canadian nation-building—if we understand them as informed by their ability to orient us—engage in the representation of Aboriginality? How do we make sense of their careful and conscious incorporation of Aboriginality? How has Aboriginality been mobilized in the context of airport terminals and to what ends?

What makes YVR stand out has been the effort it has made to integrate visual markers of Aboriginality into its passenger terminal. From the 1990s until a few years ago (as I have identified elsewhere in this book, the peak era of Aboriginality), when the mandate was reframed and the overall relationship to the xʷməθkʷəy̓əm shifted, the non-profit YVR Art Foundation operated under a mandate to pursue the accumulation of what it referred to as Northwest Coast Aboriginal art for placement within terminal space. The decision to pursue such artwork is undoubtedly linked to the discussions in the previous chapter on the growing interest in tourism-related Aboriginal experiences and is inseparable from practices of destination marketing intended to enhance local tourism. But it is also, crucially, a narrative battleground amid the experience of place-branding. The Aboriginalization of the airport terminal through strategic measures is, to a large degree, a pacifying process consistent within the larger temporal turn towards showcasing constructions of Aboriginal people and Aboriginal cultures as a part of Canada's multicultural fabric in a manner that purposefully glosses over such local histories of dispossession and violence; it subsequently obfuscates aviation's involvement in the colonization of land and the colonization of the sky.

Commercial air travel plays a significant role in many people's lives today. It is a part of everyday life and has become one of the primary ways in which people move across Indigenous homelands and the wider world. Air travel has intensified and quickened the pace of people's movements, as well as transplanted animal and plant life forms, non-sentient materials, and consumer products, across the earth. What does it mean to take aviation, its grounded forms, and Indigenous entanglements with it, seriously? To address this question, this chapter examines the Vancouver International Airport's Aboriginalization of the airport terminal. I contend that YVR's airport authority, in its taking up of Aboriginality, enacted a performative inclusion for the purposes of place-branding; the airport simultaneously marketed an image of Aboriginalized multiculturalism and sidestepped deeper questions related to the airport's role in colonization and the dispossession of local First Nations.

From Technological Nationalism to Technological Colonization

Air travel relies on mechanized transportation that falls into two broad categories: ground transportation, including machinery such as trains and cars, and air transportation, including airplanes, jets, and helicopters. Scholarship on Canada's overall transportation infrastructure has clearly situated the former of these mechanized forms of transportation—ground transportation—as most important. The railway has played a particularly significant role historically and up to the present day. The building and expansion of the trans-Canada railway system was crucial in nineteenth- and twentieth-century Canadian nation-building.[3] According to rhetoric scholar Maurice Charland the railway "was built on with a combination of public and private capital for the advantage of the state and merchants, and the former, like the latter, saw its interests in terms of economic development."[4] The railway effectively made the expansion of the nation possible in a number of ways: encouraging and transporting colonists to move to the Prairies, extending Canada's military presence, stemming American migration northward, facilitating travel and the shipment of goods from coast to coast, and serving as a rhetorical tool for promoting the supposed unification of the nation-state.

In the wake of the building of the CPR, which connected Ottawa with the colony of British Columbia, discussions around the railroad about Canada's territorial claims ceased and concerns about the railway shifted to the enhancement of the public infrastructure of the nation, a nation that was assumed to have staked its claim to finite territorial boundaries.[5] The legitimacy of the nation's claims are, however, contestable, given that much of the land claimed by Canada has never been ceded to it and the very notion of cession is itself contentious.[6] Moreover, some Indigenous peoples were coerced into signing treaties with Canada,[7] and/or Canada failed to uphold its part of the treaty.[8] Such critiques rarely appear in literature principally concerned with emphasizing the successes of Canada's first mass transportation system.

The bulk of scholarship on the CPR focuses on shoring up what Charland refers to, in his essay of the same name, as "technological nationalism." Technological nationalism binds technology and rhetoric, and in the context of the railroad is evinced by "the myth of the railroad, or of the binding of space technologically to create a nation" that "places Canadians in a very particular relationship to technology."[9] Prime Minister John A. Macdonald was the primary political force driving both railway development and the attending rhetoric that Canada could not *be* Canada without its railway.[10] At the same time, Macdonald was directly responsible for enforcing policies aimed at the dispossession and oppression of Indigenous peoples of the Prairies in order to facilitate the building of the CPR.[11] The policies were not simply concerned with moving and relocating people; they also involved the deprivation and starvation of Indigenous peoples.[12] Further to this, treaty-making led to the establishment of the reserve system, a system used for confining Indigenous peoples to what Howard Adams (1989) termed "prisons of grass," subject to successive waves of Indian Act policies aimed at "civilizing" and assimilating Indigenous peoples into British-Canadian life. Indigenous peoples were confined to reserves via legal and pseudo-legal mechanisms such as the pass system.[13] What might be called technological nationalism was more than rhetoric—it was an exercise in nation-building; the railway was accompanied by policies enacted by Macdonald and others that were intended to (to borrow from Daschuk again) clear the Plains.

The coast-to-coast system of train travel that would link colonists in the East with those in the West was devised and carried out at the expense of First Nations and Métis people. The railway would contribute to settlers peopling the lands to which Canada sought to lay claim. Yet Charland demonstrates, as one of many scholars writing on the implications of the CPR and rhetoric surrounding it, there is little awareness of or interest in discussing the role of racism in making Canada's technological nationalism possible. The campaign to increase the population of colonists was explicitly racialized and racist, invested in building a particular kind of Canada with the "right kind" of people—those who met standards of British whiteness.[14] Those who did not meet this socio-cultural, linguistic, religious, and/or racial standard were categorized as "Indians" or as "immigrants."[15] Among those categorized as immigrants were African-Canadian and African-American descendants of enslaved indigenous Africans who took up homesteading on the Prairies and Chinese labourers who built the railroad.[16] The realities of anti-Black and anti-Asian racism and racialization ensured their perpetual displacement from Canadianness. This is the reality through which railroads, the extension of an ethos of Canadianness, and the Canadian nation came into existence.

First Nations and Métis peoples in the Northwest and across the Prairies were considered unsuited to the task of nation-building. The newly forming state instead developed policies and projects intended to assimilate Indigenous peoples into the highly policed, invisibilized normativity of Canadianness and white civility.[17] A fuller account of the CPR's role in nation-building, like the one that Daschuk offers, challenges Charland's glib assertion that the CPR project was undertaken across an undeveloped wilderness.[18] The railroad was *not* built across an undeveloped wilderness; the lands the railroad tracks would be laid over were occupied by people—people with sophisticated ways of living in balance with the sentient and non-sentient beings around them.

Charland does not appear to take issue with conceptualizations of space as wilderness, yet "wilderness is a social category that works alongside other social categories such as race and gender, gaining legitimacy through its appearance as self-evident, or natural."[19] The formation of wilderness as a social category is rooted in the perpetuation of another social category, that of Indigenous peoples as Indians, as uncivilized, and of Indigenous homelands as uncultivated, and thus as terra nullius, as empty land—ideas foundational to discovery narratives such as the Doctrine of Discovery.[20] The notion that the West was undeveloped relied on the construction of its Indigenous caretakers as less civilized beings, beings who did not properly develop the land. These ideas are the very foundation on which technological nationalism was built. Technological nationalism, then, cannot be decoupled from colonization; it might therefore be more accurately termed "technological colonization," accounting for transportation technology's role in the colonization of Indigenous peoples and lands.

The establishment of the CPR was vital to Canada's colonization of Indigenous peoples and to its nation-building efforts. Yet the railway was not the only technology used to achieve these ambitions. Aviation would come to provide the Canadian state with another weapon of transportation in its arsenal, allowing it, its citizens, and its business interests to reach into areas not easily accessed via ground transportation.[21] In this sense, although air transport arose under slightly different circumstances from train travel, it too is heavily implicated in Canadian nation-building. It is more than fair to say that airstrips, airfields, and airport terminals have been constructed without regard for Indigenous peoples. Airfields were not, despite arguments to the contrary, constructed in undeveloped wilderness but were, like the railway, built in and across Indigenous lands.

Technological Colonization, Resource Capitalism, and (White) Peopling of the North

Prevailing research on the development of aviation tends to position it as a positive process in the growth of travel infrastructure within Canada.[22] Rather than offering a linear history of aviation, I will instead contextualize the industry as it has most directly impacted Indigenous peoples. Doing so also recognizes the fact that aviation, unlike rail transport, has not been developed in a linear manner but has rather been developed piecemeal in response to a constellation of interests and perceived needs. Most of its forms of development have nevertheless come to impact Indigenous peoples in direct and indirect ways.

Through the mid-twentieth century, as it developed in Canada, civil aviation "was to be the glue by which the nation was held together."[23] Proponents of aviation argued that it would "break down national boundaries, improve communications, introduce a universalistic culture and make war too terrible to contemplate."[24] It was the ultimate technological achievement of modern nations. This is evident in the gradual adoption of aviation within Canada to expand and consolidate its territorial reach. Within a capitalist framework, aviation provided Canada with the means to "people" remote regions with white, Anglo-Saxon Canadians. Canada's Department of Transportation (DOT) supported the steady increase of aviation aided by the further development of air bases during the Second World War. Throughout the war, the government hoped that the creation of routes to bring passenger travel to the North, to places such as the Yukon, would encourage greater permanent settlement of Canadians there: "More modestly, aviation companies and DOT officials hoped that it would help to maintain and encourage northern settlements. Although bush planes had been flying into the area as early as the 1920s, lack of airports precluded scheduled service."[25]

Aviation would become the new technology of nation-building in the sense that its strategic use to people northern and Arctic regions would shore up Canadian borders and thus assert Canadian sovereignty. The increased attention towards northern and Arctic regions emerged for two reasons. First, the interest in northern regions was expressly tied to the belief that such places held known and unknown material resources (such as the forests and minerals) that were considered valuable in the landscape of Canada's capitalist economy. Second, the Canadian govenrment was increasingly concerned with fending off potential US and Russian territorial claims in northern regions. Although northern and Arctic regions are clearly Inuit, Dene, and other Indigenous peoples' lands, Indigenous claims to sovereignty in these areas are undermined by prevailing racist ideologies that insist Indigenous peoples are not fully human, properly civilized, or living within a recognizable nation-state structure. This, coupled with glossy national narratives used to market assimilation, promoted the idea that Indigenous peoples located in harsh northern regions should *want* to assimilate into Canada.[26] Air travel was thus wedded to colonization and the resource capitalism at the heart of Canada's identity and its attempts to assert territorial sovereignty.[27]

The expansion of aviation hinged on the successful construction of what E.A. Wrigley refers to as a "mineral-based energy economy."[28] This system of resource capitalism, invested in extracting minerals from the earth and transforming organic matter into a material commodity, saw companies like

Imperial Oil manage a good portion of the twenty-three private/commercial airfields constructed as a part of the Trans-Canada Airway.[29] Aviation assisted Imperial Oil in its quest for new oil wells, providing ease of access to northern regions. As early as 1918, Imperial Oil was drilling near Fort McMurray in Alberta, and in three locations in the Northwest Territories—near Great Slave Lake and Peace River, and at Norman Wells.[30] It was not long before Imperial Oil located substantial oil deposits. While drilling on 24 August 1920, Imperial Oil hit oil at Norman Wells (present-day Tulit'a).[31] Such moments mark a significant shift in the Canadian state's interest in relations with northern and Arctic regions. To this point, when air travel had facilitated access to the North and the introduction of domestic and international companies to a new stock of purported resources, Canada had been largely uninterested in what, and who, lay within and beyond the boreal forest. Although it is true that the fur trade continued to be important in northern and Arctic regions, the early twentieth century saw an overall decline in the market demand for fur.

Until the 1920s, the Canadian state had deployed an informal policy of avoiding treaty-making with Indigenous peoples in the region; the consensus was that the North did not consist of particularly arable land, that the climate was too harsh, and that building a railroad to encourage settlement would be too expensive.[32] Instead of establishing a comprehensive administrative system, Canada formed a small territorial government through the North-West Territories Act of 1875. As Peter Kulchyski and Frank Tester note, the commissioner and four council members hardly met, with primary colonial administration handled by members of the RCMP.[33] Although local Indigenous leaders had repeatedly asked for a treaty since as early as 1903, one concerned with devising terms for the relationship between their peoples and Canada, it was not until 1920 that Canada began to seriously consider entering into treaty.[34] While up to this point there had been little interest in treaty-making or in the administration of peoples or lands, the federal government by and large assumed ownership of the homelands of Indigenous peoples, their kinship groups, and communities in the North. By 1920-21, however, the state recognized that a small, haphazard territorial government would not be sufficient to protect the lands, waters, and resources it was claiming for itself and thus needed to obtain land surrenders from Indigenous peoples in order to firm up its claims and further coordinate its administrative oversight.

While Canada's sudden renewed interest in treaty-making did not arise directly out of a desire to build airfields or airstrips, it was undoubtedly tied to something that aviation enabled—the locating of new resource deposits. Kulchyski and Tester argue that Canada's change in governance structure of what it termed the Northwest Territories was spurred by "a renewed interest in both the mineral [such as gold] and petroleum resources of the Mackenzie Basin" and with the identification of oil by Imperial Oil and their subsequent interest in extracting it for commercial use.[35] Revisions were made to the Northwest Territories Act on 16 June 1921, with six Canadians appointed as councillors to work with the commissioner in a more hands-on administration of the NWT.[36] Meanwhile, treaty-making had been approved in January 1921 and negotiations began the following summer. Negotiations and signing of Treaty 11 would continue through 1922 but it is clear that the treaty was not entered into with the best interests of the Dene and other Indigenous peoples in mind. Negotiations for Treaty 11 were undertaken in order to serve government interests and to secure, with support of the Canadian legal system, its right to lands for mineral development in particular regions of the North. By the late 1920s, the increase in the number of bush planes and the development of related infrastructure enticed mining companies to set a foothold in the Northwest Territories, just as they were entering into other northern regions. Airplanes supported this expansion, bringing in greater numbers of "trappers, traders, prospectors, and miners."[37] Imperial Oil, which had briefly halted operations for a time, reactivated its Norman Well refinery in 1932, while "gold fever" around Yellowknife brought dramatic increases in many types of exploration and mining.[38]

In response to these developments, in 1926, the City of Edmonton appealed to the Air Board that it was the best major city to function as a hub for flights into and beyond the boreal forest, situating both the North and the sky as extensions of a new frontier to be explored and conquered. Proponents of establishing Blatchford Field, what would later come to be known as the Edmonton City Centre Airport (closed November 2013), pitched it in such a way as to claim that it was vital for "opening the Canadian north."[39] Frontierism was therefore reinvigorated with the development of aviation technology. Historian David T. Courtwright argues that, in the context of the United States, the "frontier did not close. It became multidimensional, with continuous, technologically premised, socially constructed, and mutually reinforcing movement on the land, in the nighttime, and through the sky."[40] For First Nations, Métis, and Inuit in northern and Arctic regions, the impacts of this multidimensional rendering of frontierism means that colonization, too, became multidimensional, as air travel facilitated colonization in a way that train travel had previously done for more southerly First Nations and Métis. In providing access to the next major frontier for Canada, it has likewise meant the intrusion of colonists and the Canadian state into Indigenous lives in often damaging ways. Edmonton's successful bid for the first federal licence for a commercial airport set a precedent, demonstrating the undeniable links between air travel, frontier capitalism, resource extraction, and nation-building.

For the most part, Canada's aviation efforts have not been seen as the concern of Indigenous peoples. For example, the Lake of Two Rivers airfield was built on unceded Omàmiwininiwak land currently under land claim, the Malton Airport (later Toronto Pearson International Airport) was built on land subject to a land claim by the Mississaugas of the Credit River, and Vancouver's Sea Island Airport is on unceded xʷməθkʷəy̓əm territory. The earlier development of airfields and airports all proceeded without regard for Indigenous peoples. The land used to support aviation was assumed to be Canadian; there has never been serious consideration of questions of Indigenous land and sovereignty with respect to airfields, airport building, and the objectives of reinvigorated frontierism.

The advent of aviation technology therefore played a crucial role in the colonization of northern and Arctic regions. This is directly linked to Canadian attempts to assert sovereignty over less populated places. Military programs continued to push airport construction northward into the 1950s, and, with the construction of the Distant Early Warning Line in the mid-1950s, Canada clearly identified the Arctic as a place bounded by its claims to sovereignty. To be sure, all attempts at "settling the North" are directly linked to Canada's efforts to assert Arctic sovereignty and to further its national interest.[41] But Canada's national interest was furthered without regard for the Indigenous nations over which Canada was laying its aviation infrastructure. In this sense, the development of aviation broadly resembled the earlier construction of a trans-Canada railway. Unlike the construction of the railway, however, the development of airfields, airstrips, and, later, airports did not generally involve the direct displacement of people for their construction. However, the building of the infrastructure for both was for the benefit of white Canadians and in the context of supporting a white vision of Canada, one based on the brutal regimes of dispossession of Indigenous peoples.

Aviation historian Jennifer Van Vleck argues, in the context of the United States, that aviation as both hard and soft power has been a tool of American hegemony.[42] Drawing on the work on imagining nationhood by Benedict Anderson, Van Vleck writes that aviation made it possible to "'think' the nation," but that in the context of state aggression "it was also an instrument and symbol of national power, which could be deployed to lethal effect."[43] In this sense, aviation is therefore also directly linked to the nation's policies and practices of assimilation intended to eliminate Indigenous peoples. This is perhaps nowhere more evident than in the role of aviation relative to residential schools. As renowned Inuk artist Michael Kusugak recalls, it was by plane that he was taken away from his home and placed in a residential school: "When you're seven years old and hauled away from your parents, it's very hard. I cried the whole year I was there—that's all I remember. The following fall, when the airplane came again, I went and hid in the hills. I didn't go to school that year."[44] Airplanes have been both a site and symbol of immeasurable trauma.

Likewise, many Inuit were relocated by plane to southern Canada for treatment in tuberculosis hospitals; while the experience was traumatic for most, for those families of children, adults, and older people who did not return, airplanes were again a site and symbol of incredible trauma. Aircraft and systems of aviation also enabled the Canadian government to forcibly relocate Inuit through programs such as the High Arctic Relocation.[45] The memory of this pain lingers; today aviation continues to signal both despair and hope—it has not shaken off these dark histories. Inuit are still often forced to leave their communities to seek medical treatment. At the same time, in a vastly changed physical environment, aviation allows for the shipment of food and other commodities to the Arctic. While prices of basic consumer goods are exorbitant, in the absence of other infrastructure, without aviation shipments into many of these regions might not be possible. Much work needs to be done to develop a fuller understanding of how aviation impacts Inuit and other northern people—and all Indigenous peoples. Much has been written about Canadian aviation history, but it has ignored the fact that aviation, as much as the railway, has been a central tool of genocide.

From Nowhere to the Passenger Terminal

The development of passenger terminals would transform the aviation industry's engagement with Indigenous peoples from one based on ignorance to one of limited engagement. With the arrival of aviation's golden age in the 1960s, there was growing concern for passenger safety. Passenger terminals were initially developed to protect passengers from the pollution of planes, and also to provide insulation from the extreme noise of plane engines and turbines. Passenger terminals also functioned to "move passengers and their baggage from ground transportation to the check in, through security, and onto their plane."[46] Norwegian social anthropologists Thomas Hylland Eriksen and Runar Døving argue that the compression of time during air travel and the effects of time zone differentials lead to an impression of "the air journey as unreal and somewhat marginal: it transcends nature—it brackets and relativises time and space."[47] The terminal is the "waiting-room between two places."[48] The terminal itself may be considered a cultural void (a "transit lounge") and not really a place of its own; most travellers would not feel that they have seen a place if they have only been to the airport.[49] The terminal is therefore a potent anchor for those in transit. It provides solidity and reassurance that makes air travel less disconcerting. The terminal reminds us that in spite of being jarred by the compression of time and space, beyond the terminal's doors we are *somewhere*—that whether leaving or arriving, we are given a sure foothold.

Since the early development of terminals, art was conceptualized as a wayfinding tool for passengers. In 1952, DOT began to develop plans to update airport terminals across Canada, and major terminals contracted architectural firms for assistance in design-planning.[50] While most terminals were devised to share some core elements that would facilitate moving people through the airport, airport authorities also began to espouse the idea that the interior of the terminal could function as an art space—a gallery, of sorts.[51] Working in concert with the National Gallery in Ottawa and DOT, airport authorities in Toronto, Winnipeg, and Edmonton commissioned and incorporated twenty works of painting and sculpture into their terminals. The works were intended to "project a national image."[52] The incorporation of artwork into other Canadian passenger terminals followed.

One rationale for incorporating artwork into passenger terminals was that it promoted national unity by exposing "audiences from one part of the country to artworks produced in another. The political underpinnings of the program, a conscious effort by the Canadian government to represent a shared national culture, are part of the legacy of the Royal Commission on National Development in the Arts, Letters, and Sciences."[53] There was marked tension between "those who promoted a national perspective that was largely based on international modernist ideas of abstract expressionism and those who preferred to project a regionalist image, synonymous with representation of folk art."[54] What was then known as the Cape Dorset Eskimo Cooperative, a cooperative of Inuit artists, was included within the landscape of artists chosen to evoke Canadianness, presumably in relation to Canada's preoccupation with firming up its claims to Arctic sovereignty.

The Canadian nationalist perspective also increasingly aligned with its new national narrative—that of multiculturalism. Multiculturalism was fast becoming a cornerstone of Canada's self-image and its projection of the meaning of Canada and Canadianness throughout the 1970s. Flaman argues that there was some "declarative nature in this pursuit of Canadianism; if artists from all regions of the country participate, including First Nations, then it must be Canadian!"[55] Indigenous peoples were drawn into Canada's multiculturalist narrative into the 1980s, and this trend of emphasizing Aboriginality in an effort to convey Canadian multiculturalism, openness, and hospitality, is something that would become increasingly clear with the inclusion of First Nations art in airport terminals like YVR. As with the shifts discussed in earlier chapters with regard to the Olympics and to tourism, authenticity became a significant buzzword with respect to Aboriginal inclusion in airport terminals. It would lead to, in part, the removal of such installations as non-Indigenous artist Walter Yarwood's metal sculpture *Totem*, which had been installed in the interior courtyard of the Winnipeg airport terminal in 1963.[56]

By 1985, the federal government owned and administered 122 airports; it also owned another 1,133 that were administered by the provinces, and continued to focus on establishing and integrating nationally coordinated routes.[57] Overall, the federal government's efforts to guide the aesthetic design of airport terminals continued without disruption. Gradually, however, new ideas about the placement of art and imagery within airports began to take hold, especially in the 1980s with the expansion of global consumer capitalism. The placement of art within passenger terminals became increasingly strategically managed to "draw passengers towards retail stores and restaurants."[58] Interestingly, the public display of art declined even though capitalism intensified the focus on using passenger terminals to foment Canada's national identity. Flaman writes that in the 1990s displays of art in the public spaces of airports were gradually replaced by retail shops.[59] This coincided with both an increase in numbers of passengers and a shift from government to private ownership of airport facilities.

The shift from public to private ownership and administration saw a turn towards regional marketing with an emphasis on landscape and authenticity. As airport terminals were employed less as tools for knitting together national identity across disparate regions and populations and more as sites and spaces of consumerism, art was replaced with shops and ads intended to "evoke [marketable] regional symbol[s] inside the shells of the modernist buildings, mainly through themed retail concepts."[60] Destination marketing, as discussed in the preceding chapter, infiltrated the airport and upended the aesthetic design of terminals. Airport authorities aggressively sought to engage in place-branding for the express purpose of generating revenue.

Inasmuch as terminals were designed to keep people safe and move them along, they were also intended to influence traveller behaviour and, generally speaking, to encourage people to spend money.[61] This shift was concretized from the 1980s and into the 1990s, when airports increasingly shifted their attention from fostering national identity to fostering a localized identity that feeds into growing desires for differentiation and uniqueness. This, in turn, would foster consumer spending. Strategic decisions would be made to bring together the marketing of local identities with retail marketing. With the growth of the tourism industry and experiential tourism, terminal design gradually shifted from emphasizing national identity to associating with the local. While this has occurred in airports throughout Canada, it had taken on a distinct pattern in Vancouver, where the Vancouver International Airport Authority took deliberate and concerted steps to incorporate First Nations art as part of its destination marketing. The effort to market the region by drawing on the distinctiveness of Pacific coast First Nations visual culture was accompanied by an insidious, though not entirely misplaced, belief that exposing travellers to First Nations art would increase consumer spending within airports.

The commercialization of Indigeneity within YVR is a clear example of the logic of Aboriginalization at work. It promises some measure of inclusion in exchange for contributing to the profits of the airport and its associated businesses. It is, to a large extent, about window-dressing—giving the illusion of Aboriginal inclusion while ensuring that the relationship between Indigenous peoples and the airport is a largely superficial one. As artist and art historian Rosalind Alix Rorke writes, "YVR's presentation of native culture as non-confrontational, homogeneous and transhistorical has the effect of eliding the ongoing social and political challenges which native individuals and communities currently face."[62] YVR's incorporation of First Nations art commits to an Aboriginalization process that accords the First Nation on whose land the airport sits with limited ability to intervene in the substantive issues at work with respect to the airport itself—that it sits on unceded land and that its ongoing presence is severely damaging to the surrounding ecosystem.

YVR

After extensive lobbying by the Aero Club of British Columbia and the municipality for the construction of an airport in Vancouver, work began on Vancouver's Sea Island Airport in 1930, with the airport officially opening on 22 July 1931. According to the YVR website, "Our story began with a single runway and a small, wood-frame administration building that welcomed 1,072 passengers in 1931."[63] The airport enabled the grounding of land and seaplanes and would come to serve as a hub for cargo, mail, and passenger services for Alaska Washington Airways, United Airlines, and Canadian Airways. Historical accounts indicate that the Vancouver Sea Island Airport (also known as Seaplane Harbour) was built on 475 acres "purchased by the city" from government.[64]

In spite of glib, celebratory narratives of Vancouver's entrance into civil aviation as beginning with the airport's construction, however, its story begins further back, in its complicity in the dispossession of xʷməθkʷəy̓əm of their lands and waterways. Much of Vancouver and surrounding areas, including the lands of the airport, were never part of a formal land cession treaty-signing process and agreement; insofar as land cession is ever truly possible, ownership or stewardship was never ceded by the original people of the land to the Canadian and/or provincial government. YVR's real story begins with its construction on unceded xʷməθkʷəy̓əm land. As with a number of Canadian airports, including those mentioned earlier, YVR sits on land Canada claims ownership of through its violent dispossession of local Indigenous peoples.

A photograph taken at the launch of Sea Island Airport's transcontinental service in 1939 shows Basil Point, Dominic Point, and Tsimele'nuxw (Chief Jack Stogen) standing in front of a teepee. The caption for the image reads: "Musqueam Reservation Indians, Basil Point, Chief Semilhano and Dominic Pint took part in ceremonies at departure from Vancouver of Lockheed 14-H-2-CF-TCK on April 1, 1939 inaugurating regular passenger service on the transcontinental."[65] The juxtaposition of the three men against a teepee, a structure that is indigenous to Prairie-based and other Indigenous peoples but *not* to xʷməθkʷəy̓əm, gives some insight into processes that may have been at work in the airport's staging of the ceremonies. While it is noteworthy that local First Nations were able to find pathways to involvement in such key moments in aviation's development on their lands, companies like the CNR and CPR, along with various levels of government, often invited (non-paying) or hired Indigenous peoples to perform at events but required that participation be in keeping with prevailing stereotypes of Indigeneity—or to use Francis's expression, in keeping with the "imaginary Indian."

While in the image all three were wearing dress pants and shiny shoes, along with traditional tops, the orchestrated pose of all three men, arms crossed and standing in front of the teepee, suggests that insofar as they exercised agency over how they appeared and what they wore, they would conform to expectations in keeping with stereotypes of Indianness. As Rorke explains, those interested in marketing Vancouver drew on the "idea of Vancouver as a frontier settlement in close proximity to native peoples."[66] Frontierism was then invoked not only in the explicit context of resource capitalism but also in the thinking around how to market the growing capacity for passenger air travel to Vancouver and to promote the city as a destination for tourists. Frontierism, inasmuch as it was about resource extraction to serve capitalist interests, was also about mining "the frontier" as an adventure in and of itself. This kind of frontierist ideology, however, was, as with tourism developed in accord with expanded train travel, primarily interested in emphasizing industrial progress and technological nationalism.

Through the 1950s and into the golden age of aviation, also known as the jet age, local Indigenous peoples continued to be pushed to the background as airport proponents emphasized technological progress and Vancouver's desirability as an international destination. Following the sale of the airport to the federal government in 1962, the airport would itself undergo a significant remodel, with greater attention to the construction and enhancement of the passenger terminal itself.[67] As discussed earlier, a substantial focus was placed on using art to publicly narrate Canadian national identity. At the same time, and especially in Vancouver, there was a growing desire and push for the creation of a distinctive "sense of place" through the use of art and architectural design.[68] Drawing on the work of Umberto Eco, Rorke argues that architecture and aesthetics in the context of the Vancouver airport had everything to do with communicating "a certain image or fiction of the 'local'" that had absolutely nothing to do with the act of flying itself.[69] To this end, she argues, airport design "should be considered as an ideologically embedded statement representing aspects of locality that are important to the dominant cultural group."[70]

Vancouver, and the Vancouver represented within the airport, were increasingly framed as a colonial frontier, a "village on the edge of a rainforest."[71] Representations of "Northwest Coast Indian art" were intended to invoke the absorption of Indigenous peoples "into the dominant mainstream without constituting a threat."[72] Inasmuch as Indians were imagined to be dying out, art would be the thing that would survive and connect Canada to its imagined ancestral past. When plans for the redesign of the Vancouver airport became public knowledge, local groups and individuals pushed for the incorporation of pan-Northwest Coast artworks—in particular totem poles and carvings—to signal something distinctive about Vancouver's, and British Columbia's, identity. The push for inclusion, it should be noted, was primarily born from the belief that Northwest Coast Indigenous art *was* British Columbian. Harold Merilees, as Tourist Bureau manager, wrote a series of letters, published in the *Vancouver Sun*, pushing for the incorporation of Northwest Coast artwork in the airport's design. He argued on 6 September 1968, following successful lobbying, that "this is the culmination of a four year fight to have something in the terminal that will identify it with Vancouver rather than Toronto or with Tel Aviv."[73] In spite of this early push for representation, Indigenous peoples themselves were largely absent from processes at work. It was not until the airport was redesigned in the early 1990s that the incorporation and inclusion of Indigenous artworks would more directly engage with local Indigenous communities and with other Indigenous communities in British

Columbia, signalling a new era in the relationship between the airport and Indigenous peoples.

The airport underwent another major remodel in the early 1990s upon its transfer from the federal government to the Vancouver International Airport Authority (VIAA), an independent non-profit entity charged with administering the airport. The transfer from government grew from the adoption of a broader national strategy of privatization of airports and other public assets by the federal government.[74] The transfer, it was believed, would ensure greater commercial success of the airports but also of the regions themselves. With greater input, the VIAA would be able to develop YVR in keeping with its own regional objectives—with, of course, the broader national strategy in mind. One of the central approaches to enhancing its regional image was a refining of artistic representation within the airport's terminal interior and its exterior façade.

Aboriginalization at YVR

First Nations were essential to YVR's renewed vision, yet their role would largely be, at least through the era of Aboriginality, restricted to the artistic realm. Engagement with xʷməθkʷəy̓əm and other First Nations people would be mediated through the artistic non-profit arm of YVR known as the YVR Art Foundation, founded by the airport in 1993.[75] From its inception (and until recent terminological shifts that have come to place greater emphasis on the words First Nations and Indigenous), the YVR Art Foundation's mandate was to "foster the development of Northwest Coast Aboriginal art, to broaden its markets and to promote its display in public buildings."[76] During the era of peak Aboriginality in the 1990s and 2000s, the discourse of Aboriginality was at the forefront of the work of the foundation. Its rationale for promoting Northwest Coast Aboriginal art was further elaborated on their website as follows:

> The YVRAF believes that Northwest Coast Aboriginal art plays a vital role in defining the unique character of our province and its heritage. The Vancouver Airport is committed to creating a unique sense of place within the airport where British Columbia's

distinctive cultural heritage and spectacular natural beauty are celebrated.

Every aspect of YVR's aesthetic development has been founded upon this commitment. A painting of B.C.'s forest, mountains and sea by Canadian Group of Seven artist Lawren Harris, was chosen as the colour palette from which the materials and finishes of the airport were selected. The airport is designed to reveal spectacular views of the ocean and the mountains, and the building's finishing materials serve to showcase British Columbia's natural resources.

Nowhere is YVR's unique sense of place more alive than [in] its spectacular display of Northwest Coast Aboriginal art. This magnificent artwork has driven the vision for the airport. In fact, the aesthetic development of the airport was based on the vital role public art can play in defining its spaces.[77]

The YVR Art Foundation is unequivocal about their interest in Northwest Coast Aboriginal art as an expression of BC's character and heritage but also as a tool in the aid of "creating a unique sense of place"; Northwest Coat Aboriginal art, as they imagine it, lends an essential aspect of originary diversity to the BC brand.

While YVR's International Terminal already housed a work by Nuu-chah-nulth artist Joe David and by Roy Henry Vickers, a Tsimshian, Haida, and Heiltsuk artist, the Pacific Northwest Coast Aboriginal art was centred in the redesign of the International Terminal because of a belief that it signalled something about the "authenticity" and uniqueness of the city of Vancouver lying beyond the airport's boundaries: "According to a YVR promotional CD-ROM, native art is featured specifically because it 'honours' the natural geographical beauty which the terminals themselves 'celebrate.'"[78] Waisman Dewar Grout Carter Inc. was contracted to design the airport's International Terminal in 1993:

> Clive Grout, the architect in charge of the terminal's interior design, noted that "the materials are green and blue, very natural, reflecting the water and the foliage that we have around here."

Figure 5. Susan Point's *Flight (Spindle Whorl)*. It is located in the International Terminal of the Vancouver International Airport, and serves to welcome travellers upon their arrival to the airport, to Vancouver, to British Columbia, and to Canada. Photo by Andrew Magill, https://www.flickr.com/photos/amagill/29628849.

His firm also included ample amounts of wood, a staple of the province's resource-based economy, as well as rock facing and ceramic tiles. Grout designed the restaurant and retail spaces such that they resemble popular tourist destinations within the region: Steveston Waterfront, Granville Island, and Whistler Village ... the terminal is encased in glass and incorporates elevated walkways that allow passengers to look out toward the impressive coastal mountain landscape ... During the planning phase, the VIAA championed this design aspect and the vistas it offered, and they noted how it would improve the experience of international travellers arriving in Vancouver ... Like the numerous First Nations artworks installed in the terminal, this view of a distinctive landscape also calls to mind that the passenger has arrived at a specific place—the Pacific Northwest Coast.[79]

The architectural firm also designed the interior of the building with consideration to "how the VIAA-commissioned artworks would be positioned in the space."[80] Prior to the YVR Art Foundation's establishment, the VIAA (then the YVRAA) had already begun forming a working relationship with the xʷməθkʷəy̓əm to secure locally relevant artworks. For their part, the xʷməθkʷəy̓əm established the Musqueam Cultural Committee, responsible for negotiating with YVRAA "around the inclusion and placement of their work and on issues of the type of work to be displayed."[81] The Musqueam Cultural Committee subsequently selected artists and arranged commissions.[82]

The result of the engagement process was the designation of a portion of the third level of the terminal, after security checkpoints, that would become known as the Musqueam Welcome Area. It consists of a number of large-scale installations by xʷməθkʷəy̓əm artists: Susan A. Point, Shane A. Pointe, Krista Point, Robyn Sparrow, Debra Sparrow, Gina Grant, and Helen Callbreath. The latter five women wove four large tapestries, collectively titled *Out of the Silence*, suspended from above. Susan A. Point's massive sculpture titled *Flight (Spindle Whorl)* welcomes travellers at the top of stairs and an escalator that run parallel to two small waterfalls (Figure 5); travellers pass by two welcome figures situated at the bottom (separately carved by Point and Pointe) (Figure 6).[83] The artists all felt that the most important aspect of the inclusion of their work was the creation of a space for recognition of xʷməθkʷəy̓əm culture.

Some xʷməθkʷəy̓əm interviewed by Métis scholar Shannon Leddy expressed discomfort with YVR's Aboriginalization process, specifically noting the prominent placement of Haida artist Bill Reid's piece *The Jade Canoe*. While the Musqueam Welcome Area is only accessible post-security, Reid's work sits in the pre-security part of the terminal, accessible to all who enter the terminal. As Haida art had grown to international prominence and recognition, and as the calling card of Pacific Northwest Coast Indigenous art, Reid's well-known work was considered highly desirable by YVRAA. Originally created by Reid for the Canadian Embassy in Washington, DC, a new version, *The Spirit of Haida Gwaii: The Jade Canoe*, was commissioned by the YVRAA from Reid in 1993 for $3 million (Figure 7). While Reid "wanted the second cast to have a brown patina," Frank O'Neill, the president of YVR Visitor Services, disliked the colour and "advised against this choice."[84] The jade-green sculpture, the most expensive artwork purchased by YVRAA, would be located where it would be easily seen near the proposed International Food Court and Public Market and "could act as a landmark and a meeting point."[85] O'Neill viewed the Musqueam Welcome Area and Reid's installation as anchorpoints within the terminal, with the latter "designed to be reminiscent of a European Square."[86]

YVRAA secured consent from xʷməθkʷəy̓əm to place Reid's piece within the terminal: "In order to install the sculpture in the airport, permission and blessing had to be asked of the Musqueam people since the airport sits on their land. Permission was officially granted by Musqueam elders in the dedication ceremony at the airport on the night of April 18th, 1996."[87] It is worth noting that consent was granted at the dedication ceremony, held in 1996, even though YVRAA purchased the sculpture a full three years earlier, with the intention of placing it within the terminal. This suggests pushback by xʷməθkʷəy̓əm, and their ability to educate YVRAA, to some extent, on meaningful inclusion and consent, and the importance of honouring local protocols. In spite of the embrace of Reid's work, Leddy uncovered through her interviews that the artists and band council members had some reservations about the prominent placement of Reid's piece.

While xʷməθkʷəy̓əm band manager Howard Grant expressed mild concern with the relative placement of Reid's piece, he did not feel that its presence

Figure 6. Once visitors exit the security clearance line-ups, the Musqueam Welcome Area figures stand at the base of the escalator, which transports them up to level three and face-to-face with Point's spindle whorl. Photo by TagaSanPedroAko, https://en.wikipedia.org/wiki/File:2019-07-20_International_arrivals_hall_of_Vancouver_International_Airport_0935.jpg.

undermined the community's intended message; rather, as Leddy notes, he and others viewed its installation by YVRAA as marking a new beginning—one of inclusion, and as a stage in what would surely be a long future of negotiating.[88] While Leddy does a remarkable job of honouring the perspectives of xʷməθkʷəy̓əm about the relationship, she also poses vital questions about what goes unnoticed in the struggle to be seen within an already skewed politics of recognition.[89] The monumental shift in political relationships precipitated by the legal entrenchment of Aboriginal rights within the Constitution, ongoing Constitutional negotiations, the earlier mass mobilization of First Nations from British Columbia in the form of the Constitution Express, and the growing formalization of land claims processes sent a strong message to YVRAA that to draw on "Aboriginal art" for the purposes of marketing the airport and surrounding region would require some measure of engagement with xʷməθkʷəy̓əm.

The new runway constructed for the International Terminal the year after its 1996 opening was created without meaningful consultation or regard for xʷməθkʷəy̓əm: "The new runway abuts an historic Musqueam burial site. In addition, there are a number of invaluable midden sites in the region (essentially garbage dumps or 'toss zones' used historically by the Musqueam people)."[90] That xʷməθkʷəy̓əm would be included in processes of Aboriginalization in the context of the artistic expression of the airport terminals but ignored in the context of meaningful consultation and consent around land use practices reveals the gaping hole at the heart of Aboriginality. Here, the word Aboriginal once again reflects a carefully depoliticized articulation of Indigenous existence and of Indigenous-Canada relations. This is compounded in the fact that, as Leddy notes, information about the proximity of burial and midden sites to the new runway "has not been released in a publicly meaningful way."[91] This, along with the hierarchization of the early YVR website that placed great emphasis on Reid's sculpture and little on the works within the Musqueam Welcome Area, as well as the physical placement of the Musqueam Welcome Area in a restricted area, raises questions as to the true nature and intent of YVRAA's efforts.

The significance—and irony—of the creation of a welcome area within the airport filled with xʷməθkʷəy̓əm artwork, in consultation with xʷməθkʷəy̓əm, on the unceded land of the xʷməθkʷəy̓əm, cannot be overstated. Neither can the role that capitalism played in the acquisition of artwork and the processes of consultation, inclusion, and recognition. Leddy cites an interview in the

Vancouver Sun on 26 April 1996 in which O'Neill affirmed that the intent in purchasing and placing art within the airport was "to stimulate economic profits at the airport"; he believed that Aboriginal artwork would "provide a competitive advantage over an airport that looks upon itself as a processing factory... What art can do is create an ambience and a feeling that puts people in a good mood. That, by the way, has great commercial spinoff."[92] Competition is a core element of capitalism, and branding and marketing—both of which hinge on the notion of distinction—are key strategies to enhancing competitiveness.

With focus shifting from national unity to regional marketing, YVR sought strategies to maximize its revenue by attracting more travellers and by encouraging those travellers to spend more money while in the airport terminal. YVRAA worked to "construct Vancouver as a distinctive destination *and* reinforce a particular identity. This representational strategy has been aimed primarily at travelers arriving from the United States and other international points of departure."[93] Distinction and authenticity sell with respect to the branding of place. Authenticity became increasingly marketable and marketed throughout the 1990s, and so the appeal to Aboriginal artwork as a way to market authenticity served the function of distinguishing YVR from other airports.

Airport planners also conceived of the placement of local Aboriginal artwork within the space of the International Terminal as part of a strategy to attract passengers to spend more money while inside it. As art, architecture, and design scholar Menno Hubregtse notes in their research, Reid's *The Jade Canoe* was calculatedly placed because the Vancouver International Airport Authority (VIAA) believed that "Northwest Coast First Nations artworks such as this will encourage passengers to spend."[94] As of 2017, it was located near a Starbucks coffee shop and a gift shop (Figure 8).[95] The gift shop sells Canadiana with an emphasis on First Nations artwork, items made for mass consumption (like First Nations–designed, Chinese-made wallets), and tourist kitsch (Figures 9 and 10).[96] In May 1996, the month following his initial statements to media about the role of art in generating consumer spending at YVR, O'Neill reiterated his stance that the installation of First Nations artworks in the airport would encourage travellers to spend more money in airport shops and restaurants.[97] In this sense, YVR is not just the transitional space but part of the destination itself.

Figure 7. Bill Reid's *The Spirit of Haida Gwaii: The Jade Canoe* is still one of the most popular and recognizable sculptures within the Vancouver International Airport. Located in the International Terminal of YVR, it sits in front of Lutz Haufschild's *The Great Wave*, which is an installed glass wall whose design mimics the waves of the Pacific Ocean, 25 October 2010. Photo by Jennifer Adese.

Figure 8. Looking into the front of the gift shop in the International Terminal, next to Reid's *The Jade Canoe*, with Haufschild's *The Great Wave* in the background, 25 October 2010. Photo by Jennifer Adese.

Rorke prompts us to consider important questions that highlight the extent to which Aboriginalization is resonant with Aboriginalized multiculturalism. She questions whether First Nations are being used as a less threatening stand-in for a multicultural identity, one that might stem or divert anxieties of anti-Asian racists. Rorke asks, "If the socio-political position of B.C. First Nations peoples has not substantially improved in recent decades, then why have aspects of their cultural heritage *now* been harnessed at the airport to promote the British Columbian tourist industry? Is the relative position of native people sufficiently non-threatening to the established order that their culture can be appropriated freely without reproducing the anxiety that the presence of newer immigrant cultures may cause?"[98] While Rorke reads the inclusion of Aboriginal artworks and imagery as a possible response to a fear of Asian immigration—using Indigenous peoples to capitalize on a diverse identity while sidestepping the tension and white panic about non-white immigration, and to deny the "internationalization of the city"[99]—I would argue that it is also a response to a more long-standing anxiety that envelops the entire province related to the fact that not only the airport but the majority of the province continue to sit on unceded land. While anti-Asian racists draw on an arsenal of xenophobic comments and strategies to deny Asian immigrants a place within Vancouver and British Columbia more widely, no such comparable strategies aimed at dislocation can be launched towards First Nations. Instead, the airport, as with other entities tenuously occupying unceded Indigenous lands, must tangle with the question about its place and position in the landscape of colonization.

At the same time, First Nations artists were included insofar as they did not challenge the state's objectives or question the legitimacy of the state itself. As discussed in relation to the Olympics, this translated into the splitting of Aboriginal people into good and bad—or for inclusion or exclusion. This was evident in decisions made around whose art and which art to display in YVR for the Olympics. Rita Beiks, the curator of YVR's collection and the program manager for the entire collection, was the person charged with selecting artists whose work would be on display at the 2010 Olympics.[100] She indicated in a 2008 interview with Megan Stewart for *The Thunderbird*, the student publication of the Graduate School of Journalism at the University of British Columbia, that controversial artworks would not be selected. Beiks clarified, "Because the airport is not an art gallery, people aren't making the choice to come here to

Figure 9. Another gift shop within YVR, featuring dream catchers (which are not indigenous to xʷməθkʷəy̓əm and other Coast Salish peoples) alongside quintessential Canadiana—maple leaf flag socks, moose socks, and other markers of "wilderness," 25 October 2010. Photo by Jennifer Adese.

see art... They are making the choice to travel and if they're confronted—and I deliberately use the word confront—with work that could be offensive to them, I have to be sensitive to that."[101]

The kind of tension this creates became evident over the work of Lawrence Paul Yuxweluptun and Glen Wood. An initiative called "Orcas in the City" was established in 2004: its promotional material stated that local artists, "in partnership with sponsoring individuals or organizations, will create a unique design and apply it to the surface of a life size (approx. 8ft with base) custom formed fibreglass Orca calf. The Orca becomes the artist's canvas. Once the work is complete, the Orca will be displayed in prominent public spaces around Vancouver."[102] As a public art project, it was geared towards fundraising for the local BC Lions Society's Easter Seal Operations and the Vancouver Canucks for Kids Fund. YVR-sponsored Lawrence Paul Yuxweluptun (Coast Salish and Okanagan) and Glen Wood (Tsimshian) to create what would come to be named the *Northwest Coast Killer Whale*. Following its installation in the airport, "two aboriginal women complained about his black-and-white, Native-themed design."[103] Beiks elaborates: "These women were very upset and it was very clearly First Nations imagery that I wasn't sensitive to... But when they pointed it out to me, I could see what they were talking about. They were really offended, and the airport never bought the piece at the end of the day."[104] Beiks does not offer insight into the exact nature of the critique from the two women who brought their concerns forward, and while there are no details as to the motives or specific backgrounds of the women, what is clear is that this moment was used as a catalyst to stifle ideas which might be deemed controversial.

While Yuxweluptun indicates that he might be willing to work with YVR in future, he also asserts his sovereignty as an artist: "I can't be contained... They don't know if I would embarrass them."[105] Beiks affirms that his perception, that the airport might be less than interested in working with him in the future, is true: "He's correct... I do feel a sense of distrust about what he might actually do in the future. He's very political and that would be one of the questions. He'd have to be very careful what he does."[106] The threats within the statement are obvious. If Yuxweluptun wants to be a venerated YVR-affiliated artist, he would have to stifle his political voice and stick to giving non-Indigenous peoples what they want—pretty things to look at that feed into a desire for depoliticized Aboriginal art. For Yuxweluptun this is not an option. The resilient and resistant nature of his work reflects that he is principally concerned "with the colonial mentality that is directly responsible for the toxicological disaster... the European ethos—your utilitarian, imperious, imperialistic power and your capitalistic value of authoritarianism [that has] destroyed First Nations ancestral sacred lands in fewer than five hundred years."[107] Yuxweluptun's frank critique of colonization and capitalism also lead him to speak unfavourably about the First Nations leaders behind the Four House First Nations who acted as partners with provincial and federal governments on the 2010 Olympics.[108]

The criticism of the Olympic partnership all but ensured that YVR would not commission Yuxweluptun to create work for the Olympics—or any time thereafter. Beiks indicated that "the airport is unlikely to commission Yuxweluptun to create an original piece of work" but "they may still opt for a finished painting" such as *New Chiefs on the Land* or a similarly less political piece. While Beiks indicates that YVR's art *can* have a message, it cannot be one that would be offensive to people.[109] What this struggle over Yuxweluptun's work (Wood is not mentioned in the articles available in relation to this) reveals is what is at the core of YVR's Aboriginalization. During this period only art that did not disrupt the status quo of YVR, Vancouver's, and BC's identity was sought. This is consistent with the cases examined in previous chapters, whereby non-Indigenous peoples, even in post-Constitutional times, determine the parameters of Aboriginal inclusion. As Coulthard has identified, a subjugated politics of recognition, in spite of rhetoric espousing an ethic of inclusion, has resulted in a strategic stifling of dissent.

Conclusion: Aboriginalization and the Colonization of the Sky

Both the intent and effect of Aboriginalization was a freezing of Indigenous peoples into the past.[110] Drawing on the work of Adriana Barton, Rorke writes that the narrow lens through which YVR approached the purchase and incorporation of Indigenous artworks perpetuates the myth that Indigenous peoples remain fixed in the past. While Aboriginalization may have made room for "neo-traditional" artwork that may fit into YVR's brand for the airport and the region, Indigenous peoples and cultures are rendered "nearly synonymous with the rainforest, the exhibition of numerous larger-than-life works reinforces the location of indigenous culture outside modern civilization, technology, and rationality."[111] Indigenous peoples are also erased

Figure 10. Additional gift shop display shelves within YVR, this time selling "Made in Canada" wooden necklaces alongside "authentic" dolls that play into international travellers' fantasies of Indianness—buckskin, feathered headbands, and cherub-faced figures with "Mohawk" hairstyles. Photo by Jennifer Adese.

from the city of Vancouver by being refused the ability to contribute art that reflects the difficult reality of contemporary Indigenous life, as reflected in YVR's anxiety over Yuxweluptun's artwork. What is unmarketable—like Vancouver's "urban sprawl, environmental pollution and unresolved land claims"—is elided.[112]

To be sure, in its quest for a non-threatening brand image, YVR purchased Indigenous art with an emphasis on First Nations (but also with a later acquisition of a sizeable collection of Inuit artwork), continuing through the late 1990s and into the 2000s and 2010s. As previously discussed, Rorke argues that the primary rationale for Indigenous inclusion is anti-immigration, and in doing so poses an important question. If immigration is the threat, does this mean that Aboriginalization reflects a landscape where Indigenous peoples are no longer seen as a threat to the nation? I would say, firmly, no. In fact, it may very well be that YVR's desire for Aboriginalization led it down a path it had not intended to be set upon, for a decade after quivering at the thought of Yuxweluptun's purportedly controversial work, YVR is now deeply entangled in relations with xʷməθkʷəy̓əm that ensure that YVR moves beyond the narrow confines of a relationship solely mediated by narrow definition of artistic inclusion. In the 2010s, the gradual decline of the use of the term Aboriginal, and the death of Aboriginalization, gave way to a new set of dynamics organized around the rhetoric of Indigeneity and, most recently, of Indigenization. In light of the findings of the Truth and Reconciliation Commission about Canada's shameful past and systemically entrenched anti-Indigenous racism, it appears that, at least in the context of YVR, few things remain as they were. It is to this discussion I turn in the next and final chapter of the book.

The development of aviation in terms of its direct relationship to Indigenous peoples has been largely connected to airports and the land they are built on; however, the colonization of the sky must also be considered an "instrument and symbol of national power."[113] To fully interrogate the relationship of Indigenous peoples to airports, it is necessary to consider that if the land, in the case of YVR, is unceded, what does that mean about the sky? Courtwright reminds us that "while there were no human populations in the sky, there were insects and birds. Their presence would be affected by, and sometimes catastrophically affect, mechanical flight. It is a mistake to conceive the sky as entirely empty."[114] Air travel has undoubtedly facilitated the advance of land-based processes of dispossession—deforestation to resource extraction—and is an industry highly dependent on oil and other minerals for its very existence. Air travel is also responsible for the generation of new, albeit invisible, borders that have very real impacts as airplanes cross through the sky and above the clouds, and as they pollute the air.[115]

The disruption caused by air travel, however minor it might appear from the ground, drastically impedes the natural flow of wind, birds, pollen, and insects across the sky. For however numerous governmental agencies have attempted to control and mitigate it, air travel has grave impacts on air quality and on sky beings. The term "bird strike" is industry shorthand for the death of a bird that has collided with an aircraft—something that happens with alarming frequency. We rarely talk about colonization and the sky, unless we are speaking directly to the impacts of manufacturing and resource extraction on air quality. It is difficult to talk about what Aboriginalization covers over when we have scarcely begun to interrogate it, but if we extend our critique of YVR to thinking in terms of the actual *life* of the sky, then we see a lifeworld that has been targeted for colonization in a manner linked to, but also separate from, colonization on the ground. According to Courtwright, the sky cannot be settled "like land"; however, in the transient nature of the relationship between humans in flight and the sky world, aviation has contributed to the "colonization of the world after dark."[116]

From another angle, we might consider Treaty 4 (Tipahamatoowin) as concerned only with the top six inches of soil—or "the depth of a place . . . for the whiteman to farm."[117] Likewise, Nehiyaw lawyer Sharon Venne reminds us that, in the context of Treaty 6, Indigenous peoples, as caretakers of the birds, "never agreed that birds come under the jurisdiction of the state of Canada."[118] Do treaties extend to the sky, and have any Indigenous peoples, *could* any Indigenous peoples, cede sovereignty of the sky to Canada? Canada has operated under the assumption that land and sky are linked, and that claiming sovereignty over the land translates to automatic sovereignty of the sky. Milloy and Venne demonstrate that there were bounded limits to what Indigenous consent to British and Canadian land use looked like—and that this did not include permitting resource extraction or aviation. Treaties were created in a time before flight. What does raising questions about sovereignty and the sky tell us about what Aboriginalization is also trying to conceal? Can Indigenous peoples cede the sky? Can the sky be subdivided? Who owns airspace? Might this be the next stage of the relationship to be addressed? This is not only a question YVR may be pressed to address.

Airport development is not often discussed in the context of dispossession and treaty-making, yet it is undeniable that the development of, for example, Blatchford Field (in what is now a part of North Central Edmonton) was made possible by successive waves of displacement of the Siksika, Nakoda, Métis, and Nehiyawak. Anywhere you find an airfield, airstrip, or airport, you will find that dispossession is a part how these places have come to be. And yet it is not a part of the story told by governments and airport authorities who uphold a national narrative of unity, while trading in regional narratives, to drive local (primarily non-Indigenous) economies.

Given that one of the functions of the terminal is to locate travellers, the incorporation of any kind of representations of Indigeneity appears, to the fleeting and uncritical gaze, to be telling travellers something *real* about their destination. There is a pedagogical function to the terminal: travellers are reoriented to place by something *real*, and for those new to a particular place, the terminal is the anchor for producing the new reality of the place in which they have arrived. Inasmuch as airports rely on core elements which are indeed uniform—signs, layout, and so on—the aesthetic design of terminals has increasingly rendered them locally specific. Travellers to a particular airport, perhaps those returning home, are comforted by the familiarity of the displays they see. Whether the associated meanings of the displays are present, understood, or critiqued by travellers, the very act of Aboriginalizing the airport does in fact then signal something about place—and in the effort to use passenger terminals as vehicles for tourism destination marketing, representations of Indigeneity within airports *are* very much tied to place.

It has not been my intention here to analyze individual artworks within the airport in depth, but to briefly discuss their presence to highlight, through the different stages of YVR's existence, how what is now VIAA has or has not engaged with the question of its placement on the unceded homeland of the xʷməθkʷəy̓əm. It is my contention that the conscious incorporation of artwork by xʷməθkʷəy̓əm and other Indigenous artists is very much in keeping with an Aboriginalization in which non-Indigenous corporate entities engage in a relationship of representation that detracts from larger questions around meaningful consultation, inclusion, and, crucially, decolonization. While the significance of the creation of the Musqueam Welcome Area can only truly be understood through acknowledging how xʷməθkʷəy̓əm feel about the installation, it remains that the motivation behind the inclusion of xʷməθkʷəy̓əm arose largely from a desire for artwork—artwork that would signal something about place, about nature, about British Columbia, and that this something would encourage passengers to spend money. In the wake of the passage of the Constitution in 1982 and the Supreme Court rulings in the *Van der Peet* and the *Sparrow* cases, as discussed in the Introduction, and with growing awareness about the experiences and realities of First Nations, Métis, and Inuit, Aboriginalization emerged as a form of superficial inclusion that detracted attention from the real issues and from a deeper sense of responsibility to the people on whose unceded land the airport exists.

Conclusion: Thoughts on the End of Aboriginalization and the Turn to Indigenization

Capitalism has given rise to a disarticulated form of Aboriginality; spinning off from the pages of the Constitution, it is an Aboriginality that promotes essentially its own idiosyncratic vision of what and who the Aboriginal is, and that ultimately circulates outside of the use of Aboriginal in the legal and political realms. While formerly the Indian was constructed through paintings, film, and literature, the Aboriginal is a much more subtle entity that peeks through from the (re)presentations in the tourism industry, from the Olympics, and within the Vancouver Airport. It may seem that at times I am more focused on the representations of Indigenous peoples than on the actions and responses of Indigenous peoples to such representations. This is true, although that is not to elide the agency of Indigenous peoples in participating in narrative constructions of Aboriginality. I am well aware that our various peoples are capable of a wide range of responses and that Indigenous peoples can and do respond in vastly different ways to the conditions in which we find ourselves.

Some may elect to participate in the narratives in hopes of reclaiming them or aiding in the construction of more accurate representations, while others may launch outright resistances to the state's imagineering of them. What I have offered here are some thoughts about the ways that neoliberalism and colonialism are inextricably linked and how in the rush to contain its colonial history while capitalizing on Indigenous peoples as resources, a diverse state of actors—and the Canadian state—have pulled Aboriginal out from the Constitution to foster the development of an Aboriginal multicultural brand. Here also are my ruminations on the changing shape of state anti-Indigenous racism, a neoliberal racism that at times can so effectively invisibilize its deep investments in the oppression of Indigenous peoples that it appears as exactly the opposite. The Aboriginal is thus effectively imagineered by the state as a signpost of a reconciled relationship between the state and Indigenous peoples.

There is no specific image of the Aboriginal that I have identified here and in our minds which can be conjured in the imaginative sense of the Indian—I cannot simply call out "Look at the woman on buckskin and on horseback, that's an Aboriginal!" There seems to be a disjuncture between the older and more entrenched racial presentations and what is instigated by the new language of Aboriginality. Perhaps this is due to the articulation of Aboriginal as including a wider range of people, including Inuit and Métis. Possibly, then, an imaginative rendering of the Aboriginal would see the more stereotypical representations of Indianness alongside that which is deemed to be more culturally specific and authentic. Such a tie is reflected in the stereotypes of Indianness that are placed alongside culturally specific and nation-specific imagery.

Visualizing of the Aboriginal involves a commitment to assimilation that the very term implies. For many settler Canadians, even though they are aware that "wild Indians" no longer roam the Plains on horseback, their visions of Aboriginality are still rooted in stereotypes about Indigenous peoples. This "new racism" has not displaced earlier racist representation of Indigenous peoples. The Aboriginal (like the Indian) can be seen as carrying the cumulative weight of both negative and positive characterizations of Indigenous peoples. Settlers desperately want to "move past" their own racism (and bury the evidence of its existence), espousing the multiculturalism rhetoric that the state has encouraged—that Indigenous peoples are like "everybody else." The Aboriginal is permitted enough Aboriginality to be different (and to be marketable), but not enough to pose a threat to the state's agendas, ones which often involve the continued violation of Indigenous human rights, treaty rights, and land rights. This is evident in the Indigenous Youth Gathering's preference for "certain types" of Aboriginal youth for the Olympic Opening Ceremonies, and for "certain types" of Aboriginal people for the purposes of marketing tourism.

When figured within the national narrative and as a core part of Canada's self-branding exercises, the Aboriginal is a symbol of forgiveness, reconciliation, the state's purported post-racial status, and the assimilative success of multicultural policy. The Aboriginal conceals a more insidious agenda, namely the state's commitment to a distinctly neoliberal form of assimilation—through rhetoric and through economic rather than explicitly legal or political means. The crux of the matter is that the state no longer needs assimilative legislation as it has in the past. The state's earlier political manoeuvring tried to keep Indigenous peoples in a constant state of deprivation. As many Indigenous peoples (particularly on-reserve and rural peoples) find themselves in desperate need of employment; suffering from the intergenerational effects of deprivation, many look towards corporate opportunities and the language of economic development as an antidote to poverty. This is, as I have argued, a manifestation of neoliberal colonialism.

The implementation of corporate control and the language of "economic development" (particularly as put forth by the oil and mining industries) has made it easier to entice Indigenous peoples away from traditional economic practices and values. With the state's relationship to Indigenous peoples mediated through market logic, the state as a corporation itself has begun to wield its paternalistic control over Indigenous peoples in entirely new ways. I attended to some of the ways that Aboriginality has furthered the state's colonialist and assimilationist agenda, albeit through appeals to the (ir)rationality of neoliberal economic thought. In a time when Aboriginal is the nomenclature to describe state-mediated Indigenous relations, the Aboriginal has come to signify particular things about Indigenous peoples. Throughout this book I have reflected on a few of the many ways that Indigenous peoples have navigated, and at times counteracted, the tightening hold of Aboriginality.

Indigeneity: A New Era

As Indigenous peoples grew increasingly disillusioned with the rhetoric of Aboriginality and the markedly problematic relations it signals, more and more people have turned away from Aboriginal and asserted themselves outside of the constraints of the politics of recognition. Instead of Aboriginal, both Indigenous peoples and non-Indigenous peoples, in everyday life, across corporations, non-profits, educational institutions, and throughout government, have turned to Indigenous. I was reminded of the significance of this when, on 8 July 2020, the Toronto Aboriginal Support Services Council (TASSC) made an Instagram post somewhat paradoxically titled "Why We Say 'Indigenous' Instead of 'Aboriginal.'" The eight images shared in effect condense and summarize Animikii's post of the same name, discussed in the opening pages of this book. As of 29 July 2020, the post has received 24,126 "Likes" on Instagram alone—and an incalculable number on other social media platforms such as Facebook and Twitter. The post reiterates some of the same ideas discussed in the Introduction: that Aboriginal is an English word, that the prefix can render it to mean "not original," and that it is homogenizing.[1] The post insists that Indigenous is a preferable term because with "peoples" coming afterwards, it "succeeds" by recognizing that "there is more than just one group of Indigenous individuals," and the term's meaning "is internally consistent."[2] The council likewise acknowledges that "Indigenous peoples" is still "not a perfect term" because it is an umbrella term, and states that nation-specific terms are always preferable.[3]

As discussed in the Introduction, in its early uses, Indigenous was nearly always used in relation to the environment, for instance in relation to the classification of plants, as in books such as John White's *An Essay on the Indigenous Grasses of Ireland* (1808).[4] Into the mid-nineteenth century it was used primarily to refer to plants, insects, and animals, and only occasionally to people, unless in the description of a state of relationship as in "those people aren't indigenous to there." By contrast, at that point in time, Aboriginal had already been transformed from a verb to a noun. While Indigenous does not mean being *from* a place in the way that Aboriginal has been taken to mean, it gets closer to the prefix "ab" in that it does mean *of* a place and, in that, not just *of* a place but inseparable from it. In this sense it is more fitting—it actually moves us away from a hierarchical ordering that separates us from the natural world—that we are, like the grasses, attached to/born from/derived from the landscape. At its heart this reflects the integrative worldview of Indigenous peoples from around the world that still remembers, as Haudenosaunee and Anishinaabe scholar Vanessa Watts-Powless writes, drawing on the work of Anishinaabe scholar Leanne Simpson, that "the land is our first mother."[5] This resonates with the way Indigenous peoples have taken up the term and what we have been trying to simultaneously signal and challenge with our use of it.

In some ways it would be fine to end my book here. But given the central premise I outlined at the beginning, that it is not as much about the original definition of a term or even how it has been used over time but that it is about a more expansive, functional view, we need to consider what Indigenous has been made to mean. Has this shift from Aboriginal to Indigenous really resulted in something significantly different for Indigenous peoples? Once again, the terrain of engagement between Indigenous and non-Indigenous peoples has ruptured and shifted in such a manner as to have ripple effects outwards to nation-branding, economic-branding, and branding of place. It has altered consumer relations and corporate strategies of engagement. Eventually, it precipitated yet another change in government terminology.

Canadian public policy scholar Mathieu Landriault writes that the shifts in government terminology have had a profound impact on the media, which in turn shapes the terms used within public discourse. Landriault notes that, prior to the 2015 federal election, which saw Harper's Conservative government lose a re-election bid to the Liberals, Aboriginal was the dominant term used by reporters. After the election and over the following year, the situation began to dramatically shift, with use of the word Indigenous tripling in televised news reports on CBC and CTV.[6] The use of Indigenous as well doubled in newspapers surveyed. By contrast, Aboriginal gradually declined across all formats. In that same period, a parallel shift took place on social media, as evidenced by elected officials eschewing Aboriginal in favour of Indigenous.[7]

Much of this change was driven by initiatives undertaken by the Trudeau government soon after taking power in 2015. By the first week of November 2015, newspaper outlets were reporting that following the corporate title name change undertaken by the Conservative federal government during Stephen Harper's reign as prime minister—from Indian to Aboriginal—the Trudeau Liberal government renamed AANDC as Indigenous and Northern Affairs Canada, thus restoring its acronym as INAC. To Trudeau and his ministerial appointee, Carolyn Bennett, the name change was consistent with what Indigenous peoples wanted while also indicating a transition to a new era of reconciliation that would break with the controversial direction of the Harper government vis-à-vis Indigenous peoples. This marked the beginning of the end of Aboriginality—both as a term and as an era.

In August 2017, the Trudeau government initiated a wholesale revision of the name and administrative structure of INAC. The department was split into two and each division was given its own distinctive name: the legal titles are the Department of Crown-Indigenous Relations and Northern Affairs, and the Department of Indigenous Services. The applied titles are Crown-Indigenous Relations and Northern Affairs Canada (CIRNAC) and Indigenous Services Canada (ISC). This shift in corporate language coincides with a government shift in approach in dealing with Indigenous peoples. In splitting the department, the federal government separated out "government programs mainly geared toward status Indians, including welfare, education, infrastructure—including the move to end long-term water advisories—housing and the non-insured health benefits program," allocating them to ISC, along with "the First Nations and Inuit Health Branch (FNIHB) [which] has also been formally transferred from Health Canada to the new department."[8] The other department, CIRNAC, has been charged with "settling outstanding comprehensive land claims ... clearing a backlog of grievances at the Specific Claims Tribunal and generally fostering a new era of self-governance."[9] CIRNAC was also charged with pushing ahead the federal government's attempt "to dismantle the Indian Act," something promoted as "helping more communities opt out of provisions that date back to the 19th century."[10] This new structure was intended to herald further change in the direction of reconciliation.

At the government level, some of this change has been precipitated by the discursive groundwork laid by the Truth and Reconciliation Commission. Arising from within the Royal Commission on Aboriginal People's recommendations was the establishment, in 2001, of the federal Office of Indian Residential Schools Resolution Canada, to deal with the numerous claims of abuse made by former students during the course of RCAP. It was also established to respond to the growing number of court cases brought by former students and a coalition of survivors to pressure the federal government for accountability. Following negotiations with the federal government, the largest class-action lawsuit that Canada has ever negotiated was settled with overly eighty thousand survivors, with terms outlining a number of different mechanisms, responses, and commitments. Taking effect on 19 September 2007, it involved "five main components: the Common Experience Payment, Independent Assessment Process, the Truth and Reconciliation Commission, Commemoration, and Health and Healing Services."[11] The TRC was therefore born in 2008 out of the settlement agreement. The TRC took place over five years and involved a number of public gatherings and private processes intended to "facilitate reconciliation among former students, their families, their communities and all Canadians."[12] It would provide a forum for survivors to share their stories, an opportunity for settler Canadians to listen and learn, and would promote education about the history and ongoing impact of residential schools.

As a multi-pronged initiative, it ultimately resulted in the production of a six-volume final report, released in December 2015. The TRC final report included ninety-four "calls to action."[13] Of direct relevance to this book, within the final report, the word Aboriginal appears 1,836 times while Indigenous appears roughly 539 times. While the report still ultimately outlines reconciliation through the language of Aboriginal reconciliation, the use of Indigenous and the tone of the report itself gesture towards the changes being birthed. In particular, the report is frank in its condemnation of things such as the Doctrine of Discovery and the notion of *terra nullius*, with Call to Action #47 summoning all levels of government to "repudiate concepts used to justify European sovereignty over Indigenous peoples and lands . . . and to reform those laws, government policies, and litigation strategies that continue to rely on such concepts."[14] This strikes at the heart of colonization; the tacit entrenchment of these ideologies sits at the very base of the colonial project and of Canada's assertion of sovereignty on Indigenous lands. By invoking "Indigenous peoples" the report affirms Indigenous nationhood and the right of self-determination, and it repudiates the dehumanizing structures that have had such devastating impacts on Indigenous peoples the world over.

The TRC also links to the UN Declaration on the Rights of Indigenous peoples and the global discourse on Indigenous rights. Canada threw up a number of roadblocks to this discourse, including its long-standing refusal to adopt UNDRIP. From 2007 until 2016, when the Canadian government finally endorsed UNDRIP, its refusal seemed, in some ways, to only further Indigenous peoples' commitment to using a discourse of Indigeneity that reminded Canada of the higher level of rights recognition which Indigenous peoples were cultivating. Canada has continued to construct a number of roadblocks to the meaningful implementing of UNDRIP and has insisted that anything contained within UNDRIP would be reconciled *to* Canada's sovereignty.[15] In spite of this, the adoption of UNDRIP by the vast majority of the global community in 2007 empowered Indigenous peoples to continue to confront Canada's attempts to deny Indigenous peoples' inherent right to self-determination. The delayed adoption of UNDRIP is but the tip of the iceberg with respect to the Trudeau government's failure to meaningfully demonstrate its purported commitment to reconciliation with Indigenous peoples. While it is outside of the scope of this concluding chapter to fully account for the myriad ways that the Trudeau-led government's approach to Indigenous-Canada relations has perpetuated the status quo of previous governments, a discussion of two recent areas of contention highlights the limitations of the current government's approach: the federal government's response to the Wet'suwet'en opposition to the Coastal GasLink Pipeline and its proposed "Recognition and Implementation of Indigenous Rights Framework."

Wet'suwet'en

The Coastal GasLink pipeline, which is owned by TC Energy, is a planned 670-kilomtre pipeline that "would connect natural gas producers in the province's northeast with the LNG Canada facility currently under construction in Kitimat."[16] Yet the Coastal GasLink pipeline will run through unceded Wet'suwet'en lands; while the Indian Act-elected band council has signed on with support for the pipeline, the hereditary chiefs of the Wet'suwet'en Nation continue to stand up to "exercise their unbroken, unextinguished, and unceded right to govern and occupy their lands by continuing and empowering the clan-based governance system to this day. Under Wet'suwet'en law, clans have a responsibility and right to control access to their territories."[17] Gidimt'en "is one of the five clans of the Wet'suwet'en Nation"; in December 2018, the RCMP was granted an injunction by the BC Supreme Court to "forcibly clear a path through the Wet'suwet'en Access Point on Gitdumden territory and the Unist'ot'en Healing Centre on Unist'ot'en territory."[18] On 14 December 2018, all five clans of the Wet'suwet'en Nation came together and agreed to support the Gidimt'en Yintah Access camp.

In response to the Wet'suwet'en Nation's assertion of their sovereignty and UNDRIP-protected rights, the RCMP notified the hereditary chiefs in early 2019 that they would deploy "specially trained tactical forces" to the site to enforce the injunction.[19] In January of 2019, the RCMP "trespassed on the land of the Wet'suwet'en people and arrested 14 land defenders in heavily militarized fashion, following the orders of fossil fuel behemoth TransCanada to enforce the injunction."[20] This was not the beginning or the end of RCMP action against Wet'suwet'en people who are refusing, as Audra Simpson writes, "to consent to the apparatus of the state" and refusing to consent to elimination.[21] For the past three years, Wet'suwet'en people have continued to refuse the pipeline and their elimination, only to be met with a series of armed police interventions. The RCMP has launched frequent charges against the Wet'suwet'en land protectors and has stood by and allowed Coastal GasLink to damage Wet'suwet'en resources and land in hopes of driving the people out through fear and intimidation tactics.[22] The RCMP has likewise engaged in various practices of surveillance, intimidation, and manipulation, intent on removing the people from their land.

While it is outside of the scope of this chapter to offer fulsome discussion of Wet'suwet'en opposition to the pipeline and police and government responses, it is important to highlight that police response to Wet'suwet'en refusal has been heavy.[23] As CBC News has reported, between January 2019 and March 2020, the RCMP spent $13 million in policing actions targeting the Wet'suwet'en people and their allies who have shown up to stand alongside them.[24] Yet Canada has no legal right to the land, as clearly determined by the landmark Supreme Court *Delgamuukw* decision of 1997, which recognized that Wet'suwet'en "and Gitxsan peoples had never surrendered their land or had their title extinguished through treaties, or otherwise."[25] Rather than ensuring that rulings made by its own settler legal system are honoured and upheld, and rather than acknowledging that Canada is in violation of UNDRIP, Trudeau instead audaciously demanded that Wet'suwet'en and other Indigenous nations take down their "barricades"; more to the point of this chapter, he accused Indigenous peoples of failing to advance reconciliation: "Hurting Canadian families from coast to coast does nothing to advance the cause of reconciliation . . . Canadians have been patient, our government has been patient. But it has been two weeks and the barricades need to come down now."[26] In his clear weaponization of the discourse of reconciliation and all that the state perceives it to stand for, Trudeau highlights just how suffocating the discourse of reconciliation, in the era of Indigeneity/Indigenization, is intended to be.

Much is revealed by Trudeau's failure to redirect the RCMP and his government's refusal to accept the fact that the land is *unceded* and what that means. Instead, Trudeau uses Indigenous and Indigenous reconciliation as a weapon with which to continue to bludgeon First Nations into submission. As with Aboriginal, the language of Indigenous promised a new era of relations but, in reality, its use more accurately reflects the ongoing attempt to force Indigenous peoples into nation-state frameworks; it reflects continued attempts to brand Canada vis-à-vis Indigenous peoples by promising reconciliation while bypassing hard truths and denying meaningful and substantive restitution. The refusal of the Wet'suwet'en, then, exposes the rotting heart of reconciliation. As Simpson asks: "How, then, do those who are targeted for elimination, those who have had their land stolen from them, their bodies and their cultures worked on to be made into something else articulate their politics? How can one articulate political projects if one has been offered a half-life of civilization in exchange for land? These people have preexisting political traditions to draw from—so how do they, then, do things?"[27] They do so by refusing the logic of elimination via neoliberal colonialism delivered via the discourses of "Indigenous reconciliation" and "reconciliation with Indigenous peoples." This was made palpably clear when, following a series of RCMP raids and arrests throughout the winter of 2020, Wet'suwet'en and their allies engaged in a number of solidarity actions—including blockading railways and streets—declaring via social media that #RECONCILIATIONISDEAD.

Termination Tables

The foregoing resonates with the federal government's approach to what, as I will discuss shortly, Kahnawake Mohawk policy analyst Russ Diabo refers to as "Termination Tables." In 2018 the Trudeau government announced the "Recognition and Implementation of Indigenous Rights Framework" (RIIRF) as a pathway for reconciling its existing obligations under section 35 of the Constitution of Canada with Canadian law and policy. The government's perspective is that the agreements resulting from this framework would entrench section 35 "in federal law and aim to fill the gap between federal government policies and multiple court decisions on Indigenous rights," the effect of which would be ultimately putting an end to the existence of the *Indian Act*.[28] As Diabo points out, however, this policy mechanism continues the previous Conservative federal government's use of negotiating tables to terminate Canada's moral, ethical, and legal obligations to Indigenous peoples and to negate Indigenous sovereignty, and it looks eerily similar to the White Paper policy framework of Trudeau's father, Pierre Elliot Trudeau.[29] Termination thus refers to "the ending of First Nations pre-existing sovereign status through federal coercion of First Nations into Land Claims and Self-Government Final Agreements."[30]

Negotiations with First Nations, Métis, and Inuit at "recognition and self-determination tables," Diabo argues, will ultimately transform First Nations, particularly, into "ethnic municipalities, with their reserve lands converted into private property and their rights to the overwhelming bulk of their traditional territories extinguished in perpetuity."[31] The objective is to extinguish Aboriginal title and to end federal responsibilities to First Nations via the Indian Act. The proposal promises a renewed relationship based on Indigenous reconciliation; yet it appears as only a slightly modified version of what came before it under the banner of Indigenous reconciliation, that of the "inherent right to self-government policy" that would effectively have turned "First Nations into municipal, fourth-order governments without any significant powers."[32] Moreso, as mentioned, it appears as a modified version of White Paper assimilationist policy.

The insidious nature of such policy agendas is revealed in the shadow of the COVID-19 pandemic. When its attempts to force the RIIRF on Indigenous peoples without substantive consultation or consent stalled negotiations, the government shifted to one-on-one negotiation tables with individual nations (bypassing larger collective organized collectives, such as those discussed in Chapter 1). It has continued to pursue negotiations in spite of the significant threat that COVID-19 has posed to systemically marginalized Indigenous communities. As Diabo notes, the federal government has continued in-the-shadows negotiations over Zoom and other business networking mediums.[33] Further to this, in the midst of the pandemic both federal and provincial governments declared that resource extraction projects were of an essential nature, "meaning construction of several fiercely contested projects is moving ahead, including the Site C dam, the Trans Mountain expansion and the Coastal GasLink pipeline."[34] In spite of a shiny new discourse that takes on the language of Indigeneity and an emphasis on reconciliation (but not truth or justice), this is just the latest iteration of what Diabo refers to as "zombie policies": "unwanted policies are clothed in the new rhetoric of the day, then defeated, then they rise yet again, like colonial zombies that will not die."[35] When these policies are challenged and rejected, and when Indigenous peoples draw on the strength of international legislation to show that another way is possible, Indigenous peoples are instead criminalized, heavily surveilled, arrested and detained, and/or aggressively delegitimized in political and public discourse.

These cracks within Indigenous, Indigeneity, and Indigenization propped up by the stifling bind of reconciliation may portend another shift. However, we need to consider if it is the relationship itself that needs shifting; and if that is the case, what was wrong with it before? What did Aboriginalization fail to do? Does Indigenization provide a better pathway forward? By returning here to the discussions within each of the preceding chapters, and by offering a brief discussion of what I argue is the turn away from Aboriginalization and the turn towards Indigenization in areas outside of the expressly political, some of the relationships and distinctions become even clearer. How has the turn manifested beyond the obviously political?

Indigeneity as a National Brand

It is a fair argument, given the trajectory of discursive change in successive Canadian-hosted Olympics, that should Canada eventually host another Olympic Games, it will not be doing so with Aboriginality in mind. The 2015 Pan Am/Parapan Am Games hosted in Toronto revealed an international spectacle in transition. According to media sources, the Aboriginal Pavilion was the main site for "Indigenous music and arts festivals" for the Games and Indigenous peoples.[36] The shifting terminology itself punctuates this transition. Although the site has sinced changed, during the Games, the Mississaugas of the Credit First Nation (MCFN), on whose territories the Games were hosted, likewise promoted on their website that "Aboriginal culture" was showcased throughout the Games, including in the opening ceremony, while at the same time identifying their people as an Indigenous people. The shifting language from Aboriginal to Indigenous, alongside clear engagement with local communities and frequent direct references to MCFN's name, highlights a transition period—one in which Aboriginal will eventually entirely fall from favour. Were there to be another bid for a Canadian-hosted Olympic Games, bid committees and organizing committees would likely follow this example.

This trend is also demonstrated by the successful shift towards marketing Indigeneity as a national brand. On 21 June 2017, Trudeau announced that the name of National Aboriginal Day would be changed to National Indigenous Peoples Day.[37] By making the name internally consistent with other shifts, and by insisting that the change in name is also what Indigenous peoples want, the federal government is able to deflect previous criticism regarding National Aboriginal Day—that it was a state-driven and -dominated day that was tokenistic in its acknowledgement of Indigenous peoples. In bringing the terminology in line, Indigenous peoples are positioned as partners and as *consenting* to the day and its associated meetings. Yet the position of the day alongside other Celebrate Canada days has not changed. Its position reflects its use now as a mark of *Indigenized* multiculturalism. It is also "on-brand" for the federal government in the sense that as it emphasizes National Indigenous Peoples Day as a reflection of its commitment to building "a nation-to-nation, Inuit-Crown, government-to-government relationship—one based on respect, partnership, and recognition of rights," however contingent on either Indigenous assimilation through "termination tables" or acquiescence to a relationship prefaced on the reconciliation of Indigenous peoples *to* Canada.[38] Indigenous has in effect served as a seamless substitute for Canada's Aboriginalized multicultural brand.

Indigeneity as an Economic Brand

Indigenous has as well been incorporated, with relative ease, into the language of various non-profit and for-profit organizations. In particular, universities have moved from a non-specific practice of Aboriginalization to a concerted process of Indigenization.[39] In the context of post-secondary institutions, Indigenous is often used to refer to "Indigenizing the academy," which is taken, fairly often, as being synonymous with decolonizing the academy and with decolonization generally. Again, this process mirrors, as laid out above, processes of incorporating Indigenous peoples into university spaces while enhancing the institutions' capacity to in turn market themselves as leaders in Indigenization, attracting Indigenous (and non-Indigenous allied) students, faculty, and staff. These efforts, consequently, draw money to the institution under the auspices of Indigenization. Funds are also generated via accessing provincial and federal dollars intended to enhance Indigenous research and presence within academic institutions. This has led to a rise in the number of people claiming an Indigenous identity. Recently universities such as Queen's University in Kingston, Ontario, have come under heavy criticism for hiring, promoting, and supporting non-Indigenous peoples who self-identify as Indigenous with little context (or evidence) to substantiate their claims.[40]

The use of Indigenous for revenue generation is also reflected in the changes undertaken by business entities such as ATBC, who in recent years have shifted their brand to focus on Indigenous tourism. Their website has been changed— www.indigenousbc.com—to reflect their new name of Indigenous Tourism BC (ITBC), and they have reframed Aboriginal tourism experiences as Indigenous ones. Indigenous is thus industrialized and economized through the refashioning of the Aboriginal tourism industry as the Indigenous tourism industry. Indigenous Tourism BC likewise rebranded its authenticity program in May 2019 with the Authentic Indigenous designation.[41] Those whose businesses were designated as Authentic Aboriginal would be grandfathered in, while new businesses seeking designation as Authentic Indigenous would need to meet a new set of criteria. The Authentic Indigenous designation is identified as helping "travelers identify these experiences throughout the province and acknowledges that they are contributing to the revitalization and preservation of local Indigenous cultures and languages."[42] A series of survey questions outlines the standard that companies must meet. As with the Authentic Aboriginal label, they must in one way or another be, as mentioned earlier, 51 per cent owned by Indigenous peoples. There appears to be no direct qualification as to what Indigenous means other than self-identification. To be certified a business must also be a stakeholder in ITBC, meaning it must apply to become a member and pay a membership fee, a common practice among non-profit organizations looking to skirt for-profit status and regulations.

The application also asks a number of more specific questions, centred on Indigenous nationhood and precise cultural contexts, which are in turn connected to place. The questions include the following: "What Indigenous Nation do you present or share in your tourism business?"; "For the Indigenous cultural activity or activities offered, have you gained approval or recognition from the Indigenous Nation (or the Cultural Keepers of this culture) to offer these activities?"; and "Are you sharing this cultural activity within the traditional territory where the culture originates?" There are also questions about what "era" the "traditional activities represent," with the option to select either "Modern" or "Pre Contact," and whether/how the business "is preserving Indigenous cultures."[43] Questions of sustainability are subdivided around employment, community, and the environment, and, while responses to questions regarding employment and community are required, questions pertaining to environmental sustainability are optional.[44]

Despite the lack of emphasis placed on environmental sustainability, which belies the public-facing marketing of eco-friendliness and environmental caretaking, the overall shift in the tone of the program's language is remarkable. The language of Indigeneity moves us closer to insisting on the recognition of the diversity of Indigenous peoples; while acting as a generalizing term, Indigenous is also clearly signposted as a placeholder for diverse local communities. It emphasizes the role of tourism experiences in *revitalization* and *preservation*, as well as pointing to the way that Indigenous tourism itself may contribute to the self-determination, and survival, of Indigenous peoples. There is a notable difference between the vaguer rhetoric of Aboriginal and the increasingly precise and determined language of Indigenous.[45]

Indigeneity as a Place-Brand

Perhaps one of the most poignant shifts has been in the relationship between the Vancouver International Airport Authority and xʷməθkʷəy̓əm, on whose land the airport sits. The airport authority faced significant criticism over its ignorance of xʷməθkʷəy̓əm and the location and operation of the airport on unceded land. In the aftermath of the TRC report and the wave of Indigenous reconciliation, YVR faced mounting pressure to strengthen its relationship to xʷməθkʷəy̓əm. This shift, alongside the continued success of BC First Nations in the courts and the consistent effort of xʷməθkʷəy̓əm at relationship-building with YVR, continued to see the expansion of YVR's effort to incorporate xʷməθkʷəy̓əm artworks within airport terminal spaces but also to enter into new relationships framed on Indigenous reconciliation.

First, the YVR Art Foundation changed its language: Aboriginal art was replaced by Indigenous art. Then, and most significantly, on 21 June 2017, the xʷməθkʷəy̓əm chiefs and council and the Vancouver Airport Authority signed a massive thirty-year agreement, called The Musqueam Indian Band–YVR Airport Sustainability and Friendship Agreement, that, according to YVR, is "based on friendship and respect to achieve a sustainable and mutually beneficial future for our community."[46] Commonly known as the Musqueam-YVR Agreement, it "sets a strong precedent for how YVR honours its relationship with Indigenous peoples and how we will work together to manage the airport for the benefit of everyone."[47] The agreement focuses on what it refers to as "four pillars of Sustainability—Social, Economic, Environment and Governance" and lays out a series of commitments on the part of YVR: ten scholarships per year valued at $10,000, along with apprenticeships and jobs at YVR; giving 1 percent of YVR's annual revenue to xʷməθkʷəy̓əm (in 2017 that amount was estimated at $5 million with an expectation that YVR ultimately pay $200 million to xʷməθkʷəy̓əm over the life of the agreement); the promise that xʷməθkʷəy̓əm would be able to access business contracts; the promise that xʷməθkʷəy̓əm would be able to have input on future development projects (and this would include a job dedicated to managing the relationship between the two).[48] The agreement also provided for collaborative efforts to protect "the land and waters around Sea Island, which is directly across the river from the band's main reserve in south Vancouver. Some of that work will include restoring and enhancing areas on the land, reducing or mitigating airplane noise, and identifying and protecting historical sites of the band."[49]

On the webpage celebrating the agreement, there are links to point to YVR's past in the form of a historical narrative and video. In these nothing is said about xʷməθkʷəy̓əm. Nothing is mentioned about the processes of colonization that took place and which enabled settlers to dispossess xʷməθkʷəy̓əm of their land. There is also nothing to explicitly refer to—or apologize for—the airport's direct role in the dispossession, such as the displacement of band members "from their homes in 1931" during the construction of the first runway.[50] At the celebration and official signing of the agreement, however, band council member Wendy Grant-John ensured that the story of her nation's dispossession was at least partly told. In her comments at the event, she "shared what former Musqueam Chief Johnny told the Royal Commission on Indian Affairs in 1913. She read some of his words, which related to the way of life for Musqueam being disrupted and destroyed by 'the white man.'"[51] Yet to date the airport has no plans to tell us of this history, and if we take the YVR Art Foundation's approach to Yuxweluptun's artwork and its steadfast commitment to fostering reconciliation by avoiding showcasing "difficult" narratives, then it is, at least for now, fair to assume that no such truth-telling is forthcoming.

This reluctance is evident in the way that Vancouver Airport Authority president and CEO Craig Richmond brushed off questions as to why it has taken so long for the airport to commit to an agreement with the band. Richmond replied, "It's hard for me to go through so much history. I've only been the CEO here for four years coming up in July. But everybody on all sides recognized that it's time."[52] It is far too easy to slough off responsibility and to avoid providing a real explanation as to why the airport has been reluctant to acknowledge its problematic position and its failure to just *be* better. An agreement like this also threatens to shift the narrative out of the airport's control, in a way opening the airport up to questions, after all this time, about its ongoing presence on unceded land.

Still, in spite of possible criticism, these agreements are undeniably substantial. By drawing on the ethos of reconciliation, the Vancouver Airport Authority took unprecedented steps that have been lauded by both the xʷməθkʷəy̓əm chief and council and by non-Indigenous peoples. It is the first revenue-sharing agreement of its kind between the management of a major airport and a First Nation. Inasmuch as the agreement has been lauded, we must still be mindful of the larger context and future implications, particularly as it is held up by the airport and the media as a model for reconciliatory success. As I write this, we are in the midst of a slow and unstable economic recovery from the early stages of the COVID-19 pandemic. Travel and tourism continue to be among the hardest-hit industries. While at present the precise impact is not measurable, it is highly likely that in the face of mass layoffs from major Canadian airlines and the airports themselves that such revenue-sharing will as well drop off. That said, until this moment, the agreement has still engendered substantial hope and may still being doing so.

While there are, I am sure, a number of criticisms that could be made about this agreement (primarily about an Indigenous people having little to leverage against the airport other than the spectre of a land claim), xʷməθkʷəy̓əm have been able to use this moment to amplify their voices in significant ways. Wendy John (also referred to as Grant-John) recounts that her people "have been excluded from economic development in the city that was built on their territory without permission."[53] But in the wake of signing the agreement, xʷməθkʷəy̓əm are not just taking over control, they are also reclaiming the narrative and telling the stories YVR has been reluctant to tell. John tells about stalled processes of negotiation between Musqueam and YVR "when the airport moved to expropriate some of Musqueam's reserve land for a third runway in the 1980s. But the relationship remained dormant until a few years ago."[54] She recalls remarks made by their chief, Wayne Sparrow, while passing the airport: "those guys are making money on our land, and we need to do something about it."[55] John's reflections on the history and journey to the agreement also reveals some further underlying tenets of what Indigenous, in the context of reconciliation, is made to mean, noting that they had to work very hard for an agreement that "created true partnership and benefit-sharing" rather than one that was merely composed of platitudes, "shallow promises, and land acknowledgements."[56] There is, then, a lingering sense that Indigenous reconciliation, when in the hands of non-Indigenous peoples, will lead only to tokenistic processes of recognition and acknowledgement that do little more than *specify* the name of Indigenous peoples being recognized.

This discussion reflects one of the challenges with respect to place-focused reconciliation initiatives, ones that are directly tied up in a larger economic domain that derives its existence from its ability to effectively place-brand. Here, non-Indigenous desires for place-branding abut an Indigenous people's desire to see a large-scale declaration to arrivals that they are, indeed, on/in xʷməθkʷəy̓əm territory. Interestingly, John frames land acknowledgements, something that has become quite popular under Indigenous reconciliation, as an empty gesture; were the airport to simply acknowledge the land, it would do little more than perpetuate a non-reciprocal place-brand fairly consistent with what took place under Aboriginality. Yet YVR's CEO still has questions to answer. If this is not about seizing on Indigenous reconciliation as a new brand identity, then why did it take the airport so long to engage in a more meaningful set of negotiations?

In light of all of this, will Indigenous and Indigeneity lose their lustre when the cracks in the founding framework of reconciliation are revealed? Will Indigeneity—like Aboriginality, even within the limited zone of rights recognition—fail to meet its promise of substantive change? With a federal government still unwilling to commit to an implementation of UNDRIP that accepts Indigenous assertions of, and rights to, self-determination, will the limits of Indigeneity compel a turn elsewhere? Will we at some point in future, and especially given the pace at which government and non-Indigenous businesses, educational institutions, and everyday people have flocked to Indigenous, see a similar rejection? It seems unlikely. In de-emphasizing Aboriginal and embracing Indigenous, Indigenous peoples signal to the Canadian government that acquiescence has not, and will not happen; that in whatever form, in whatever way, and through whatever terms most strategically useful, Indigenous peoples will continue to persist, resist, and exist. At the same time, Indigenous peoples once again provide the ruptures that draw our attention to the pathway forward. By prodding at the widening gaps between truth and reconciliation, between Indigenization and decolonization, Indigenous peoples insist that locally rooted relationships that are ethical and respectful of Indigenous peoples and lands are the only way to resist the enormously damaging forces of neoliberal colonialism and globalization.

Notes

Introduction

1. Simeone, "Indigenous Peoples." The guide also issues an important reminder that "it is preferable to describe Indigenous peoples through their specific identities or nations. Examples would be 'a Haida artist,' 'a Cree pilot,' or 'a Mohawk scholar.' When in doubt, one should refer to Indigenous peoples in the way they refer to themselves."
2. Animikii Inc., "Why We Use 'Indigenous.'"
3. Ibid.
4. Ibid.
5. Ibid.
6. Ibid. See also Marks. "What's in a name."
7. *Merriam Webster Dictionary*, s.v. "Indigenous."
8. *Merriam-Webster Dictionary*, s.v. "Aboriginal." Emphasis added.
9. Amikii Inc., "Why We Use Indigenous." Emphasis added.
10. *Merriam Webster Dictionary*, s.v. "History and Etymology for ab."
11. Membean, "Ab-, Ab-, and Away!" https://membean.com/wrotds/ab-away, (accessed 26 May 2021).
12. To allay confusion and to clarify the argumentative juxtaposition, I will continue to use Indigenous to refer to Indigenous peoples—except where otherwise noted.
13. Wilton, *Word Myths*, 165-66. Wilton's argument is highly contradictory. As quickly as he advances this argument, he pivots and criticizes those who take issue with words that have been used to perpetuate racism and the hierarchical ordering and marginalizing of humans designated as "non-white"; he does so because he argues that such words are, at their origins, neutral. This leads him to proselytize that attempts to confront and weed out racist terminology have led to a "peril of political correctness." With the inanity—and racist microaggression—of such an argument noted, it is in his contradictory arguments that we can extract that which is relevant to this discussion.
14. Hall, "The West and the Rest," 205.
15. Ibid., 199.
16. Ibid., 205.
17. Ibid.
18. McChesney, "Introduction to Profit Over People," 7.
19. Bargh, *Resistance*, 1.

20　Manitowabi, "Casino Rama," 261.
21　Ibid.
22　Bradburn, "In the Mood for Cuts."
23　Little, *No Car, No Radio, No Liquor Permit*.
24　In addition to Little, *No Car*, see also Little, "A Litmus Test for Democracy."
25　For more background on the Canadian context, see Carroll and Shaw, "Consolidating a Neoliberal Policy Bloc in Canada"; Hermer and Mosher, *Disorderly People*; Keil, "'Commonsense' Neoliberalism"; Prudham, "Poisoning the Well"; Mascarenhas, *Where the Waters Divide*; Albo and Evans, *Divided Province*.
26　Dawson, *Selling British Columbia*, 16.
27　Francis, *Selling Canada*. See also Colpitts, "Wildlife Promotions."
28　Malciw, "Settling and 'Selling' Canada's West," 10.
29　Ibid. See also Owram, *Promise of Eden*.
30　Daschuk, *Clearing the Plains*, 108.
31　See Daschuk, *Clearing the Plains*.
32　Francis, *The Imaginary Indian*.
33　Olins, "Branding the Nation," 245.
34　Owram, *Promise of Eden*, 5.
35　Goldberg, *The Threat of Race*, 221.
36　Stewart-Harawira, *The New Imperial*, 18.
37　Slowey, *Navigating Neoliberalism*, xiv and xv.
38　Howard-Wagner, Bargh, and Altamirano-Jimenez, "From New Paternalism to New Imaginings," 25. For a defence of how neoliberalism can aid Indigenous peoples in the path towards self-determination, see Slowey, *Navigating Neoliberalism*; Alcantara, "Privatize Reserve Land?"; Mills and McCreary, "Negotiating Neoliberal Empowerment."
39　Howard-Wagner, Bargh, and Altamirano-Jimenez, "From New Paternalism to New Imaginings," 26. The authors also write that "Maria Bargh progresses this argument in relation to indigenous entrepreneurship and economic development, bringing to the fore critical considerations. As Bargh notes, this is not simply a case of 'a group of elite Māori recognised by the Crown as economic actors, indoctrinated in neoliberal thought and a marginalised underclass of Māori resistance.' Moving beyond the binary or conceptualisations of Māori enterprise and Māori as 'only either champions or victims of neoliberal policies and practices,' Bargh explores the 'areas of a diverse economy that are forging other alternative neoliberal or non-neoliberal worlds.' It is more instructive to consider what Māori want from economic and political activity and the ways in which they are agents in managing neoliberalism's constraints and pursuing its possibilities. . . . For example, Māori agency is evident in the non-market opportunities that Bargh shows them as pursuing, as well as in the ascription of 'legal personhood' to a mountain as part of the Tūhoe."

40 Ibid.
41 See also Cliff Atleo Jr.'s work on Aboriginal neoliberalism and the problems therein in *From Indigenous Nationhood to Neoliberal Aboriginal Economic Development*.
42 Bargh, *Resistance*, 2, 13.
43 Ibid., 1.
44 Manitowabi, "Casino Rama," 198.
45 Bargh, *Resistance*, 13.
46 Ibid., 15.
47 Ibid., 9.
48 Ibid., 10-11.
49 Ibid., 8.
50 Ibid., 13.
51 Ibid.
52 Ibid., 10.
53 For more information, see https://unistoten.camp.
54 Bargh, *Resistance*, 14.
55 For more on this in an Australian context, see Strakosch, *Neoliberal Indigenous Policy*.
56 Ibid. Bargh argues, rather, that neoliberalism is *akin* to colonialism. See also Altamirano-Jiménez, *Indigenous Encounters with Neoliberalism*; Brondo, *Land Grab*; Kirsch, *Mining Capitalism*.
57 Alfred and Corntassel, "Being Indigenous," 598.
58 Ibid., 599.
59 Coulthard, *Red Skin, White Masks*, 3.
60 Ibid.
61 Ladner, "Negotiated Inferiority."
62 Ibid.
63 See Andersen, "From Nation to Population."
64 Lambertus, "Canada's Aboriginal Peoples and Intersecting Identity Markers," 5.
65 Marcus, *Out in the Cold*. See also Tester and Kulchyski, *Tammarniit (Mistakes)*.
66 Dunning, "Reflections of a Disk-less Inuk."
67 Tester, McNicoll, and Irniq, "Writing for Our Lives." See also Tester, McNicoll, and Tran, "Structural Violence and the 1962-1963 Tuberculosis Epidemic in Eskimo Point, NWT."
68 Tester, "Mad Dogs and (Mostly) Englishmen." See also Qikiqtani Truth Commission, *Qikiqtani Truth Commission: Achieving Saimaqatigiingniq*.

69 See Tough and McGregor, "'The Rights to the Land May Be Transferred.'"
70 Qtd. in Macdougall, *Land, Family and Identity*, 15.
71 For a thorough discussion of Saskatchewan Road Allowances, see Troupe, "Mapping Métis Stories."
72 See Pocklington, *The Government and Politics of the Alberta Métis Settlements*.
73 See Burley, "Rooster Town." See also Peters, Stock, and Werner, *Rooster Town*.
74 Logan, "Settler Colonialism in Canada and the Métis."
75 Barron, "The CCF and the Development of Métis Colonies."
76 For a detailed breakdown of changes to the Indian Act in 1951 and into the 1960s and 1970s, see Parrott, "Indian Act."
77 Ibid. See also Cannon, "Race Matters"; Barker, "Gender, Sovereignty, Rights"; Green, "Canaries in the Mines of Citizenship."
78 Parrott, "Indian Act."
79 Cairns, *Citizens Plus*, 162.
80 Henderson, "Empowering Treaty Federalism," 241.
81 Ibid., 182.
82 Lagace and Sinclair, "The White Paper, 1969." See also Turner, *This Is Not a Peace Pipe*; Nickel, "Reconsidering 1969."
83 See Gemmell, "Defending Indigenous Rights against the Just Society." See also O'Bonsawin, "Indigenous Peoples and Canadian-hosted Olympic Games."
84 *Statement of the Government of Canada on Indian Policy, 1969*.
85 Cardinal, *The Unjust Society*.
86 Calliou, "The Indian Association of Alberta."
87 Sanders, "Article 27 and the Aboriginal Peoples of Canada," 156.
88 Wherrett, "The Struggle for Inclusion," 41.
89 Wherrett, "The Struggle for Inclusion"; see also Daniels, *Report of the Metis*; Jenson, Polletta, and Raibmon, "The Difficulties of Combating Inequality in Time."
90 Lambertus, "Canada's Aboriginal Peoples," 5.
91 Saul, *A Fair Country*.
92 Ibid; qtd. in Lambertus, "Canada's Aboriginal Peoples," 5.
93 Mawani, "From Colonialism to Multiculturalism?" 51.
94 Ibid., 52.
95 Housel, "Australian Nationalism and Globalization," 449.
96 Thobani, *Exalted Subjects*, 144.
97 Morgan, "Aboriginal Protest and the Sydney Olympic Games," 31.

98   Johnson, "From the Tomahawk Chop to the Road Block," 111.
99   Nimijean, "The Politics of Branding Canada," 68-69.
100 van Ham, "Branding Territory," 250.
101 Slowey, *Navigating Neoliberalism*, xiii.
102 Coulthard, *Red Skin*, 6. Italics in original.
103 Here I use postcolonialism in the most literal of meanings—as Canada's effort to market itself as "over" colonialism.
104 "Statement of Cooperation."
105 Ibid.
106 Adams, *Prison of Grass*, 35.
107 Raibmon, *Authentic Indians*, 12.
108 Francis, "Aboriginal Tourism in the Southern Interior of British Columbia," 8.
109 Werry, *The Tourist State*, x.
110 Allen, "Place Branding," 60.
111 Kavaratizis and Hatch, "The Dynamics of Place Brands," 76.
112 Ibid., 75.
113 Hodge and Mishra, *Dark Side of the Dream*, 26.

Chapter 1 - *Aboriginal, Aboriginality, Aboriginalism, Aboriginalization: What's in a Word?*

1   See Plot, *The Natural History of Oxford-Shire*, and Richards, *The Aboriginal Britons*. The name Turtle Island arises from within Haudenosaunee worldviews and in particular the Haudenosaunee creation story. It has become more widely adopted by those who acknowledge the contentious claims to land and sovereignty of Canada and the United States. While I am not Haudenosaunee, I was raised on lands that sit at a territorial transition point between the Mississauga Nation and the Haudenosaunee Confederacy. In addition, where I live and work it is common to hear "Turtle Island" used by the diverse community of Indigenous peoples that make up the Greater Toronto Area. The latter three terms refer to, respectively, the ancestral homeland of Inuit on the lands and waters colonized by Canada, the ancestral homeland of the Aztec and their related nations and descendants, and the Indigenous peoples of "Latin America." For more information, see Medina, "Indigenous Decolonial Movements in Abya Yala, Aztlán, and Turtle Island," 147-63; Mignolo, "From the 'Western Hemisphere' to the 'Eastern Hemisphere,'" 59. For the purposes of this book, when I refer to the "Americas" I will use all three, separated by a backslash.

2   Emphasis in original. Slattery, "The Metamorphosis of Aboriginal Title," 258.

3   Emphasis in original. Ibid.

4   Mayhew, *The Massachusetts Psalter*; New York Missionary Society, *The New York Missionary Magazine and Repository of Religious Intelligence for the Year 1800*; Miers, *Travels in Chile and La Plata*; Reddie, *A Letter to the Lord High Chancellor*; "Aboriginal Tribes"; Morton, *An Inquiry*.

5   See Morton and Combe, *Crania Americana*.

6   Morton, *An Inquiry*.

7   Martin, *The Hudson's Bay Company's Land Tenures*.

8   The term Indian has held less relevance to/for Inuit; however, in *Re Eskimos*, a 1939 Supreme Court of Canada decision involving the province of Quebec and the federal government determined that Inuit be considered "Indians" for the purposes of section 91(24) of the British North America Act of 1867. This section speaks to the delineation of federal and provincial responsibilities whereby "Indians" are classed as federal responsibility. See Backhouse, *Colour-Coded*, 18-55.

9   *Daniels v. Canada (Indian Affairs and Northern Development)*, https://scc-csc.lexum.com/scc-csc/scc-csc/en/item/15858/index.do. See also Adese, "A Tale of Two Constitutions."

10 See https://nunatsiaq.com/stories/article/65674natan_obed_why_the_name_edmonton_eskimos_harms_inuit/.

11 As Anishinaabe legal scholar John Borrows has compellingly pointed out, the Royal Proclamation of 1763 was only the first part of a two-part ratification process in British claims to Turtle Island; the second took place the following year and manifested in the creation of the Treaty at Niagara (1764) and reflected British acknowledgement of First Nations' nationhood and sovereignty. For further details on the Treaty at Niagara, see Borrows, "Wampum at Niagara."

12 https://www.thecanadianencyclopedia.ca/en/article/aboriginal-affairs-and-northern-development-canada.

13 https://www.aadnc-aandc.gc.ca/eng/1100100010252/1100100010254.

14 For a thorough and more recent discussion on the changing landscape of sexism of the Indian Act, see Deschambault, "An Exploration of the Colonial Impacts."

15 For a definition and debate around the origin of the term Eskimo, see https://www.merriam-webster.com/dictionary/Eskimo.

16 See https://scc-csc.lexum.com/scc-csc/scc-csc/en/item/5113/index.do.

17 Ibid.

18 See https://scc-csc.lexum.com/scc-csc/scc-csc/en/item/5113/index.do.

19 See https://indigenousfoundations.arts.ubc.ca/calder_case/.

20 While prior to the early 1900s Indigenous peoples, the Canadian government, and British colonial administrators often interacted with one another in the form of nation-to-nation (and in some cases Indigenous confederacy-to-nation) diplomacy, the effects of residential schooling, land dispossession, the pass system, the consolidated Indian Act, and other measures intended to disappear Indigenous peoples via aggressive assimilation policy

impeded the continuance of such approaches. Following Canada's confederation in 1867, the first major "Indian legislation" Parliament passed was the Gradual Enfranchisement Act of 1869. Building from earlier acts and programs focused on civilization and assimilation, the Gradual Enfranchisement Act specifically targeted the governing structures of Indigenous nations in an effort to undermine their distinct nationhood and to curb Indigenous peoples' abilities to resist assimilation and elimination as Indigenous peoples. The act implemented "a male-only elective system largely under the control of the local Indian agent" (Milloy, *Indian Act Colonialism*, 6; Poucette, "Spinning Wheels," 503). By imposing the elected band council system on Indigenous nations drawn in under the Gradual Civilization Act, the Canadian government also sought to eliminate the very means of Indigenous diplomatic expression and political organization. While the act had devastating impacts, with its most oppressive mechanisms refined through the 1876 consolidation of Indian legislation, and while it generated a split in many Indigenous communities between traditional governance structures and the imposed band council system, it did not completely stifle Indigenous peoples' collective repudiation of Canadian colonialism.

21 Knickerbocker and Nickel, "Negotiating Sovereignty," 71.
22 Miller, *Skyscrapers Hide the Heavens*, 214.
23 Ibid.
24 For an excellent discussion of First Nations women's activism and organizing in British Columbia, see Nickel, *Assembling Unity*.
25 Dyck and Sadik, "Indigenous Political Organization and Activism in Canada."
26 Freeman, "Inuit."
27 Miller, *Skyscrapers Hide the Heavens*.
28 It is, in fact, Native that emerges as the first pan-Indigenous term that marks different positionalities and status categories (or categories of recognition) vis-à-vis the federal government as held by Métis, non-status Indians, and status (yet mostly off-reserve) Indians. Native reached its peak in the era of Indigenous sovereignty movements of the 1960s–80s, and gradually declined in significance through the 1990s. Native was still used by some through the 1990s and 2000s and for people like myself—because it was the term of preference during my formative years—I often still use it. It is used far more frequently today in American state contexts than in Canadian state contexts (as Native American and American Indian). Its use in the context of the Native Council of Canada (NCC), as mentioned previously, speaks to the growing urbanization of Indigenous peoples of the time. It was a particularly salient term for NCC in its work representing the voice of those Indigenous peoples cut off from federal recognition by the Indian Act's stipulations around Indian status; it also signals the profound changes wrought on Indigenous families and communities via assimilatory processes that led people to leave their communities for urban areas in search for such necessities as stable work, education, and health care. As with other Indigenous peoples, for people outside of existing federal categories of recognition, and thus at least implicit if not manifest responsibility, the organizing carried out in political coalitions served as a vital channel for their voices as they fought for consultation on Canada's new Constitution.

29 Wherrett, "The Struggle for Inclusion," 28. COPE was formed in 1970 in the western Arctic to advocate regarding Indigenous peoples's land rights in the area. See also https://www.aadnc-aandc.gc.ca/eng/1100100016900/1100100016908.

30 Wherrett, "The Struggle for Inclusion," 29.

31 Ibid., 31, 49; Knickerbocker and Nickel, "Negotiating Sovereignty," 71.

32 See Wherrett, "The Struggle for Inclusion," 31.

33 Ibid., 76.

34 Special Joint Committee of the Senate, *Minutes* 12: 64.

35 Ibid., 15.

36 Wherrett, "The Struggle for Inclusion," 35.

37 Ibid., 46, drawing on Paul Williams, Union of Ontario's Indians, *Special Joint Committee*, No. 31, 5 January 1981, 29.

38 Wherrett, "The Struggle for Inclusion," 47.

39 Daniels, quoted in Canada, "Special Joint Committee of the Senate and the House of Commons of Canada on the Constitution of Canada." *Minutes of the Proceedings and Evidence*. Ottawa: Queen's Printer, 1978, no. 5, 43. See also Dodek, *The Charter Debates*.

40 Delbert Riley from NIB, qtd. in Dodek, *The Charter Debates*, 414.

41 Wherrett, "The Struggle for Inclusion," 48.

42 Ibid., 47–48.

43 Ibid., 35.

44 Ibid., 74.

45 Ibid., 49.

46 See UBCIC Aboriginal Rights Position Paper.

47 Ibid.

48 I put decolonize in quotation marks to flag that this use is, indeed, contentious. But it was precisely how the Canadian government framed/viewed what it was doing by patriating a Constitution independent of Britain. In doing so it would move from being a "colony" of Britain to a fully independent nation-state.

49 Hanson, "Constitution Express."

50 Ibid.

51 Ibid. The significance of this action cannot be overstated. According to the Indigenous Foundations website, "Despite the warm welcome and support from Ottawa citizens and mayor, the Constitution Express's arrival in Ottawa did not initially change Trudeau's position. As a result, 41 people immediately continued on to the United Nations headquarters in New York City, and presented their concerns before the United Nations to gain international attention. In 1981, the Constitution Express continued across the Atlantic to the Netherlands, Germany, France, Belgium, and then England in order to present the

concerns and experiences of Aboriginal peoples across Canada to an international audience. They were met with support and convinced many politicians and members of the House of Lords (now known as the Supreme Court of the United Kingdom) to support Indigenous rights. Subsequently, after months of international attention and pressure from Aboriginal groups across Canada, the Canadian government agreed to specifically recognize Aboriginal rights within the new Constitution.

52 Minutes of Proceedings, 9 December 1980, 144; see also Dodek, *The Charter Debates*, 409.
53 Dodek, *The Charter Debates*, 418.
54 Ibid., 66.
55 Qtd. in ibid., 400.
56 Qtd. in ibid., 349–50.
57 Ibid.
58 Ibid., 402.
59 See Roblin in ibid., 411.
60 Qtd. in ibid., 411–12.
61 Qtd in ibid., 412.
62 Qtd. in ibid., 412.
63 Ibid. For a discussion of the problems inherent in self-identification with respect to post-secondary research and hiring, see https://yellowheadinstitute.org/2019/08/20/research-ethnic-fraud-and-the-academy-a-protocol-for-working-with-indigenous-communities-and-peoples/.
64 For a thorough discussion of the rise of self-identification and the issues surrounding it, see Andersen, "From Nation to Population"; Andersen, "Moya Tipimsook "; Andersen, *Métis*; Andersen, "Residual Tensions of Empire"; Gaudry and Andersen, "Daniels v. Canada"; Gaudry and Leroux, "White Settler Revisionism"; Gaudry, "Communing with the Dead"; Leroux, *Distorted Descent*; Leroux, "'Eastern Métis' Studies and White Settler Colonialism Today"; Adese, Todd, and Stevenson, "Mediating Métis Identity"; Adese, "A Tale of Two Constitutions"; Macdougall, "The Myth of Metis Cultural Ambivalence."
65 https://www.cbc.ca/news/canada/newfoundland-labrador/labrador-s-m%C3%A9tis-nation-adopts-new-name-1.927252.
66 Qtd. in Dodek, *The Charter Debates*, 412–13.
67 Qtd. in ibid., 413–15.
68 Qtd. in ibid., 415–16.
69 Qtd. in ibid.
70 Qtd. in ibid.
71 Qtd. in ibid., 409.
72 Qtd. in ibid., 410. See also Gordon from ICNI on Inuit perspectives qtd. in ibid., 408.

73 Qtd. in ibid., 411.
74 Qtd. in ibid., 410.
75 Qtd. in ibid., 401.
76 Qtd. in ibid., 410. For more information on Sinclair, see "Jim Sinclair," *Indspire*, no date, https://indspire.ca/laureate/jim-sinclair-2/ (accessed 28 July 2021).
77 Minutes of Proceedings, 5 January 1981, 31: 86.
78 See ibid., 73–76.
79 Ibid., 77. See also Hošek, "Women and the Constitutional Process," 280, 291.
80 See https://laws-lois.justice.gc.ca/eng/const/page-16.html.
81 Hawkes, "Aboriginal Peoples and Constitutional Reform?," 7.
82 See Andersen, "Residual Tensions of Empire."
83 *R. v. Sparrow*, [1990] 1 SCR 1075. https://scc-csc.lexum.com/scc-csc/scc-csc/en/item/609/index.do; see also Andersen, "Residual Tensions of Empire."
84 See Borrows, "The Trickster," 27; Morse, "Permafrost Rights," 1011; Borrows, "Frozen Rights in Canada"; Kent, "The Van der Peet Test?"; Zalewski, "From *Sparrow* to *Van der Peet*"; Andersen, "Residual Tensions of Empire."
85 See Borrows, "The Trickster"; Morse, "Permafrost Rights"; Borrows, "Frozen Rights in Canada."
86 Zalewski, "From *Sparrow* to *Van der Peet*," 438.
87 *R. v. Powley*, 2003 SCC 43. https://scc-csc.lexum.com/scc-csc/scc-csc/en/item/2076/index.do.
88 Andersen, *Métis*, 65.
89 "Frequently Asked Questions—Powley," 2.
90 See Andersen, *Métis*.
91 Leroux, *Distorted Descent*.
92 See Andersen, *Métis*.
93 Qtd. in Aboriginal Multi-Media Society of Alberta (AMMSA), "MNA to Have Local Voting," 24 August 1984; qtd. in Sawchuk, "The Métis, Non-Status Indians and the New Aboriginality," 139.
94 See Canadaland, "From Joseph Boyden To Michelle Latimer—Why Does This Keep Happening?" For a discussion on Boyden, see Adese and Innes, *Indigenous Celebrity*.
95 Sawchuk's "The Métis, Non-Status Indians and the New Aboriginality" details the split between Métis and non-status. While I think Sawchuk's article is flawed in its inability to see that in other provinces—such as Saskatchewan and Manitoba—there were differences between Métis and non-status, and that he overlooks the way that Métis and non-status have different political objections (as in non-status seeking the restoration of Indian status),

he nevertheless provides interesting insight into a crucial shift in political articulation and aspiration in coalition organizing.

96 Shari Narine, "Dorey Dropped the Ball."
97 See http://www.abo-peoples.org/en/capaffiliates/.
98 Chris Andersen, "Underdeveloped Identities," 627.
99 Andersen, "Underdeveloped Identities," 633.
100 Andersen, "Urban Aboriginality as a Distinctive Identity, in Twelve Parts," 47.
101 Kudelik, "National Indigenous Peoples Day."
102 Zhu, "National Holidays and Minority Festivals in Canadian Nation-building," 200. See also "Public Education: Building Awareness and Understanding"; "Renewal: A Twenty-Year Commitment," 82 and 97.
103 Zhu, "National Holidays," 201. See also "First Nations in Canada."
104 "June 21 is National Aboriginal Day."
105 Zhu, "National Holidays," 204.
106 Ibid.
107 Troian, "20 years since the Royal Commission on Aboriginal Peoples."
108 *Looking Forward, Looking Back*, iii–iv.
109 Ibid.
110 Ibid.
111 Ibid.
112 Emphasis in original. Ibid., iv.
113 Saunders and Dubois, *Métis Politics and Governance in Canada*, 77. See also Andersen, *Métis*, 116–17.
114 Saunders and Dubois, Ibid.
115 See Andersen's discussion in *Métis*, 104–5.
116 Turner, "On the Idea of Reconciliation in Contemporary Aboriginal Politics," 104.
117 Emphasis in original. *Looking Forward, Looking Back*, iii.
118 Andersen, *Métis*, 105.
119 See https://www.rcaanc-cirnac.gc.ca/eng/1100100015725/1571590271585.
120 Ibid.
121 See Lawrence, "Rewriting Histories of the Land." On the violence and erasure of early colonial encounters, see also O'Brien, *Firsting and Lasting*. For a discussion of Inuit resistance, see Eber, *Encounters on the Passage*.
122 See https://www.rcaanc-cirnac.gc.ca/eng/1100100015725/1571590271585.
123 Ibid.

124 Ibid.

125 See Borrows, "Frozen Rights in Canada."

126 Irlbacher-Fox, *Finding Dahshaa*, 7; see also Jenson, Polletta, and Raibmon, "The Difficulties of Combating Inequality in Time."

127 Daytec, "Fraternal Twins with Different Mothers."

128 Ibid. See also Office for the High Commissioner of Human Rights, *Concluding Observations of the Human Rights Committee*.

129 The change was contested by Assembly of First Nations leader Shawn Atleo and a number of other Indigenous leaders. The federal government rationalized that the move was to acknowledge the relationship of the office to other Indigenous populations; however, the concerns expressed by Atleo and others hold that the change was done without consultation with Indigenous peoples—see http://www.aadnc-aandc.gc.ca/eng/1314808945787.

130 See https://www.canada.ca/en/treasury-board-secretariat/services/government-communications/federal-identity-program/manual.html.

131 Qtd. in "Indian Ministry Name-change Puzzles Some."

132 Goldberg, *The Racial State*.

133 https://www.ic.gc.ca/app/scr/cc/CorporationsCanada/fdrlCrpSrch.html?locale=en_CA.

Chapter 2 – Aboriginalized Multiculturalism™: Canada's Olympic National Brand

1 Boykoff, "Celebration Capitalism and the Sochi 2014 Winter Olympics," 42.

2 Ibid., 43.

3 Ibid., 44.

4 Tomlinson, "Olympic Spectacle," 586. See also Hogan, "Staging the Nation"; Hall, "Urban Entrepreneurship, Corporate Interests and Sports Mega-events," 59–70; O'Bonsawin, "A Coast Salish Olympic Welcome"; Adese, "Colluding with the Enemy?"; Lee and Yoon, "Narratives of the Nation in the Olympic Opening Ceremonies."

5 Nye Jr., "Public Diplomacy and Soft Power," 94. See also Potter, *Branding Canada*; Grix and Lee, "Soft Power, Sports Mega-events and Emerging States"; Grix and Houlihan, "Sports Mega-events as Part of a Nation's Soft Power Strategy"; Nauright, "Selling Nations to the World through Sports."

6 See also Borgerson, Schroeder, and Wu, "Branding as Soft Power."

7 For the Vancouver 2010 Olympics there were two Indigenous women participating in snowboard/slalom events. According to an article from *The Canadian Press* titled "Aboriginal Athletes Rare Participants at Olympics," Indigenous peoples were woefully underrepresented in the Olympics as athletes. It notes that there were two Indigenous athletes (which they referred to as "aboriginal") at the Beijing Summer Olympics. For more information, see: http://www.ctv.ca/servlet/an/local/CTVNews/20091225/091225_aboriginals_olympics?hub=CP24Bin.

8   Forsyth and Wamsley, "Symbols without Substance," 228.
9   See Bannerji, *The Dark Side of the Nation*; Mackey, *The House of Difference*; Thobani, *Exalted Subjects*.
10 Schantz, "La présidence de Avery Brundage," 77.
11 Ibid., 138.
12 Forsyth, "Teepees and Tomahawks," 72-73.
13 COJO 76, "Games," 306. The number of Indigenous participants is inconsistently reported in official Olympic materials/coverage. Some estimates say 75, some refer to 250, while other estimates put the number closer to 500. The wild discrepancies between the counts further underline the lack of concern with representations of/inclusions of Indigenous peoples.
14 Ibid.
15 Ibid., 312.
16 Ibid.
17 Ibid.
18 Forsyth, "Teepees and Tomahawks," 73.
19 COJO 76, "Games," 306.
20 Takac, *Sixty Olympic Years*.
21 Ibid.
22 Ibid.
23 Forsyth, "Teepees and Tomahawks," 72.
24 Godwell, "The Olympic Branding of Aborigines," 246.
25 Forsyth and Wamsley, "Symbols without Substance," 234.
26 Deer, "Blast From The Past."
27 Indigenous peoples had long been involved in performing "for empire." But the conditions in which, for example, an exiled Gabriel Dumont joined Buffalo Bill's Wild West show, or people participated in Banff's Indian Days, or Kwakw aka'wakw participated in the 1893 Chicago World's Fair, were markedly different from those facing Indigenous peoples in the time of the Montreal and later Olympic Games. For a more extensive account of such histories, see Raibmon, "Theatres of Contact"; Mason, "Rethinking the Banff Indian Days."
28 O'Bonsawin, "Indigenous Peoples and Canadian-hosted Olympic Games," 36.
29 Ibid., 37.
30 Forsyth, "Teepees and Tomahawks," 72.
31 Ibid.
32 Ibid.
33 Ibid., 72.

34 Ibid., 73.
35 Adams, *Prison of Grass*, 35.
36 OCO'88, "XV Olympic Winter Games Official Report," 11.
37 Ibid.
38 The contemporary Calgary Stampede evolved out of an agricultural fair that began in 1886. By 1923 it had become formalized as the Calgary Stampede and was turned into an annual event. Max Foran suggests in his work on the Calgary Stampede that "some see it as a 'ten-day party,' a Disneyesque sham, and a commercial rip-off. Others hail it as 'the greatest outdoor show on earth,' a destination event, and a world-class festival rivaling Mardi Gras, Carnivale, or Oktoberfest"; see Foran, *Icon, Myth, Brand: The Calgary*, xiv.
39 Wamsley and Heine, "'Don't Mess with the Relay," 173.
40 King, *It's How You Play the Game*, 85-86.
41 O'Bonsawin, "'No Olympics on Stolen Native Land,'" 147. "Native Indians" became an essential service category in the administration of the games, alongside "Food Services." In 1986 OCO'88 appointed Sykes Powderface of the local Stoney Nakoda as the "full time Native Liaison coordinator" and financial manager of the broader Native Participation Program (NPP). Out of this relationship grew a separate Treaty 7 chiefs committee with financial assistance redirected from Indian Affairs to offer loans and grants to support Native-initiated Olympic events as part of the NPP. Proposals approved included a cultural exhibition, Olympic powwow, fashion show, and national youth conference. According to OCO'88, the purpose of instituting NPP was to "highlight the lifestyle transition of Canada's Aboriginal peoples by focusing on their past, present, and future" (OCO'88, "Official Report," 271).
42 Crossingham, "Klein Meets with Lubicon Chief," 3.
43 Ibid.
44 Yellow Bird, "Cowboys and Indians," 43.
45 For a thorough discussion of what she calls the "Benevolent Mountie Myth," see Mackey, *House of Difference*.
46 Francis, *National Dreams*, 33.
47 Ibid.
48 Ibid., 30; for a discussion on how civility is in actuality "white civility," see Coleman, *White Civility*.
49 "1988 Winter Olympics OC Part 7-Introduction by ABC."
50 Yellow Bird, "Cowboys and Indians," 42.
51 "Natives in Olympics."
52 O'Bonsawin, "Indigenous Peoples and Canadian-hosted Olympic Games," 49.

53 Yellow Bird, "Cowboys and Indians," 43.
54 Comm. Series 15, box 8, City of Calgary Archives.
55 OCO'88, "Official Report," 277.
56 Ibid.
57 Qtd. in Sidsworth, "Aboriginal Participation," 33.
58 McLoughlin, "Of Boundaries and Borders," 366.
59 Sidsworth, "Aboriginal Participation," 32.
60 King, *It's How You Play the Game*, 258.
61 Trigger qtd. in McLoughlin, "Of Boundaries and Borders," 366.
62 Wamsley and Heine, "'Don't Mess with the Relay,'" 107–8.
63 Qtd. in ibid. See also Harrison, "The Spirit Sings," 360.
64 Qtd. in Wamsley and Heine, "'Don't Mess with the Relay,'" 107–8.
65 Ibid., 108.
66 Ibid.
67 VANOC, "Vancouver 2010 Bid Books," 63.
68 Sidsworth, "Aboriginal Participation," 124.
69 Ibid.
70 Ibid., 3.
71 Ibid., 17.
72 Ibid.
73 Sidsworth, "Aboriginal Participation," 128. See "Working Effectively with Aboriginal Peoples."
74 Forsyth, "The Illusion of Inclusion," 22–33.
75 Ibid.
76 Ibid.
77 VANOC, "Vancouver 2010 Bid Books," 19.
78 Ibid.
79 Ibid., 9.
80 Ibid.
81 Sidsworth, "Aboriginal Participation," 12.
82 "VOC1: 1723."
83 Ibid.
84 O'Bonsawin, "The Conundrum of 'Ilanaaq,'" 387.

85 In the wake of the 2010 Games, a number of residential school survivors have come forward about racism, sexual abuse, and physical abuse perpetrated by Furlong. In September 2013, a former student filed a civil lawsuit against him. While none of the accusations have been proven in court, it is important that in writing on issues related to Indigenous peoples while referring to Furlong that I acknowledge the severity of this matter. For more information, see "John Furlong."

86 Furlong, *Patriot Hearts*, 195.

87 Emphasis added in ibid. In personal communications with various friends, I have been told that instead of attending a "gathering," the young people chosen to participate were expected to partake in lengthy workout regimens in the weeks leading up to the games. Some were expected to spend significant time learning how to dance the "traditional" dances of their peoples.

88 Emphasis added in ibid.

89 http://www.youtube.com/watch?v=MxZpUueDAvc (accessed 12 November 2010).

90 Keene, "The Vancouver Opening Ceremonies."

91 Ibid.

92 Charleyboy, "2010 Olympics Token Tribute."

93 Ibid.

94 McMahon, "Canada's Aboriginal Peoples and the Vancouver 2010 Olympics."

95 Ibid.

96 "Growing Pains," 228.

97 Ranasinghe, "The Refashioning of Vagrancy," 214.

98 Brethour, "Exclusive Demographic Picture."

99 Ranasinghe, "The Refashioning of Vagrancy," 214.

100 Ibid., 239.

101 Qtd. in ibid., 235.

102 Fetrow, "Black Flags over the Olympics."

103 For an excellent discussion of this, see Hermer and Mosher, *Disorderly People*.

104 Further, in June 2008 the federal government "paid 17 million dollars each to the Musqueam and the Tsleil-Waututh, making the Musqueam one of the wealthiest tribes in Canada," while the provincial government sped up agreements and made an out-of-court cash settlement with the Musqueam "for over twenty million dollars, ending three court cases over land at the UBC golf course and Rock River Casino." Fetrow, "Black Flags over the Olympics."

105 Ibid.

106 Qtd. in Rezaee, "Olympic Countdown."

107 O'Bonsawin, "'No Olympics on Stolen Native Land,'" 148.

108 Klein, "Olympics Land Grab."
109 Four Host First Nations, "Statement."
110 Mickleburgh, "Misguided Olympic Protesters."
111 Four Host First Nations, "Statement."
112 Ibid.
113 Forsyth, "Teepees and Tomahawks," 72.
114 Forsyth and Wamsley, *Symbols without Substance*, 236.
115 Simpson, *Mohawk Interruptus*, 1.
116 Ibid.
117 Thobani, *Exalted Subjects*, 148.
118 O'Bonsawin, "No Olympics," 148.
119 Stoler, *Education of Desire*, 92–93.

Chapter 3 – Selling Aboriginal Experiences and Authenticity: Canadian and Aboriginal Tourism

1 See http://www.news.com.au/world/outrage-over-indian-islands-human-zoo-video/story-e6frfkyi-1226242317881.
2 See http://www.guardian.co.uk/world/video/2012/jan/07/andaman-islanders-human-safari-video.
3 Francis, *The Imaginary Indian*, 181.
4 Aboriginal Tourism of BC, "The Next Phase: 2012–2017," 8.
5 Moran, "The Psychodynamics of Australian Settler-Nationalism," 689.
6 Alfred, "Colonialism and State Dependency," 44.
7 For more on non-Indigenous peoples' ongoing fascination with Indigenous peoples, see Adese and Innes, *Indigenous Celebrity*; Lutz, Strzelczyk, and Watchman, *Indianthusiasm*; Thrush, *Indigenous London*; Raheja, "Reservation Reelism"; Wernitznig, *Europe's Indians, Indians in Europe*; Dyar, "Fatal Attraction."
8 Sheller, *Consuming the Caribbean*, 38.
9 Jasen, *Wild Things*, 15.
10 Jasen, "Native People and the Tourist Industry," 1.
11 Jasen, *Wild Things*, 17.
12 Ibid., 4.
13 Jasen, "Native People," 11.
14 Jasen, *Wild Things*, 3.

Notes to Pages 113 - 118

15 Jasen, "Native People," 11.
16 Ibid, 8.
17 Francis, *The Imaginary Indian*, 179.
18 Dawson, *Selling British Columbia*, 16.
19 For more on interactions between tourists and Indigenous peoples, see Jasen's *Wild Things*.
20 Dawson, *Selling British Columbia*, 72.
21 Francis, *The Imaginary Indian*, 179-81.
22 Ibid.
23 Jasen, *Wild Things*, 3. Jasen flags some of the problems inherent in her analysis, noting that the absence of oral histories from the nineteenth century, especially around Indigenous perspectives on tourism, limits a comprehensive treatment of the relationship between Indigenous peoples and tourist economies. Later in the book, she advocates (albeit briefly) the importance of oral history research in ensuring understandings of the early phenomenon of Canadian tourism are not limited.
24 Jasen, *Wild Things*, 2.
25 Raibmon, *Authentic Indians*, 158.
26 Mawani, "From Colonialism to Multiculturalism?" 40-41.
27 Ibid., 41.
28 McGinley, "Best Practices," 15.
29 Francis, *The Imaginary Indian*, 183.
30 Mawani, "From Colonialism to Multiculturalism," discusses the rise of the popularity of the totem pole in Vancouver through the 1930s, noting the complex interplay between Indigenous desires to "increase their visibility in their territories" (45) and colonial assumptions about "'uncivilized savages' who, among other things, could not protect their cultural property. Colonial authorities needed to 'save' and 'preserve' totem poles and other artifacts as evidence of a 'lost civilization'" (44).
31 Ibid., 44.
32 Jasen, "Native People," 11.
33 D'Hauteserre, "Postcolonialism, Colonialism, and Tourism," 237.
34 Jasen, "Native People," 6.
35 Milne and Ateljevic, "Tourism, Economic Development and the Global-local Nexus," 370-71.
36 Canada's Minister's Roundtable on Parks Canada qtd. in Smith, "Experiential," 5. For more on the rise of mass tourism, see Kopper, "The Breakthrough of the Package Tour in Germany after 1945."
37 See "International Recommendations for Tourism Statistics 2008."
38 Silver, "Marketing Authenticity in Third-World Countries," 306.

39 Prentice, "Experiential Cultural Tourism," 7.
40 Qtd. in Smith, "Experiential Tourism," 4.
41 Qtd. in ibid., 5.
42 Qtd. in ibid., 4-5.
43 Prentice, "Experiential Cultural Tourism," 7.
44 Roundtable qtd. in Smith, "Experiential Tourism," 4-5.
45 Ibid.
46 Smith, "Experiential Tourism, 2; Prentice, "Experiential Cultural Tourism," 10.
47 Blundell, "Riding the Polar Bear Express," 29.
48 Qtd. in ibid.
49 Ibid.
50 Ibid.
51 Theobald, *Global Tourism*, 1.
52 Dawson, *Selling British Columbia*, 2.
53 In 2015, its corporate brand was changed with the introduction of a new name, Destination Canada. For more information on this change, see https://www.tourismkelowna.com/industry/industry-news-centre/post/canadian-tourism-commission-ctc-changes-name-to-destination-canada/.
54 Qtd. in Andrew, "Federal Policies on Image-building," 30.
55 Blundell, "Riding the Polar Bear Express," 30.
56 Qtd. in Morrison, *Marketing and Managing Tourism Destinations*, 298.
57 "Canada's Tourism Brand."
58 Ibid.
59 Ibid.
60 Ibid.
61 Ibid.
62 Ibid.
63 Ibid.
64 Ibid.
65 Ibid.
66 "Traveller Types."
67 Coleman, *White Civility*, 15-16.
68 Ibid., 16.
69 Ibid.

214 Notes to Pages 123 - 129

70 Gregory, "Colonial Nostalgia and Cultures of Travel," 140.
71 Hodge and Mishra, *Dark Side of the Dream*, 27.
72 Blundell, "Riding the Polar Bear Express," 30.
73 Qtd. in Nimijean, "The Politics of Branding Canada," 68-69.
74 Ibid., 70.
75 Blundell, "Riding the Polar Bear Express," 30.
76 Abu-Laban and Gabriel, *Selling Diversity*, 110.
77 Nimijean, "The Politics of Branding," 69.
78 See the 1996 Aboriginal Business Survey conducted by Industry Canada: "Aboriginal Tourism Opportunities for Canada; see also "Aboriginal Arts and Crafts and Tourism."
79 "Canada, Aboriginal-style."
80 Pfeiff, "Go Inuit for a Weekend."
81 "Dance at Ahbee Festival."
82 Ibid.
83 "Batoche and Louis Riel."
84 Ibid.
85 Alfred, *Wasase*, 23.
86 Huhndorf, *Going Native*, 2.
87 Ibid., 6.
88 Qtd. in ibid., 172.
89 Ibid.
90 Ibid., 15.
91 Ibid., 5.
92 "Whiteshell Blockade Threat Averted . . . for Now."
93 Alfred, *Wasase*, 126.
94 Ibid., 127.
95 Ibid.
96 Ibid., xiv.
97 Huhndorf, *Going Native*, xv, 5.
98 Alfred, *Wasase*, 126.
99 To name a few, there are/have been the Canadian National Aboriginal Tourism Association (CNATA), the Aboriginal Working Group (AWG), Alberta Aboriginal Tourism (ATA), the Northern Ontario Native Tourism Association (NONTA), and Eastside Aboriginal Sustainable Tourism, Inc.

100 Roundtable qtd. in Smith, "Experiential Tourism," 5.
101 Rostum, "Review of Aboriginal Tourism Team Canada," 2. According to Rostum's review, the ATTC's mission was that it would "influence and develop policies and programs to benefit Aboriginal people in Canada" through key activity areas such as industry development, community awareness and capacity development, marketing and partnership building, human resources development, and communications and advocacy with stakeholders. The organization operated in accordance with the regulations of Corporations Canada as a non-profit organization and was structured as required by government regulations for non-profit organizations. The ATTC hosted a number of national gatherings on Aboriginal tourism and conducted industry research, although over half of Aboriginal tourism business respondents to the final review of ATTC reported never having heard of the ATTC (vi).
102 "Backgrounder."
103 Ibid.
104 Kelly, "Atiik Askii: Land of the Caribou," ii.
105 Ibid.
106 O'Neil, "Aboriginal Cultural Tourism: Checklist for Success."
107 "Aboriginal Entrepreneurs in Canada."
108 "Aboriginal Tourism Takes Flight in British Columbia."
109 Aboriginal Tourism Association of BC, "The Next Phase: 2012–2017."
110 Aboriginal Tourism Association of BC, "Aboriginal Cultural Tourism."
111 Aboriginal Tourism Association of BC, "Experience Types: Art and Culture Connoisseur."
112 Ibid.
113 Aboriginal Tourism Association of BC, "Experience Types: Authentic Experience Seeker."
114 Ibid.
115 Aboriginal Tourism Association of BC, "Experience Types: Nature and Beauty With a Twist."
116 Ibid.
117 Ibid. Although it is not the direct focus of this section, it is important to note that the first two images are of men while the third image of Native & Beauty, features a woman; the juxtaposition of these images, particularly that of the woman, does double duty in marketing the Aboriginal culture experiences along gendered lines. As Trask writes in reference to the prostitution of culture in Hawaii, women are effectively "pimped out" as hula dancers.
118 Aboriginal Tourism Association of BC, "Cultural Authenticity Program."
119 Ibid.
120 Ibid.

121 Aboriginal Tourism Association of BC, "Guide to Applying to the Authentic Aboriginal Cultural Tourism Program," 3.

122 Ibid. The program is also contingent upon businesses becoming "stakeholders": in exchange "The Marketing Program (which is largely supported by ATBC) provides thousands of dollars of national and international exposure at a small fraction of the cost to you." Aboriginal Tourism Association of BC, "ATBC Authenticity Program," 1.

123 Aboriginal Tourism Association of BC, "Guide to Applying to the Authentic Aboriginal Cultural Tourism Program," 10.

124 Laliberté, "Authenticity."

125 Ibid.

126 Ibid.

127 Ibid.

128 Raibmon, *Authentic Indians*, 7.

129 Ibid., 9.

130 Ibid., 3.

131 Ibid.

132 Borrows, "Frozen Rights in Canada," 29.

133 Verboven, "BC First Nation a Corporate Success."

134 Atleo, *From Indigenous Nationhood to Neoliberal Aboriginal Economic Development*.

135 Ibid., 23.

136 Daschuk, *Clearing the Plains*, 159. See also the work of Robert Innes, "Historians and Indigenous Genocide in Saskatchewan."

137 Daschuk, *Clearing the Plains*, 133.

138 Adese, "Behaving Unexpectedly in Expected Places."

139 Alfred, "Colonialism and State Dependency," 52.

140 Alfred, *Wasase*, 121–22.

141 Ibid., 121.

142 Ibid., 105.

143 Ibid., 105–6.

144 Ibid.

145 Aboriginal Tourism Association of BC, "Shaping the Future of Aboriginal Tourism."

146 Ruth Phillips qtd. in Raibmon, *Authentic Indians*, 11. See also Phillips and Phillips, *Trading Identities*.

147 Ibid.

148 The question here, "what kind of work" does the term do, is inspired by a talk given by David Theo Goldberg at McMaster University on 15 March 2012, as he questioned the effects of labelling American and global society as "postracial." Rather than taking an interest in what the term means, he suggested we focus on considering what it is that "postracial" does—what sorts of histories and present realities does it conceal/supplant/reimagine? This is the spirit in which I discuss "Aboriginal."

149 Sheller, *Consuming the Caribbean*, 38.

150 Ibid.

Chapter 4 – Marketing Aboriginality and the Branding of Place: The Case of Vancouver International Airport

1   Martinez, "Wrong Directions and New Maps," 556.

2   Flaman, "Public Art and Canadian Cultural Policy," 84.

3   See Charland, "Technological Nationalism"; St. Germain, *Indian Treaty-making*; Gwyn, *Nation Maker*.

4   Charland, "Technological Nationalism," 199.

5   See Nerbas, "Canadian Transportation Policy," 242.

6   Harris, "How Did Colonialism Dispossess?"; Lawrence, *Fractured Homeland*; see also Gaudry and Drake, "The Resilience of Métis Title: Rejecting Assumptions of Extinguishment for Métis Land Rights."

7   Daschuk, *Clearing the Plains*.

8   See Venne, "Understanding Treaty 6"; Krasowski, *No Surrender*.

9   Charland, "Technological Nationalism," 201.

10 Ibid.

11 Daschuk, *Clearing the Plains*, 108-9.

12 Ibid., 133-34.

13 In *Indian Treaty-making Policy in the United States and Canada, 1867-1877*, St. Germain argues that no explicit connection was "made between the Indians and the railroads in Canadian sources or literature" (42). She argues that while General Sherman on the part of the United States government viewed the railroad as a "technological solution to the Indian problem," the Dominion of Canada, insofar as it wanted to build a national railway to build the nation, did not view Indigenous peoples as enough of a threat to use the railway to suppress various peoples (ibid.). Later, however, she acknowledges that through the course of treaty signing, when First Nations sought particular lands deemed to be in the way of the path of the railroad, such as with Treaty 4, the railway's needs were given precedence over First Nations decisions (94).

14 Coleman, *White Civility*, 6-7; see also Woodsworth, *Strangers within Our Gates*.

15 Thobani, *Exalted Subjects*, 6; see also Mackey, *The House of Difference*.
16 Thomson, *Blacks in Deep Snow*; Wang, "'His Dominion' and the 'Yellow Peril,'" 91; Thobani, *Exalted Subjects*.
17 See Coleman, *White Civility*; also Tobias, "Canada's Subjugation of the Plains Cree"; Armitage, "Canada: The General Structure of Canadian Indian Policy"; Miller, *Skyscrapers Hide the Heavens*; Milloy, *A National Crime*; Sangster, "'She Is Hostile to Our Ways'"; Brownlie, "Intimate Surveillance."
18 Charland, "Technological Nationalism," 199.
19 Thorpe, *Temagami's Tangled Wild*, 29.
20 Lindberg, "The Doctrine of Discovery in Canada," 92.
21 Nerbas, "Canadian Transportation Policy," 243.
22 See Flaman, "Public Art."
23 Pigott, *Flying Canucks*, 59.
24 Paris, *From the Wright Brothers to Top Gun*, 4.
25 Harris, "Airports," 300.
26 LaRocque, *When the Other Is Me*, 39.
27 Aviation in Canada developed in step with resource extraction. Pilots with combat training returning from the First World War found work as bush pilots for small companies "involved in the exploration and development of remote northern areas" (Rorke, "Constructed Destinations," 20). In *Airport Development, Management and Operations in Canada*, Edward Syme and Alexander Wells write, "These small operators (often one pilot, one mechanic, and an airplane) gradually evolved into small air transport companies, forming the basis of Canada's air transport industry" (5); see also Rorke, "Constructed Destinations," 20. The most prominent commercial venture in so-called remote northern areas, in the wake of the decline of the fur trade, was lumbering and the industrialization of forestry. While small operators began carrying out flights to transport people into northern regions, larger companies like Southern Labrador Pulp and Lumber Co. Inc. (affiliated with an American company, the Belle Island Straits Lumber and Pulp Company Ltd. of Boston) would come to use the private and commercial airfields that had been developed for wartime aviation training to launch large-scale surveys. The largest, the H.V. Green Aerial Survey, was completed in the summer of 1919 and produced 15,000 aerial photographs covering an area of forestation and water stretching 75 by 42 miles (Shaw, *Photographing Canada*, 5). The purpose of the survey, piloted by Daniel Owen, captain with the Royal Air Force (RAF), was to access and evaluate forestation in Labrador in an area leased by the government to the company, and that on the timber market would be worth roughly $26 million (ibid.). In addition, the survey party was also tasked with searching for "other exploitable natural resources and to locate possible hydroelectric power generation sites" (ibid.). In this case, forestry provided the rationale for the introduction of aviation and its expansion to further natural resource development; these early explorations and the possibilities they promised, in turn, fuelled a desire to expand the aviation industry.

28 Wrigley, "The Mineral-Based Energy Economy," 77.
29 Harris, "Airports," 290.
30 Fumoleau, *As Long as This Land Shall Last*, 194.
31 Kulchyski and Tester, *Kiumajut (Talking Back)*, 35.
32 Coates and Morrison, "Treaty Research Report—Treaty No. 11 (1921)."
33 Kulchyski and Tester, *Kiumajut (Talking Back)*, 35.
34 Ibid.
35 Ibid. It is worth noting that while a fuller exposition is outside the immediate scope of this chapter, there is much room to be critical of our too easy reliance on the language of "natural resources." While mining is not a recent thing, nor is it unique to the nineteenth and twentieth centuries, our contemporary understanding of what is meant by the shorthand of "natural resources" is a direct result of the convergence of imperialism, scientific knowledge production, and commodification.
36 Ibid; Coates and Morrison, "Treaty Research Report–Treaty No. 11 (1921)."
37 Kulchyski and Tester, *Kiumajut (Talking Back)*, 47-48.
38 Ibid.; Zaslow, *The Northward Expansion of Canada*, 178-88.
39 Harris, "Airports," 290.
40 Courtwright, *Sky as Frontier*, 14.
41 Harris, "Airports," 300.
42 Van Vleck, *Empire of the Air*, 15.
43 Ibid., 9.
44 "Michael Kusugak."
45 See Tester and Kulchyski, *Kiumajut (Talking Back)*.
46 Hubregtse, "Passenger Movement and Air Terminal Design," 156.
47 Eriksen and Døving, "In Limbo."
48 Ibid.
49 Ibid.
50 Flaman, "Public Art," 76.
51 Ibid.
52 Ibid.
53 Ibid.
54 Ibid., 86.
55 Ibid., 87.
56 "Painting and Sculpture"; Flaman, "Public Art," 87.

57 Harris, "Airports," 286.
58 Flaman, "Public Art," 87.
59 Ibid., 90.
60 Ibid., 89.
61 Hubregtse, "Passenger Movement," 157.
62 Rorke, "Constructed Destinations," 11.
63 YVR, "Past and Future."
64 Harris, "Airports," 294.
65 Qtd. in Rorke, "Constructed Destinations," 24–25.
66 Ibid., 24.
67 Ibid., 22.
68 Ibid., 7.
69 Ibid., 5.
70 Ibid., 6.
71 Ibid., 13.
72 Ibid., 25.
73 Qtd. in ibid., 38.
74 Ibid., 40.
75 YVR Art Foundation, "About."
76 YVR Art Foundation, "The YVR Art Foundation."
77 Ibid.
78 Rorke, "Constructed Destinations," 42–43.
79 Hubregtse, "Passenger Movement," 9–10.
80 Ibid., 11.
81 Leddy, "Tourists, Art and Airports," 26.
82 Ibid., 7. Through a series of interviews with xʷməθkʷəy̓əm band council members and artists commissioned to create work for YVR's International Terminal, Shannon Leddy concludes that the effort made by YVR towards inclusion was mostly positively received (ibid., 32).
83 Ibid., 9.
84 Hubregtse, "Passenger Movement," 12.
85 Ibid., 11.
86 Leddy, "Tourists, Art and Airports," 37.
87 Ibid., 33–34.

88 Ibid., 38-39.

89 Ibid., 25.

90 Ibid., 2.

91 Ibid., 38.

92 Ibid., 52.

93 Ibid., 3.

94 Hubregtse, "Passenger Movement," 11. See also Hubregtse, *Wayfinding, Consumption, and Air Terminal Design*.

95 Ibid.

96 For more information on the legacies and harm of these stereotypes, see the Jim Crow Museum of Racist Memorabilia: https://www.ferris.edu/HTMLS/news/jimcrow/native/homepage.htm.

97 Ibid., 12.

98 Rorke, "Constructed Destinations," 55.

99 Ibid., 62.

100 Stewart, "Controversial Art Can't Land at Vancouver Airport."

101 Ibid.

102 "Orcas in the City–Vancouver."

103 Ibid.

104 Ibid.

105 Qtd. in ibid.

106 Qtd. in ibid.

107 Artist's statement in the catalogue for McMaster and Martin, *Indigena*; see also Townsend-Gault, ed., "The Salvation Art of Yuxweluptun."

108 Stewart, "Artist Lawrence Paul Yuxweluptun Speaks Out."

109 Ibid.

110 Rorke, "Constructed Destinations," 51.

111 Ibid., 53.

112 Ibid., 54.

113 Van Vleck, 9.

114 Courtwright, *Sky as Frontier*, 8.

115 I think these borders can also be understood in another way—national airlines crisscross Indigenous airways that were never ceded.

116 Courtwright, *Sky as Frontier*, 12, 17.

117 Milloy, *Indian Act Colonialism*, 106.
118 Venne, "Understanding Treaty 6," 198.

Conclusion – Thoughts on the End of Aboriginalization and the Turn to Indigenization

1 TASSOfficial, "Swipe Through and Check Out."
2 Ibid.
3 Ibid.
4 White, *An Essay on the Indigenous Grasses of Ireland*.
5 Watts, "Smudge This," 151. See also Simpson, *Dancing on Our Turtle's Back*.
6 Landriault, "From 'Aboriginal' to 'Indigenous.'"
7 Ibid.
8 Tasker, "Indigenous Affairs Is No More."
9 Ibid.
10 Ibid.
11 Marshall, "Indian Residential Schools Settlement Agreement."
12 Government of Canada, "Truth and Reconciliation Commission of Canada."
13 Ibid.
14 Truth and Reconciliation Commission of Canada, *Truth and Reconciliation Commission of Canada*.
15 Lightfoot, "A Promise Too Far?"
16 Wood, "'Dangerous Precedent.'"
17 Gidimt'en Yintah Access Point, "Wet'suwet'en Strong."
18 Gidimt'en Yintah Access Point, "History and Timeline."
19 Ibid.
20 Ibid.
21 Simpson, "Consent's Revenge."
22 Gidimt'en Yintah Access Point, "History and Timeline."
23 For more detailed information and a partial timeline, see "Timeline of the Coastal GasLink Pipeline."
24 Bellrichard, "RCMP Spent More than $13M."
25 Wood, "'Dangerous Precedent.'"
26 Berman, "Justin Trudeau Says Rail Barricades 'Need to Come Down Now.'"

27 Simpson, "Consent's Revenge," 328.
28 Barrera, "Battle Brewing Over Indigenous Rights Recognition Framework."
29 Diabo, "Trudeau's 'Zombie Policies.'"
30 Diabo, "Harper Launches Major First Nations Termination Plan."
31 Diabo, "Trudeau's 'Zombie Policies.'"
32 Ibid.
33 Ibid.
34 Ibid.
35 Ibid.
36 Steel, "The Aboriginal Pavilion."
37 "Trudeau Changes Name of National Aboriginal Day."
38 "Statement of the Prime Minister of Canada on National Aboriginal Day."
39 Macdonald, "Indigenizing the Academy." It also follows in the spirit of the work of Devon Abbott Mihesuah and Angela Cavender Wilson and their 2004 book, *Indigenizing the Academy*. See also Gaudry and Lorenz, "Indigenization as Inclusion, Reconciliation, and Decolonization."
40 See Williams and Allan, "Celebrated Artist Says He's Indigenous."
41 Indigenous Tourism Association of BC, "Authentic Indigenous."
42 Ibid.
43 Indigenous Tourism Association of BC, "Authentic Indigenous Designation Program Survey."
44 Ibid.
45 It is worth noting, too, that Destination Canada (CTC) has changed the language it uses, bringing their website in line with the current emphasis on Indigeneity; however, many of the problematic quizzes and gimmicks of pairing travellers with experiences, previously designated as Aboriginal, remain.
46 YVR, "Musqueam YVR Agreement."
47 YVR, "Musqueam–YVR."
48 Korstrom, "Musqueam's YVR Pact."
49 Howell, "Musqueam Deal."
50 "How YVR and the Musqueam Forged a Working Relationship."
51 Howell, "Musqueam Deal"; see also Grant-John in video of event: https://www.youtube.com/watch?v=dwuRAUoG_dY&feature=emb_logo.
52 Qtd. in Howell, Musqueam Deal"; Wood, "Musqueam Shows Visitors."
53 Wood, "Musqueam Shows Visitors."
54 Ibid.

55 Ibid.
56 Ibid.

Bibliography

"1988 Winter Olympics OC Part 7-Introduction by ABC." YouTube. 12 November 2010. http://www.youtube.com/watch?v=u61dC8RW4AA (accessed 14 June 2020).

"Aboriginal." *Merriam Webster*. https://www.merriam-webster.com/dictionary/aboriginal (accessed 14 April 2020).

"Aboriginal Arts and Crafts and Tourism: A Sector Analysis." *Aboriginal Tourism Team Canada (ATTC)*, August 2002.

"Aboriginal Entrepreneurs in Canada: Progress & Prospects." Micro-Economic Policy Analysis Branch and Aboriginal Business Canada, 1998. https://iportal.usask.ca/index.php?sid=538872931&id=51957&t=details (accessed 11 August 2011).

Aboriginal Multi-Media Society of Alberta (AMMSA). "MNA to Have Local Voting." 24 August 1984

Aboriginal Tourism Association of BC. "Aboriginal Cultural Tourism: Blueprint Strategy for BC." 2005. www.indigenousbc.com/assets/corporate/atbc_blueprint-strategy_full-report.pdf (accessed 11 August 2011).

———. "ATBC Authenticity Program: Frequently Asked Questions." No date. http://www.aboriginalbc.com/assets/corporate/atbc_authenticity_faqs.pdf (accessed 13 August 2011).

———. "Cultural Authenticity Program." No date. http://www.aboriginalbc.com/corporate/info/cultural-authenticity-program (accessed 11 August 2011).

———. "Experience Types: Art and Culture Connoisseur." No date. http://www.aboriginalbc.com/experience-types/art-culture-connoisseur (accessed 11 August 2011).

———. "Experience Types: Authentic Experience Seeker." No date. http://www.aboriginalbc.com/experience-types/authentic-experience-seeker (accessed 11 August 2011).

———. "Experience Types: Nature and Beauty with a Twist." No date. http://www.aboriginalbc.com/experience-types/nature-beauty-with-a-twist (accessed 11 August 2011).

———. "Guide to Applying to the Authentic Aboriginal Cultural Tourism Program." 2010. http://www.aboriginalbc.com/assets/corporate/atbc_authenticity_how-to-apply.pdf (accessed 12 August 2011).

———. "The Next Phase: 2012-2017, A Five-Year Strategy for Aboriginal Cultural Tourism in British Columbia." https://www.indigenousbc.com/assets/corporate/The%20Next%20Phase%20-%20BCs%20Aboriginal%20Cultural%20Tourism%20Strategy%20-%20AtBC.pdf (accessed 11 August 2011).

———. "Shaping the Future of Aboriginal Tourism." No date. http://www.aboriginalbc.com/media/story-ideas/revitalization (accessed 15 August 2011).

"Aboriginal Tourism Opportunities for Canada: U.K., Germany, France." *Canadian Tourism Commission (CTC)*. http://en-corporate.canada.travel/sites/default/files/pdf/Research/Product-knowledge/Aboriginal-tourism/Aboriginal_Tourism_Opportunities_eng.pdf.

"Aboriginal Tourism Takes Flight in British Columbia." *Aboriginal Affairs and Northern Development*, 2008. http://www.aadnc-aandc.gc.ca/eng/1100100021348 (accessed 11 August 2011).

"Aboriginal Tribes Resident in His Majesty's Dominions in North America, or in Any Adjacent Territories" (p. 284) – Great Britain Parliament House of Commons – H.M. Stationery Office 1834 – "Votes and Proceedings" 11th Parliament – Great Britain and Ireland.

Abu-Laban, Yasmeen, and Christina Gabriel. *Selling Diversity: Immigration, Multiculturalism, Employment Equity, and Globalization*. Peterborough, ON: Broadview Press, 2002.

Adams, Howard. *Prison of Grass: Canada from a Native Point of View*. Saskatoon: Fifth House Publishers, 1989.

Adese, Jennifer. "Behaving Unexpectedly in Expected Places: First Nations Artists and the Embodiment of Visual Sovereignty." In *More Will Sing Their Way to Freedom: Indigenous Resistance and Resurgence*, edited by Elaine Coburn, 130–49. Winnipeg: Fernwood, 2015.

———. "Colluding with the Enemy? Nationalism and Depictions of 'Aboriginality' in Canadian Olympic Moments." *American Indian Quarterly* 36, no. 4 (2012): 479–502.

———. "A Tale of Two Constitutions: Métis Nationhood and Section 35 (2)'s Impact on Interpretations of Daniels." *TOPIA: Canadian Journal of Cultural Studies* 36 (2016): 7–19.

Adese, Jennifer, Zoe Todd, and Shaun Stevenson. "Mediating Métis Identity: An Interview with Jennifer Adese and Zoe Todd." *MediaTropes* 7, no. 1 (2017): 1–25.

Adese, Jennifer, and Robert Alexander Innes, eds. *Indigenous Celebrity: Entanglements with Fame*. Winnipeg: University of Manitoba Press, 2021.

Albo, Greg, and Bryan M. Evans, eds. *Divided Province: Ontario Politics in the Age of Neoliberalism*. Montreal and Kingston: McGill-Queen's University Press, 2019.

Alcantara, Christopher. "Privatize Reserve Land? No. Improve Economic Development Conditions on Canadian Indian Reserves? Yes." *Canadian Journal of Native Studies* 28, no. 2 (2008): 421–27.

Alfred, Gerald Taiaiake. "Colonialism and State Dependency." *Journal of Aboriginal Health* (2009): 42–60.

———. *Wasase: Indigenous Pathways of Action and Freedom*. Toronto: University of Toronto Press, 2005.

Alfred, Taiaiake, and Jeff Corntassel. "Being Indigenous: Resurgences against Contemporary Colonialism." *Government and Opposition* 40, no. 4 (2005): 597–614.

Allen, George. "Place Branding: New Tools for Economic Development." *Design Management Review* 18, no. 2 (2007): 60–68.

Altamirano-Jiménez, Isabel. *Indigenous Encounters with Neoliberalism: Place, Women, and the Environment in Canada and Mexico*. Vancouver: UBC Press, 2013.

Andersen, Chris. "From Nation to Population: The Racialisation of 'Métis' in the Canadian Census." *Nations and Nationalism* 14, no. 2 (2008): 347-68.

———. *Métis: Race, Recognition, and the Struggle for Indigenous Peoplehood*. Vancouver: UBC Press, 2014.

———. "Moya Tipimsook ('The People Who Aren't Their Own Bosses'): Racialization and the Misrecognition of 'Métis' in Upper Great Lakes Ethnohistory." *Ethnohistory* 58, no. 1 (2011): 37-63

———. "Residual Tensions of Empire: Contemporary Métis Communities and the Canadian Judicial Imagination." In *Reconfiguring Aboriginal State Relations—Canada: The State of the Federation*, 295-325. Montreal: McGill-Queen's University Press, 2005.

———. "Underdeveloped Identities: The Misrecognition of Aboriginality in the Canadian Census." *Economy and Society* 42, no. 4 (2013): 626-50.

———. "Urban Aboriginality as a Distinctive Identity, in Twelve Parts." In *Indigenous in the City: Contemporary Identities and Cultural Innovation*, edited by Evelyn Peters and Chris Andersen, 46-68. Vancouver: UBC Press, 2013.

Andrew, Caroline. "Federal Policies on Image-building: Very Much Cities and Communities." In *Image-building in Canadian Municipalities*, edited by Jean Harvey and Robert Young, 27-48. Montreal and Kngston: McGill-Queen's University Press, 2012.

Animikii, Inc. "Why We Use 'Indigenous.'" 7 June 2017. http://muskratmagazine.com/why-we-use-indigenous-instead-of-aboriginal/ (accessed 21 June 2017).

Anishinabek Nation—Union of Ontario Indians. "Anishinabek Outlaw Term 'Aboriginal.'" *NationTalk*, 25 June 2008. http://nationtalk.ca/story/anishinabek-outlaw-term-aboriginal (accessed 14 April 2020).

Armitage, Andrew. "Canada: The General Structure of Canadian Indian Policy." In *Comparing the Policy of Aboriginal Assimilation: Australia, Canada, and New Zealand*, edited by A. Armitage, 70-99. Vancouver: UBC Press, 1995.

Atleo, Cliff. *From Indigenous Nationhood to Neoliberal Aboriginal Economic Development: Charting the Evolution of Indigenous-settler Relations in Canada*. Victoria, BC: Canadian Social Economy Hub, 2009.

"Backgrounder." Aboriginal Tourism Association of British Columbia. No date. https://www.indigenousbc.com/assets/media/AtBC_MediaKit.pdf (accessed 11 August 2011).

Backhouse, Constance. *Colour-Coded: A Legal History of Racism in Canada, 1900-1950*. Toronto: University of Toronto Press, 1999.

Bannerji, Himani. *The Dark Side of the Nation: Essays on Multiculturalism, Nationalism and Gender*. Toronto: Canadian Scholars' Press, 2000.

Bargh, Maria, edited by *Resistance: An Indigenous Response to Neoliberalism*. Honolulu: Huia Publishers, 2007.

Barker, Joanne. "Gender, Sovereignty, Rights: Native Women's Activism against Social Inequality and Violence in Canada." *American Quarterly* 60, no. 2 (2008): 259-66.

Barrera, Jorge. "Battle Brewing Over Indigenous Rights Recognition Framework." *CBC News*. 11 September 2018. https://www.cbc.ca/news/indigenous/indigenous-rights-framework-bennett-1.4819510 (accessed 15 January 2022).

Barron, F. Laurie. "The CCF and the Development of Métis Colonies in Southern Saskatchewan during the Premiership of TC Douglas, 1944–1961." *Canadian Journal of Native Studies* 10, no. 2 (1990): 243–70.

"Batoche and Louis Riel." Canadian Tourism Commission. No date. http://caen.canada.travel/experience/batoche-and-louis-riel (accessed 12 August 2013).

Bellrichard, Chantelle. "RCMP Spent More than $13M on Policing Coastal GasLink Conflict on Wet'suwet'en Territory." *CBC News*. 21 October 2020. https://www.cbc.ca/news/indigenous/rcmp-wetsuweten-pipeline-policing-costs-1.5769555.

Berman, Sarah. "Justin Trudeau Says Rail Barricades 'Need to Come Down Now.'" *Vice*, 21 February 2020. https://www.vice.com/en_ca/article/qjdwb3/justin-trudeau-says-rail-barricades-need-to-come-down-now (accessed 31 July 2020).

Blundell, Valda. "Riding the Polar Bear Express: And Other Encounters between Tourists and First Peoples in Canada." *Journal of Canadian Studies* 30, no. 4 (Winter 1996): 28–43.

Borgerson, Janet, Jonathan Schroeder, and Zhiyan Wu. "Branding as Soft Power: Brand Culture, Nation Branding and the 2008 Beijing Olympics." In *Soft Power with Chinese Characteristics: China's Campaign for Hearts and Minds*, edited by Ying Zhu, Kingsley Edney, and Stanley Rosen, 117–32. London: Routledge, 2019.

Borrows, John. "Frozen Rights in Canada: Constitutional Interpretation and the Trickster." *American Indian Law Review* 22, no. 1 (1997): 37–64.

———. "The Trickster: Integral to a Distinctive Culture." *Constitutional Forum* 8 (1996).

———. "Wampum at Niagara: The Royal Proclamation, Canadian Legal History, and Self-government." In *Aboriginal and Treaty Rights in Canada: Essays on Law, Equity, and Respect for Difference*, edited by Michael Ash, 155–72. Vancouver: UBC Press, 1997.

Boykoff, Jules. "Celebration Capitalism and the Sochi 2014 Winter Olympics." *Olympika* XXII (2013): 39–70.

Bradburn, Jamie. "In the Mood for Cuts: How the 'Common Sense Revolution' Swept Ontario in 1995." *TVO*, 6 June 2018. https://www.tvo.org/article/in-the-mood-for-cuts-how-the-common-sense-revolution-swept-ontario-in-1995 (accessed 23 July 2021).

Brethour, Patrick. "Exclusive Demographic Picture: A Comparison of Key Statistics in the DES, Vancouver, BC and Canada." *Globe and Mail*. 13 February 2009. http://www.globeandmail.com/incoming/exclusive-demographic-picture/article4277604 (accessed 15 July 2010).

Brondo, Keri Vacanti. *Land Grab: Green Neoliberalism, Gender, and Garifuna Resistance in Honduras*. Tucson: University of Arizona Press, 2013.

Brownlie, Jarvis. "Intimate Surveillance: Indian Affairs, Colonization, and the Regulation of Aboriginal Women's Sexuality." In *Contact Zones: Aboriginal and Settler Women in Canada's Colonial Past*, edited by Myra Rutherdale and Katie Pickles, 160–78. Vancouver: UBC Press, 2005.

Burley, David. "Rooster Town: Winnipeg's Lost Métis Suburb, 1900–1960." *Urban History Review/Revue d'histoire urbaine* 42, no. 1 (2013): 3–25.

Cairns, Alan. *Citizens Plus: Aboriginal Peoples and the Canadian State.* Vancouver: UBC Press, 2011.

Calliou, Brian. "The Indian Association of Alberta: A History of Political Action." *Canadian Ethnic Studies Journal* 35, no. 2 (2003): 141–43.

"Canada, Aboriginal-style." *Canadian Tourism Commission.* No date (accessed 12 August 2011).

Canadaland (website). "From Joseph Boyden to Michelle Latimer—Why Does This Keep Happening?" 15 February 2021. https://www.canadaland.com/inconvenient-truth-michelle-latimer/ (accessed 29 July 2021).

"Canada's Tourism Brand." *Canadian Tourism Commission.* No date (accessed 12 August 2011).

Cannon, Martin J. "Race Matters: Sexism, Indigenous Sovereignty, and McIvor." *Canadian Journal of Women and the Law* 26, no. 1 (2014): 23–50.

Cardinal, Harold. *The Unjust Society: The Tragedy of Canada's Indians.* Edmonton: M.G. Hurtig, 1969.

Carroll, William K., and Murray Shaw. "Consolidating a Neoliberal Policy Bloc in Canada, 1976 to 1996." *Canadian Public Policy/Analyse de Politiques* (2001): 195–217.

Charland, Maurice. "Technological Nationalism." *Communications Theory* 10, no. 1–2 (1986): 196–220.

Charleyboy, Lisa. "2010 Olympics Token Tribute." *Urban Native Girl*, 14 February 2010. https://www.straight.com/blogra/2010-winter-olympics-token-tribute-and-memorial-march-indigenous-women (accessed 24 February 2010).

Coates, Kenneth S., and William R. Morrison. "Treaty Research Report – Treaty No. 11 (1921)." Treaties and Historical Research Centre, Indian and Northern Affairs Canada, 1986. http://www.aadnc-aandc.gc.ca/eng/1100100028912/1100100028914.

COJO 76. "Games of the XXI Olympiad Montréal 1976 Official Report." Ottawa: COJO 76, 1978.

Coleman, Daniel. *White Civility: The Literary Project of English Canada.* Toronto: University of Toronto Press, 2006.

Colpitts, George. "Wildlife Promotions, Western Canadian Boosterism, and the Conservation Movement, 1890–1914." *American Review of Canadian Studies* 28, nos. 1–2 (1998): 103–30.

Comm. Series 15, box 8, City of Calgary Archives, Calgary, Alberta

Constitution Act, 1982, being Schedule B to the Canada Act 1982 (U.K.), 1982, c. 11.

Coulthard, Glen Sean. *Red Skin, White Masks: Rejecting the Colonial Politics of Recognition.* Minneapolis: University of Minnesota Press, 2014.

Courtwright, David T. *Sky as Frontier: Adventure, Aviation, and Empire.* College Station: Texas A and M University Press, 2005.

Crossingham, Lesley. "Klein Meets with Lubicon Chief." *Windspeaker*, 20 March 1987, 3.

———. "Natives in Olympics: Frank King—'OCO Is Not a Funding Agency." *Windspeaker*, 10 May 1987. https://ammsa.com/publications/windspeaker/natives-olympics-frank-king-oco-not-funding-agency (accessed 17 February 2010).

"Dance at Ahbee Festival." Canadian Tourism Commission. No date. http://caen.canada.travel/experience/dance-ahbee-festival (accessed 12 August 2013).

Daniels, Harry. *Report of the Metis and Non-Status Indian Constitutional Commission*. Native Council of Canada. Ottawa: Mutual Press, 1981.

Daschuk, James William. *Clearing the Plains: Disease, Politics of Starvation, and the Loss of Aboriginal Life*. Regina: University of Regina Press, 2013.

Dawson, Michael. *Selling British Columbia: Tourism and Consumer Culture, 1890–1970*. Vancouver: UBC Press, 2005.

Daytec, Cheryl. "Fraternal Twins with Different Mothers: Explaining Differences between Self-Determination and Self-Government Using the Indian Tribal Sovereignty Model as Context." *Minnesota Journal of International Law* 29 (2013).

Deer, Jessica. "Blast from the Past: Onkwehón:We at the Olympics in Montreal 40 Years Ago." *The Eastern Door*, 1 August 2016. https://www.easterndoor.com/2016/08/01/blast-from-the-past-onkwehonwe-at-the-olympics-in-montreal-40-years-ago/ (accessed 19 July 2020).

Deschambault, Mackenzie. "An Exploration of the Colonial Impacts of the Indian Act on Indigenous Women in Canada." PhD diss., Carleton University, 2020.

D'Hauteserre, Anne Marie. "Postcolonialism, Colonialism, and Tourism." In *A Companion to Tourism*, edited by Alan Lew, C. Michael Hall, and Allan M. Williams, 235–45. Malden: Blackwell, 2004.

Diabo, Russ. "Harper Launches Major First Nations Termination Plan: As Negotiating Tables Legitimize Canada's Colonialism." *Intercontinental Cry*. 9 November 2012. https://intercontinentalcry.org/harper-launches-major-first-nations-termination-plan-as-negotiating-tables-legitimize-canadas-colonialism/ (accessed 15 January 2022).

———. "Trudeau's 'Zombie Policies' Threaten Indigenous Rights.' *The Tyee*, 5 May 2020. https://thetyee.ca/Analysis/2020/05/05/Trudeau-Pandemic-Indigenous-Rights-Approach/ (accessed 31 July 2020).

Dodek, Adam. *The Charter Debates: The Special Joint Committee on the Constitution, 1980–81, and the Making of the Canadian Charter of Rights and Freedoms*. Toronto: University of Toronto Press, 2018.

Dunning, Norma. "Reflections of a Disk-less Inuk on Canada's Eskimo Identification System." *Études/Inuit/Studies* 36, no. 2 (2012): 209–26.

Dussault, René, and Georges Erasmus. *Report of the Royal Commission on Aboriginal Peoples*. 5 vols. Ottawa: Royal Commission on Aboriginal Peoples, 1996.

Dyar, Jennifer. "Fatal Attraction: The White Obsession with Indianness." *The Historian* 65, no. 4 (2003): 817–36.

Dyck, Noel, and Tonio Sadik. "Indigenous Political Organization and Activism in Canada." *The Canadian Encyclopedia*. 6 June 2011. https://www.thecanadianencyclopedia.ca/en/article/aboriginal-people-political-organization-and-activism (accessed 14 June 2020).

Eber, Dorothy. *Encounters on the Passage: Inuit Meet the Explorers*. Toronto: University of Toronto Press, 2008.

Eriksen, Thomas Hylland, and Runar Døving. "In Limbo: Notes on the Culture of Airports." *2nd EASA Conference, Prague*, vol. 30. 1992. No page.

Fetrow, Karla. "Black Flags over the Olympics." *Subversify*, 26 February 2010. http://subversify.com/2010/02/26/black-flags-over-the-olympics (accessed 22 November 2011).

"First Nations in Canada." Government of Canada (website). 12 May 2017. https://www.rcaanc-cirnac.gc.ca/eng/1307460755710/1536862806124 (accessed 13 July 2020).

Flaman, Bernard. "Public Art and Canadian Cultural Policy: The Airports." *Public Art in Canada: Critical Perspectives*, edited by Annie Gérin and James S. McLean, 75–94. Toronto: University of Toronto Press, 2009.

Foran, Max, ed. by *Icon, Myth, Brand: The Calgary Stampede*. Edmonton: Athabasca University Press, 2008.

Forsyth, Janice. "The Illusion of Inclusion: Agenda 21 and the Commodification of Indigenous Culture in Olympic Games." PUBLIC 53 (Spring 2016): 22–33.

———. "Teepees and Tomahawks: Aboriginal Cultural Representation at the 1976 Olympic Games." In *The Global Nexus Engaged: Past, Present, Future Interdisciplinary Olympic Studies*, edited by K.B. Wamsley, R.K. Barney and S.G. Martyn, 71–76. London, ON: International Centre for Olympic Studies, University of Western Ontario, 2002.

Forsyth, Janice, and Kevin B. Wamsley. "Symbols without Substance: Aboriginal Peoples and the Illusions of Olympic Ceremonies." In *Global Olympics: Historical and Sociological Studies of the Modern Games*, edited by Kevin B. Wamsley and Kevin Young, 227–48. Oxford: Elsevier Press, 2005.

Four Host First Nations. "Statement from the FHFN Chiefs—Protocols and Traditional Territories." 15 February 2010. http://www.fourhostfirstnations.com/statement-from-the-fhfn-chiefs-protocols-and-traditional-territories (accessed 13 October 2010).

Francis, Daniel. *The Imaginary Indian: The Image of the Indian in Canadian Culture*. Vancouver: Arsenal Press, 1992.

———. *National Dreams: Myth, Memory, and Canadian History*. Vancouver: Arsenal, 1997.

———. *Selling Canada: Three Propaganda Campaigns That Shaped the Nation*. Vancouver: Stanton Atkins and Dosil, 2011.

Francis, Jessica. "Aboriginal Tourism in the Southern Interior of British Columbia: Identities, Representations, and Expectations." MA thesis, York University, 2011.

Freeman, Minnie Aodla. "Inuit." *The Canadian Encyclopedia*. 8 June 2010. https://www.thecanadianencyclopedia.ca/en/article/inuit (accessed 14 June 2020).

"Frequently Asked Questions—Powley." Crown-Indigenous Relations and Northern Affairs Canada (website). Ottawa: Government of Canada, 2015. https://www.rcaanc-cirnac.gc.ca/eng/1100100014419/1535469560872.

Fumoleau, René. *As Long as This Land Shall Last: A History of Treaty 8 and Treaty 11, 1870–1939*. Calgary: University of Calgary Press, 2004.

Furlong, John, with Gary Mason. *Patriot Hearts: Inside the Olympics That Changed a Country*. Vancouver: Douglas and McIntyre Publishers, 2011.

Gaudry, Adam. "Communing with the Dead: The 'New Métis,' Métis Identity Appropriation, and the Displacement of Living Métis Culture." *American Indian Quarterly* 42, no. 2 (2018): 162–90.

Gaudry, Adam, and Chris Andersen. "Daniels v. Canada: Racialized Legacies, Settler Self-Indigenization and the Denial of Indigenous Peopleshood." TOPIA: *Canadian Journal of Cultural Studies* 36 (2016): 19–30.

Gaudry, Adam, and Karen Drake. "The Resilience of Métis Title: Rejecting Assumptions of Extinguishment." In *Bead By Bead: Constitutional Rights and Métis Community*, edited by Yvonne Boyer and Larry Chartrand, 71–93. Vancouver: UBC Press, 2020.

Gaudry, Adam, and Darryl Leroux. "White Settler Revisionism and Making Métis Everywhere: The Evocation of Métissage in Quebec and Nova Scotia." *Critical Ethnic Studies* 3, no. 1 (2017): 116–42.

Gaudry, Adam, and Danielle Lorenz. "Indigenization as Inclusion, Reconciliation, and Decolonization: Navigating the Different Visions for Indigenizing the Canadian Academy." *AlterNative: An International Journal of Indigenous Peoples* 14, no. 3 (2018): 218–27.

Gemmell, Andres. "Defending Indigenous Rights against the Just Society." In *1968 in Canada: A Year and Its Legacies*, edited by Michael K. Hawes, Andrew C. Holman, and Christopher Kirkey. Ottawa: University of Ottawa Press, 2021.

Gidimt'en Yintah Access Point. "Wet'suwet'en Strong." No date. https://www.yintahaccess.com/ (accessed 30 July 2020).

———. "History and Timeline." No date. https://www.yintahaccess.com/historyandtimeline (accessed 30 July 2020).

Godwell, Darren J. "The Olympic Branding of Aborigines: The 2000 Olympic Games and Australia's Indigenous Peoples." In *The Olympics at the Millennium: Power, Politics and the Games*, edited by K. Schaffer and S. Smith, 234–57. New Brunswick, NJ: Rutgers University Press, 1999.

Goldberg, David Theo. *The Racial State*. Malden: Blackwell Publishing, 2001.

———. *The Threat of Race: Reflections on Racial Neoliberalism*. Malden: Wiley-Blackwell, 2008.

Government of Canada. "Truth and Reconciliation Commission of Canada." No date. https://www.rcaanc-cirnac.gc.ca/eng/1450124405592/1529106060525 (accessed 30 July 2020).

Green, Joyce. "Canaries in the Mines of Citizenship: Indian Women in Canada." *Canadian Journal of Political Science/Revue canadienne de science politique* 34, no. 4 (2001): 715–38.

Gregory, Derek. "Colonial Nostalgia and Cultures of Travel: Spaces of Constructed Visibility in Egypt." In *Consuming Tradition, Manufacturing Heritage: Global Norms and Urban Forms in the Age of Tourism*, edited by Nezar AlSayyad, 111–51. New York: Routledge, 2001.

Grix, Jonathan, and Barrie Houlihan. "Sports Mega-events as Part of a Nation's Soft Power Strategy: The Cases of Germany (2006) and the UK (2012)." *British Journal of Politics and International Relations* 16, no. 4 (2014): 572–96.

Grix, Jonathan, and Donna Lee. "Soft Power, Sports Mega-events and Emerging States: The Lure of the Politics of Attraction." *Global Society* 27, no. 4 (2013): 521–36.

"Growing Pains." *The Economist.* 6 July 2006. https://www.economist.com/the-americas/2006/07/06/growing-pains (accessed 20 July 2021).

Gwyn, Richard J. *Nation Maker: Sir John A. Macdonald: His Life, Our Times. 1867–1891.* Toronto: Random House Canada, 2011.

Hall, Michael C. "Urban Entrepreneurship, Corporate Interests and Sports Mega-events: The Thin Policies of Competitiveness within the Hard Outcomes of Neoliberalism." *Sociological Review* 54, no. 2 suppl. (2006): 59–70.

Hall, Stuart. "The West and the Rest: Discourse and Power." In *Modernity: An Introduction to Modern Societies,* edited by Stuart Hall, 185–227. Cambridge: Blackwell Publishing, 1996.

Hanson, Eric. "Constitution Express." https://indigenousfoundations.arts.ubc.ca/constitution_express.

Harris, Cole. "How Did Colonialism Dispossess? Comments from an Edge of Empire." *Annals of the Association of American Geographers* 94, no. 1 (2004): 165–82.

Harris, Julie. "Airports." In *Building Canada: A History of Public Works,* edited by Norman R. Ball, 286–312. Toronto: University of Toronto Press, 1988.

Harrison, Julia D. "The Spirit Sings: The Last Song?" *International Journal of Museum Management and Curatorship* 7, no. 4 (1988): 353–63.

Hawkes, David C. *Aboriginal Peoples and Constitutional Reform: What Have We Learned?* Kingston, ON: Institution of Intergovernmental Relations, 1989.

Heinz Housel, Teresa. "Australian Nationalism and Globalization: Narratives of the Nation in the 2000 Sydney Olympics' Opening Ceremony." *Critical Studies in Media Communication* 24, no. 5 (2007): 446–61.

Henderson, James Youngblood. "Empowering Treaty Federalism." *Saskatchewan Law Review* 58, no.2 (1994): 241–329.

Hermer, Joe, and Janet E. Mosher. *Disorderly People: Law and the Politics of Exclusion in Ontario.* Winnipeg: Fernwood Publishing, 2002.

"History and Etymology for ab." *Merriam Webster.* https://www.merriam-webster.com/dictionary/ab-#etymology (accessed 14 April 2020).

Hodge, Bob, and Vijay Mishra. *Dark Side of the Dream: Australian Literature and the Postcolonial Mind.* Sydney: Allen and Unwin, 1991.

Hogan, Jackie. "Staging the Nation: Gendered and Ethnicized Discourses of National Identity in Olympic Opening Ceremonies." *Journal of Sport and Social Issues* 27, no. 2 (2003): 100–23.

Hošek, Chaviva. "Women and the Constitutional Process." In *And No One Cheered: Federalism, Democracy and the Constitution Act,* edited by Keith Banting and Richard Simeon, 280–300. Toronto: Methuen, 1983.

Housel, Teresa Heinz. "Australian Nationalism and Globalization: Narratives of the Nation in the 2000 Sydney Olympics' Opening Ceremony." *Critical Studies in Media Communication* 24, no. 5 (2007): 446–61.

"How YVR and the Musqueam Forged a Working Relationship." *CBC News.* 22 June 2019. https://www.cbc.ca/news/canada/british-columbia/musqueam-airport-yvr-indigenous-agreement-1.5184284 (accessed 31 July 2020).

Howard-Wagner, Deirdre, Maria Bargh, and Isabel Altamirano-Jimenez. "From New Paternalism to New Imaginings of Possibilities in Australia, Canada and Aotearoa/New Zealand: Indigenous Rights and Recognition and the State in the Neoliberal Age." In *The Neoliberal State, Recognition and Indigenous Rights: New Paternalism to New Imaginings*, 1–42. Canberra: ANU Press, 2018.

Howell, Mike. "Musqueam Deal with YVR Could Be Worth $300 Million." *Vancouver Courier*, 21 June 2017. https://www.vancourier.com/news/musqueam-deal-with-yvr-could-be-worth-300-million-1.20706153 (accessed 31 July 2020).

Hubregtse, Menno. "Passenger Movement and Air Terminal Design: Artworks, Wayfinding, Commerce, and Kinaesthesia." *Interiors* 7, nos. 2–3 (2016): 155–79.

———. *Wayfinding, Consumption, and Air Terminal Design*. London: Routledge, 2020.

Huhndorf, Shari M. *Going Native: Indians in the American Cultural Imagination*. Ithaca: Cornell University Press, 2001

"Indian Ministry Name-change Puzzles Some." *CBC News*. 18 May 2011. https://www.cbc.ca/news/canada/saskatchewan/indian-ministry-name-change-puzzles-some-1.1119673.

"Indigenous." *Merriam Webster*. https://www.merriam-webster.com/dictionary/indigenous (accessed 14 April 2020).

Indigenous Tourism Association of BC. "Authentic Indigenous." No date. https://www.indigenousbc.com/authentic-indigenous/ (accessed 31 July 2020).

———. "Authentic Indigenous Designation Program Survey." No date. https://www.surveymonkey.com/r/authentic-indigenous (accessed 31 July 2020).

Innes, Alexander. "Historians and Indigenous Genocide in Saskatchewan." *Shekon Neechie*, 21 June 2018. https://shekonneechie.ca/2018/06/21/historians-and-indigenous-genocide-in-saskatchewan/ (accessed 27 July 2021).

"International Recommendations for Tourism Statistics 2008." World Tourism Organization. United Nations: New York, 2008. https://unstats.un.org/unsd/publication/seriesm/seriesm_83rev1e.pdf (accessed 31 July 2020).

Irlbacher-Fox, Stephanie. *Finding Dahshaa: Self-government, Social Suffering, and Aboriginal Policy in Canada*. Vancouver: UBC Press, 2010.

Jasen, Patricia. "Native People and the Tourist Industry in Nineteenth-Century Ontario." *Journal of Canadian Studies* 28 (1993): 5–27.

———. *Wild Things: Nature, Culture, and Tourism in Ontario, 1790–1914*. Toronto: University of Toronto Press, 1995.

Jenson, Jane, Francesca Polletta, and Paige Raibmon. "The Difficulties of Combating Inequality in Time." *Dædalus* 148, no. 3 (2019): 136–63.

"John Furlong, Former VANOC CEO, Faces 3rd Sex Abuse Lawsuit." *Canadian Press*, 23 September 2013. http://www.cbc.ca/news/canada/british-columbia/john-furlong-former-vanoc-ceo-faces-3rd-sex-abuse-lawsuit-1.1865603.

Johnson, Daniel Morley. "From the Tomahawk Chop to the Road Block: Discourses of Savagism in Whitestream Media." *American Indian Quarterly* 35, no. 1 (2011): 104–34.

"June 21 Is National Aboriginal Day." Manitoba Government and General Employees' Union (website). 18 June 2013. https://www.mgeu.ca/news-and-multimedia/news/read,article/1033/june-21-is-national-aboriginal-day (accessed 13 July 2020).

Kavaratzis, Mihalis, and Mary Jo. Hatch. "The Dynamics of Place Brands: An Identity-based Approach to Place Branding Theory." *Marketing Theory* 13, no. 1 (2013): 69-86.

Keene, Adrienne. "The Vancouver Opening Ceremonies: Honoring Canadian First Nations?" *Native Appropriations*, 18 February 2010. http://nativeappropriations.com/2010/02/the-vancouver-opening-ceremonies-honoring-canadian-first-nations.html (accessed 24 February 2010).

Keil, Roger. "'Common-sense' Neoliberalism: Progressive Conservative Urbanism in Toronto, Canada." *Antipode* 34, no. 3 (2002): 578-601.

Kelly, Michael E. "Atiik Askii: Land of the Caribou." In *Indian and Northern Affairs Canada*. Ottawa: Minister of Public Works and Government Services Canada, 2005.

Kent, Alexandra. "The Van der Peet Test: Constitutional Recognition or Constitutional Restriction?" *Arbutus Review* 3, no. 2 (2012): 20-36.

King, Frank. *It's How You Play the Game: The Inside Story of the Calgary Olympics.* Calgary: Script/The Writer's Group, 1991.

Kirsch, Stuart. *Mining Capitalism.* Berkeley: University of California Press, 2014.

Klein, Naomi. "Olympics Land Grab." *Naomi Klein* (blog). 16 July 2013. https://naomiklein.org/olympics-land-grab (accessed 22 August 2013).

Knickerbocker, Madeline Rose, and Sarah Nickel. "Negotiating Sovereignty: Aboriginal Perspectives on a Settler-Colonial Constitution, 1975-1983." *BC Studies: The British Columbian Quarterly* 190 (2016): 67-88.

Kopper, Christopher M. "The Breakthrough of the Package Tour in Germany after 1945." *Journal of Tourism History* 1, no. 1 (2009): 67-92.

Korstrom, Glen. "Musqueam's YVR Pact Could Be Native Partnership Template." *BIV*, 4 July 2017. https://biv.com/article/2017/07/musqueams-yvr-pact-could-be-native-partnership-tem (accessed 31 July 2020).

Krasowski, Sheldon. *No Surrender: The Land Remains Indigenous.* Regina: University of Regina Press, 2019.

Kudelik, Gail. "National Indigenous Peoples Day." *The Canadian Encyclopedia.* 5 January 2012. https://www.thecanadianencyclopedia.ca/en/article/national-aboriginal-day (accessed 13 July 2020).

Kulchyski, Peter, and Frank James Tester. *Kiumajut (Talking Back): Game Management and Inuit Rights, 1950-70.* Vancouver: UBC Press, 2008.

Ladner, Kiera L. "Negotiated Inferiority: The Royal Commission on Aboriginal People's Vision of a Renewed Relationship." *American Review of Canadian Studies* 31, nos. 1-2 (2001): 241-64.

Lagace, Naithan, and Niigaanwewidam James Sinclair. "The White Paper, 1969." *The Canadian Encyclopedia.* 24 September 2015. https://www.thecanadianencyclopedia.ca/en/article/the-white-paper-1969 (accessed 21 July 2021).

Laliberté, Michèle. "Authenticity–What Do They (Tourists) Really Want?" Montreal: Tourism Intelligence Network, University of Quebec, 2006.

Lambertus, Sandra. "Canada's Aboriginal Peoples and Intersecting Identity Markers: Research and Policy Implications for Multiculturalism." In *Paper Commissioned for Seminar on Intersections of Diversity*. 2002. https://citeseerx.ist.psu.edu/viewdoc/download?doi=10.1.1.477.2198&rep=rep1&type=pdf (accessed 13 July 2020).

Landriault, Mathieu. "From 'Aboriginal' to 'Indigenous' in the Justin Trudeau Era." *The Conversation*, 22 October 2018. https://theconversation.com/from-aboriginal-to-indigenous-in-the-justin-trudeau-era-105204 (accessed 22 July 2020).

LaRocque, Emma. *When the Other Is Me: Native Resistance Discourse, 1850–1990*. Winnipeg: University of Manitoba Press, 2011.

Lawrence, Bonita. *Fractured Homeland: Federal Recognition and Algonquin Identity in Ontario*. Vancouver: UBC Press, 2012.

——. "Rewriting Histories of the Land: Colonization and Indigenous Resistance in Eastern Canada." In *Race, Space, and the Law: Unmapping a White Settler Society*, edited by Sherene H. Razack, 22–47. Toronto: Between the Lines, 2002.

Leddy, Shannon C. "Tourists, Art and Airports: The Vancouver International Airport as a Site of Cultural Negotiation." PhD diss., University of British Columbia, 1997.

Lee, Jongsoo, and Hyunsun Yoon. "Narratives of the Nation in the Olympic Opening Ceremonies: Comparative Analysis of Beijing 2008 and London 2012." *Nations and Nationalism* 23, no. 4 (2017): 952–69.

Leroux, Darryl. *Distorted Descent: White Claims to Indigenous Identity*. Winnipeg: University of Manitoba Press, 2019.

——. "'Eastern Métis' Studies and White Settler Colonialism Today." *Aboriginal Policy Studies* 8, no. 1 (2019).

Lightfoot, Sheryl. "A Promise Too Far? The Justin Trudeau Government and Indigenous Rights." In *Justin Trudeau and Canadian Foreign Policy*, edited by Norman Hillmer and Phillippe Lagasse, 165–85. London: Palgrave Macmillan, 2018.

Lindberg, Tracey. "The Doctrine of Discovery in Canada." In *Discovering Indigenous Lands: The Doctrine of Discovery in the English Colonies*, edited by Robert J. Miller, Jacinta Ruru, Larissa Behrendt, and Tracey Lindberg, 89–125. Oxford: Oxford University Press 2010.

Little, Margaret, and Jane Hillyard. "A Litmus Test for Democracy: The Impact of Ontario Welfare Changes on Single Mothers." *Studies in Political Economy* 66, no. 1 (2001): 9–36.

——. *No Car, No Radio, No Liquor Permit: The Moral Regulation of Single Mothers in Ontario, 1920–1997*. Oxford: Oxford University Press, 1998.

Logan, Tricia. "Settler Colonialism in Canada and the Métis." *Journal of Genocide Research* 14, no. 4 (2015): 433–52.

Looking Forward, Looking Back. Report of the Royal Commission on Aboriginal Peoples, Vol. 1. Ottawa: Royal Commission on Aboriginal Peoples, 1996.

Lutz, Hartmut, Florentine Strzelczyk, and Renae Watchman, eds. *Indianthusiasm: Indigenous Responses*. Waterloo: Wilfrid Laurier University Press, 2020.

Macdonald, Moira. "Indigenizing the Academy." *University Affairs*, 6 April 2016. https://www.universityaffairs.ca/features/feature-article/indigenizing-the-academy/ (accessed 30 July 2020).

Macdougall, Brenda. *Land, Family and Identity: Contextualizing Metis Health and Well-Being*. Prince George: National Collaborating Centre for Aboriginal Health, 2017.

———. "The Myth of Metis Cultural Ambivalence." In *Contours of a People: Metis Family, Mobility, and History*, edited by Nicole St-Onge, Carolyn Podruchny, and Brenda Macdougall, 422–64. Norman: University of Oklahoma Press, 2012.

Mackey, Eva. *The House of Difference: Cultural Politics and National Identity in Canada*. Toronto: University of Toronto Press, 2002.

Malciw, J.A. "Settling and 'Selling' Canada's West: The Role of Immigration." MA thesis, Ryerson University, 2009.

Manitowabi, Darrel. "Casino Rama: First Nations Self-Determination, Neoliberal Solution or Partial Middle Ground." In *First Nations Gaming in Canada*, edited by Yale Belanger, 255–78. Winnipeg: University of Manitoba Press, 2011.

Marcus, Alan R. *Out in the Cold: The Legacy of Canada's Inuit Relocation Experiment in the High Arctic*. Copenhagen: International Work Group for Indigenous Affairs, 1992.

Marks, Don. "What's in a name: Indian, Native, Aboriginal or Indigenous?" *CBC News*. 2 October 2014. https://www.cbc.ca/news/canada/manitoba/what-s-in-a-name-indian-native-aboriginal-or-indigenous-1.2784518 (accessed 11 July 2021).

Marshall, Tabitha. "Indian Residential Schools Settlement Agreement." *The Canadian Encyclopedia*. 11 July 2013. https://www.thecanadianencyclopedia.ca/en/article/indian-residential-schools-settlement-agreement (accessed 30 July 2020).

Martin, Archer. *The Hudson's Bay Company's Land Tenures and the Occupation of Assiniboia*. London: W. Clowes and Sons, 1898.

Martinez, Doreen E. "Wrong Directions and New Maps of Voice, Representation, and Engagement: Theorizing Cultural Tourism, Indigenous Commodities, and the Intelligence of Participation." *American Indian Quarterly* 36, no. 4 (2012): 545–73.

Mascarenhas, Michael. *Where the Waters Divide: Neoliberalism, White Privilege, and Environmental Racism in Canada*. Lanham: Lexington Books, 2012.

Mason, Courtney W. "Rethinking the Banff Indian Days as Critical Spaces of Cultural Exchange." In *Spirits of the Rockies: Reasserting an Indigenous Presence in Banff National Park*, 107–38. Toronto: University of Toronto Press, 2018.

Mawani, Renisa. "From Colonialism to Multiculturalism? Totem Poles, Tourism and National Identity in Vancouver's Stanley Park." *ARIEL: A Review of International English Literature* 35, nos. 1–2 (2004): 31–57.

Mayhew, Experience. *The Massachusee Psalter: Or, Psalms of David With the Gospel According to John – also known as "An Introduction for Training up the Aboriginal Natives, in Reading and Understanding the Holy Scriptures.*" Boston: Honourable Company for the Propagation of the Gospel in New-England and Company, 1709.

McChesney, Robert W. "Introduction." In *Profit over People: Neoliberalism and Global Order*, by Noam Chomsky, 7–18. New York: Seven Stories Press, 1999.

McGinley, Robin. "Best Practices: A Planned Approach to Developing a Sustainable Aboriginal Tourism Industry in Mistissini." *Journal of Aboriginal Economic Development* 3, no. 2 (2003): 12–19.

McLoughlin, Moira. "Of Boundaries and Borders: First Nations' History in Museums." *Canadian Journal of Communication* 18, no. 3 (1993): 365–85.

McMahon, Ryan. "Canada's Aboriginal Peoples and the Vancouver 2010 Olympics—Unprecedented Inclusion?" *Ryan McMahon Comedy.* 16 February 2010. http://www.rmcomedy.com/2010/02/16/canadas-aboriginal-peoples-the-vancouver-2010-olympics-unprecedented-inclusion/ (accessed 24 February 2010).

McMaster, Gerald, and Lee-Ann Hunt, eds. *Indigena: Contemporary Native Perspectives.* Hull: Canadian Museum of Civilization, 1992.

Medina, Néstor. "Indigenous Decolonial Movements in Abya Yala, Aztlán, and Turtle Island: A Comparison." In *Decolonial Christianities: Latinx and Latin American Perspectives*, edited by Raimundo Barreto and Roberto Sirvent, 147–63. Cham, Switzerland: Palgrave Macmillan, 2019.

Membean (website). "Ab-, Ab-, and Away!" https://membean.com/wrotds/ab-away (accessed 26 May 2021).

"Michael Kusugak." *Strong Nations.* No date. https://www.strongnations.com/gs/show.php?gs=6&gsd=6446 (accessed 12 July 2020).

Mickleburgh, Rod. "Misguided Olympic Protesters Have Nothing to Teach Natives, One Leader Argues." *Globe and Mail*, 22 October 2009. http://www.theglobeandmail.com/news/british-columbia/misguided-olympicprotesters-have-nothing-to-teach-natives-one-leaderargues/article1345833 (accessed 24 June 2010).

Miers, John. *Travels in Chile and La Plata: Including Accounts Respecting the Geography, Geology, Statistics, Government, Finances, Agriculture, Manners, and Customs, and the Mining Operations in Chile.* Vol. 1. London: Baldwin, Cradock, and Joy, 1826.

Mignolo, Walter D. "From the 'Western Hemisphere' to the 'Eastern Hemisphere.'" In *The Routledge Companion to Inter-American Studies*, edited by Wilfried Raussert, 59–67. New York: Routledge, 2017.

Mihesuah, Devon Abott, and Angela Cavender Wilson, eds. *Indigenizing the Academy: Transforming Scholarship and Empowering Communities.* Lincoln: University of Nebraska Press, 2004.

Miller, James Rodger. *Skyscrapers Hide the Heavens: A History of Native-Newcomer Relations in Canada.* 4th edited by Toronto: University of Toronto Press, 2018.

Milloy, John Sheridan. *Indian Act Colonialism: A Century of Dishonour, 1869–1969.* West Vancouver: National Centre for First Nations Governance, 2008.

———. *A National Crime: The Canadian Government and the Residential School System, 1879 to 1986.* Winnipeg: University of Manitoba Press, 1999.

Mills, Suzanne E., and Tyler McCreary. "Negotiating Neoliberal Empowerment: Aboriginal People, Educational Restructuring, and Academic Labour in the North of British Columbia, Canada." *Antipode* 45, no. 5 (2013): 1298–317.

Milne, Simon, and Irena Ateljevic. "Tourism, Economic Development and the Global-local Nexus: Theory Embracing Complexity." *Tourism Geographies* 3, no. 4 (2001): 369–93.

Minutes of Proceedings and Evidence of the Special Joint Committee of the Senate and of the House of Commons on the Constitution of Canada, 32nd Parl., 1st Sess., No. 22 (9 December 1980), 144.

Minutes of Proceedings and Evidence of the Special Joint Committee of the Senate and of the House of Commons on the Constitution of Canada, 5 January 1981. Issue No. 31 (31: 86).

Mississaugas of the Credit First Nation. Website. No date. http://www.newcreditfirstnation2015.com/ (accessed 31 July 2020).

Moran, Anthony. "The Psychodynamics of Australian Settler-Nationalism: Assimilating or Reconciling with the Aborigines?" *Political Psychology* 23, no. 4 (2002): 667–701.

Morford, Ashley Caranto. "'This Is an Indigenous City': Un-Firsting Early Representations of Vancouver." In *Firsting in the Early-Modern Atlantic World*, edited by Lauren Beck, 218–40. New York: Routledge, 2020.

Morgan, George. "Aboriginal Protest and the Sydney Olympic Games." OLYMPIKA: *The International Journal of Olympic Studies* (2003): 23–38.

Morrison, Alastair M. *Marketing and Managing Tourism Destinations*. London: Routledge, 2018.

Morse, Bradford W. "Permafrost Rights: Aboriginal Self-Government and the Supreme Court in R. v. Pamajewon." *McGill Law Journal* 42 (1996): 1011.

Morton, Samuel George. *An Inquiry into the Distinctive Characteristics of the Aboriginal Race of America: Read at the Annual Meeting of the Boston Society of Natural History, Wednesday, April 27, 1842*. Vol. 1, no. 5. Tuttle and Dennett, Printers, 1842.

Morton, Samuel George, and George Combe. *Crania Americana; Or, a Comparative View of the Skulls of Various Aboriginal Nations of North and South America: To Which Is Prefixed an Essay on the Varieties of the Human Species*. Philadelphia: J. Dobson; London: Simpkin, Marshall, 1839.

Narine, Shari. "Dorey Dropped the Ball on Daniels, Says New CAP National Chief." *Windspeaker*, 11 October 2016. https://www.windspeaker.com/news/windspeaker-news/dorey-dropped-the-ball-on-daniels-says-new-cap-national-chief (accessed 14 June 2020).

"Natives in Olympics: Frank King—OCO Is Not a Funding Agency." *Windspeaker*, 10 May 1987. https://ammsa.com/publications/windspeaker/natives-olympics-frank-king-oco-not-funding-agency (accessed 17 February 2010).

Nauright, John. "Selling Nations to the World through Sports: Mega-events and Nation Branding as Global Diplomacy." *Public Diplomacy Magazine* 9 (2013): 22–27.

Nerbas, Grant H. "Canadian Transportation Policy, Regulation, and Major Problems." *Journal of Air Law and Commerce* 33 (1967): 242.

New York Missionary Society. *The New York Missionary Magazine and Repository of Religious Intelligence for the Year 1800*. New York: T and J Swords, 1800.

Nickel, Sarah A. *Assembling Unity: Indigenous Politics, Gender, and the Union of BC Indian Chiefs*. Vancouver: UBC Press, 2019.

———. "Reconsidering 1969: The White Paper and the Making of the Modern Indigenous Rights Movement." *Canadian Historical Review* 100, no. 2 (2019): 223–38.

Nimijean, Richard. "The Politics of Branding Canada: The International-Domestic Nexus and the Rethinking of Canada's Place in the World," *Mexican Journal of Canadian Studies* 11 (2006): 67-85.

Nye, Joseph S., Jr. "Public Diplomacy and Soft Power." *The Annals of the American Academy of Political and Social Science* 616, no. 1 (2008): 94-109.

O'Bonsawin, Christine M. "A Coast Salish Olympic Welcome: The 2010 Vancouver Opening Ceremony and the Politics of Indigenous Participation." In *Proceedings: International Symposium for Olympic Research*, 255-65. London, ON: International Centre for Olympic Studies, 2010.

——. "The Conundrum of 'Ilanaaq'—First Nations Representation and the 2010 Vancouver Winter Olympics." In *Proceedings: International Symposium for Olympic Research*, 387-95. London, ON: International Centre for Olympic Studies, 2006.

——. "Indigenous Peoples and Canadian-hosted Olympic Games." In *Aboriginal Peoples and Sport in Canada: Historical Foundations and Contemporary Issues*, edited by Audrey R. Giles and Janice Forsyth, 35-63. Vancouver: UBC Press, 2013.

——. "'No Olympics on Stolen Native Land': Contesting Olympic Narratives and Asserting Indigenous Rights within the Discourse of the 2010 Vancouver Games." *Sport in Society* 13, no. 1 (2010): 143-56.

O'Brien, Jean M. *Firsting and Lasting: Writing Indians Out of Existence in New England*. Minneapolis: University of Minnesota Press, 2010.

OCO'88, "XV Olympic Winter Games Official Report." Calgary: XV Olympic Winter Games Organizing Committee, 1988.

Office for the High Commissioner of Human Rights. *Concluding Observations of the Human Rights Committee*. Australia, U.N. Doc. A/55/40, 498-538 (24 July 2000).

Olins, Wally. "Branding the Nation—The Historical Context." *Journal of Brand Management* 9, no. 4 (2002): 241-48.

O'Neil, Beverly, edited by "Aboriginal Cultural Tourism: Checklist for Success." Aboriginal Tourism Team Canada/Canadian Tourism Commission, 2000.

"Orcas in the City—Vancouver." Orcas in the City. No date. http://www.orcasinthecity.com/index.cfm?fuseaction=vancouver.description (accessed 29 July 2020).

Owram, Doug. *Promise of Eden*. Toronto: University of Toronto Press, 2016.

"Painting & Sculpture." *Maclean's*, 24 August 1963. https://archive.macleans.ca/article/1963/8/24/painting-sculpture (accessed 13 July 2020).

Paris, Michael. *From the Wright Brothers to Top Gun: Aviation, Nationalism, and Popular Cinema*. Manchester: Manchester University Press, 1995.

Parrott, Zach. "Indian Act." *The Canadian Encyclopedia*. 7 February 2006 https://www.thecanadianencyclopedia.ca/en/article/indian-act (accessed 21 July 2021).

Paul, Lawrence, Charlotte Townsend-Gault, and Scott Watson. *Lawrence Paul Yuxweluptun: Born to Live and Die on Your Colonialist Reservations: June 20-September 16, 1995*. Exhibition catalogue. Morris and Helen Belkin Art Gallery, University of British Columbia, 1995.

Peters, Evelyn, Matthew Stock, and Adrian Werner. *Rooster Town: The History of an Urban Métis Community, 1901-1961*. Winnipeg: University of Manitoba Press, 2018.

Peters, Michael A., and Carl T. Mika. "Aborigine, Indian, Indigenous or First Nations?" *Educational Philosophy and Theory* (2017): 1229-34.

Phillips, Ruth Bliss. *Trading Identities: The Souvenir in Native North American Art from the Northeast, 1700-1900*. University of Washington Press, 1998.

Pigott, Peter. *Flying Canucks: Famous Canadian Aviators*. Toronto: Hounslow Press, 1996.

Pfeiff, Margo. "Go Inuit for a Weekend." Canadian Tourism Commission. 9 February 2009. http://mediacentre.canada.travel/content/travel_story_ideas/kimmirut_homestay (accessed 12 August 2011).

Plot, Robert. *The Natural History of Oxford-Shire: Being an Essay toward the Natural History of England*. Oxford, 1676.

Pocklington, Thomas C. *The Government and Politics of the Alberta Métis Settlements*. Regina: University of Regina Press, 1991.

Potter, Evan H. *Branding Canada: Projecting Canada's Soft Power through Public Diplomacy*. Montreal and Kingston: McGill-Queen's Press, 2008.

Poucette, Terry Lynn. "Spinning Wheels: Surmounting the Indian Act's Impact on Traditional Indigenous Governance." *Canadian Public Administration* 61, no. 4 (2018): 499-522.

Prentice, Richard. "Experiential Cultural Tourism: Museums and the Marketing of the New Romanticism of Evoked Authenticity." *Museum Management and Curatorship* 19, no. 1 (2001): 5-26.

Prudham, Scott. "Poisoning the Well: Neoliberalism and the Contamination of Municipal Water in Walkerton, Ontario." *Geoforum* 35, no. 3 (2004): 343-59.

"Public Education: Building Awareness and Understanding." In *Report of the Royal Commission on Aboriginal Peoples*, vol. 5. Ottawa: Royal Commission on Aboriginal Peoples, 1996.

Qikiqtani Truth Commission. *Qikiqtani Truth Commission: Achieving Saimaqatigiingniq*. Iqaluit, Nunavut: Qikiqtani Inuit Association, 2010.

Raheja, Michelle H. *Reservation Reelism: Redfacing, Visual Sovereignty, and Representations of Native Americans in Film*. Lincoln: University of Nebraska Press, 2011.

Raibmon, Paige. *Authentic Indians: Episodes of Encounter from the Late-Nineteenth-Century Northwest Coast*. Durham: Duke University Press, 2005.

———. "Theatres of Contact: The Kwakwa̱ka̱'wakw Meet Colonialism in British Columbia and at the Chicago World's Fair." *Canadian Historical Review* 81, no. 2 (2000): 157-90.

Ranasinghe, Prashan. "The Refashioning of Vagrancy and the (Re) Ordering of Public Space." PhD diss., University of Toronto, 2009.

Reddie, John. *A Letter to the Lord High Chancellor of Great Britain, on the Expediency of the Proposal to Form a New Civil Code for England*. London: J. and W.T. Clarke, 1828.

"Renewal: A Twenty-Year Commitment." In *Report of the Royal Commission on Aboriginal Peoples*, Vol. 5. Ottawa: Royal Commission on Aboriginal Peoples, 1996.

Rezaee, Jasmine. "Olympic Countdown: Aboriginal Groups Clash with the Games—and with Each Other." THIS, 13 January 2010. https://this.org/2010/01/13/olympics-aboriginal-land-claims (accessed 24 February 2010).

Richards, George. *The Aboriginal Britons: A Poem*. 1791.

Rorke, Rosalind Alix. "Constructed Destinations: Art and Representations of History at the Vancouver International Airport." PhD diss., University of British Columbia, 2001.

Rostum, Hussein. "Review of Aboriginal Tourism Team Canada." *Industry Canada*, 2002. http://torc.linkbc.ca/torc/downs1/ReviewOfAboriginalTourismTeamCanada.pdf (accessed 11 August 2011).

Said, Edward W. *Orientalism*. New York: Vintage, 1979.

Sanders, Douglas. "Article 27 and the Aboriginal Peoples of Canada." In *Multiculturalism in Canada: A Legal Perspective*, edited by Canadian Human Rights Foundation, 155-66. Toronto: Carswell, 1987.

Sangster, Joan. "'She Is Hostile to Our Ways': First Nations Girls Sentenced to the Ontario Training School for Girls, 1933-1960." *Law and History Review* 20, no. 1 (2002): 59-96.

Saul, John Ralston. *A Fair Country: Telling Truths about Canada*. Toronto: Penguin Canada, 2009.

Saunders, Kelly, and Janique Dubois. *Métis Politics and Governance in Canada*. Vancouver: UBC Press, 2019.

Sawchuk, Joe. "The Métis, Non-Status Indians and the New Aboriginality: Government Influence on Native Political Alliances and Identity." *Canadian Ethnic Studies / Études ethniques au Canada* 17, no. 2 (1985): 135-46.

Schantz, Otto. "La présidence de Avery Brundage (1952-1972)." *Un siècle du Comité International Olympique: L'Idée-Les Présidents-L'Œuvre* 2 (1995): 77-200.

Shaw, S. Bernard. *Photographing Canada from Flying Canoes*. Burnstown: General Store Publishing House, 2001.

Sheller, Mimi. *Consuming the Caribbean: From Arawaks to Zombies*. New York: Routledge, 2003.

Sidsworth, Robin. "Aboriginal Participation in the Vancouver/Whistler 2010 Olympic Games: Consultation, Reconciliation and the New Relationship." LLM thesis, University of British Columbia, 2010.

Silver, Ira. "Marketing Authenticity in Third-World Countries." *Annals of Tourism Research* 20 (1993): 302-18.

Simeone, Tonina. "Indigenous Peoples: Terminology Guide." *HillNotes*. Ottawa: Library of Parliament. https://hillnotes.ca/2020/05/20/indigenous-peoples-terminology-guide/ (accessed 3 June 2020).

Simpson, Audra. "Consent's Revenge." *Cultural Anthropology* 31, no. 3 (2016): 326-33.

———. *Mohawk Interruptus*. Durham: Duke University Press, 2014.

Simpson, Leanne Betasamosake. *Dancing on Our Turtle's Back: Stories of Nishnaabeg Re-creation, Resurgence and a New Emergence*. Winnipeg: Arbeiter Ring, 2011.

Slattery, Brian. "The Metamorphosis of Aboriginal Title." *Canadian Bar Review* 85, no. 2 (2006): 255-86.

Slowey, Gabrielle. *Navigating Neoliberalism: Self-Determination and the Mikisew Cree First Nation.* Vancouver: UBC Press, 2008.

Smith, William L. "Experiential Tourism around the World and at Home: Definitions and Standards." *International Journal of Services and Standards* 2 (2006): 1–14.

Special Joint Committee of the Senate, and of the House of Commons on the Constitution of Canada. Minutes of Proceedings and Evidence of the Special Joint Committee of the Senate and the House of Commons on the Constitution of Canada: Procès-verbaux et Témoignages du Comité Spécial Mixte du Sénat et de la Chambre des Communes sur la Constitution du Canada. Nos. 31–37. Queen's Printer, 1981.

"Statement of Cooperation." The Four Host First Nations: Lil'wat, Musqueam, Squamish, Tsleil-Waututh and the Canadian Tourism Commission. 13 November 2007. http://encorporate.canada.travel/system/files/Statement_of_Cooperation-CTC_indd.pdf.

Statement of the Government of Canada on Indian Policy, 1969. Ottawa: Government of Canada, 1969). https://publications.gc.ca/site/eng/9.700112/publication.html.

"Statement of the Prime Minister of Canada on National Aboriginal Day." 21 June 2017. https://pm.gc.ca/en/news/statements/2017/06/21/statement-prime-minister-canada-national-aboriginal-day (accessed 30 July 2020).

Steel, Debora. "The Aboriginal Pavilion for the TORONTO 2015 Pan Am/Parapan Am Games Is Lone 'Official' Indigenous Music and Arts Festival." *Windspeaker* 33, no. 4 (2015). https://ammsa.com/publications/windspeaker/aboriginal-pavilion-toronto-2015-pan-amparapan-am-games-lone-%E2%80%9Cofficial%E2%80%9D-ind.

Stewart, Megan. "Artist Lawrence Paul Yuxweluptun Speaks Out." *The Thunderbird*, 23 November 2008. https://thethunderbird.ca/2008/11/23/lawrence-paul-yuxweluptun-outspoken-and-out-raged-2/ (accessed 29 July 2020).

———. "Controversial Art Can't Land at Vancouver Airport." *The Thunderbird.* 23 November 2008. https://thethunderbird.ca/2008/11/23/airport-says-yes-to-controversial-artists-no-to-their-art/ (accessed 29 July 2020).

Stewart-Harawira, Makere. *The New Imperial Order: Indigenous Responses to Globalization.* London: Zed Books, 2005.

St. Germain, Jill. *Indian Treaty-making Policy in the United States and Canada, 1867–1877.* Lincoln: University of Nebraska Press, 2001.

Stoler, Ann Laura. *Education of Desire: Foucault's History of Sexuality and the Colonial Order of Things.* Durham: Duke University Press, 1995.

Strakosch, Elizabeth. *Neoliberal Indigenous Policy: Settler Colonialism and the 'Post-Welfare' State.* New York: Springer, 2016.

Syme, Edward R., and Alexander T. Wells. *Airport Development, Management and Operations in Canada.* Scarborough: Prentice Hall Canada Career and Technology, 2000.

Takac, Jan. *Sixty Olympic Years.* Biel, Switzerland: Courvoisier-Attinger SA, 1998.

Tasker, John Paul. "Indigenous Affairs Is No More–Department Split Is Underway, Liberal Government Says." *CBC News.* 4 December 2017. https://www.cbc.ca/news/politics/indigenous-affairs-dissolution-two-new-departments-1.4432683 (accessed 30 July 2020).

TASSO official. "Swipe Through and Check Out Why We Use the Word 'Indigenous' Instead of 'Aboriginal.'" *Instagram*, 8 July 2020. https://www.instagram.com/p/CCY53Mhnsrq/ (accessed 8 July 2020).

Tester, Frank. "Mad Dogs and (Mostly) Englishmen: Colonial Relations, Commodities, and the Fate of Inuit Sled Dogs." *Études/Inuit/Studies* 34, no. 2 (2010): 129-47.

Tester, Frank, and Peter Kulchyski. *Tammarniit (Mistakes): Inuit Relocation in the Eastern Arctic, 1939-63*. Vancouver, UBC Press, 2011.

Tester, Frank James, Paule McNicoll, and Peter Irniq. "Structural Violence and the 1962-1963 Tuberculosis Epidemic in Eskimo Point, NWT." *Études/Inuit/Studies* 36, no. 2 (2012): 165-85.

——. "Writing for Our Lives: The Language of Homesickness, Self-esteem and the Inuit TB Epidemic." *Études/Inuit/Studies* (2001): 121-40.

Theobald, William F., edited by *Global Tourism*. London: Routledge, 2012.

Thobani, Sunera. *Exalted Subjects: Studies in the Making of Race and Nation in Canada*. Toronto: University of Toronto Press, 2007.

Thomson, Colin A. *Blacks in Deep Snow: Black Pioneers in Canada*. Toronto: Dent, 1979.

Thorpe, Jocelyn. *Temagami's Tangled Wild: Race, Gender, and the Making of Canadian Nature*. Vancouver: UBC Press, 2012.

Thrush, Coll. *Indigenous London*. New Haven: Yale University Press, 2016.

"Timeline of the Coastal GasLink Pipeline in British Columbia." *The Canadian Press*. 24 January 2021. https://vancouversun.com/business/energy/timeline-of-the-coastal-gaslink-pipeline-in-british-columbia (accessed 14 January 2022).

Tobias, John L. "Canada's Subjugation of the Plains Cree, 1879-1885." In *Sweet Promises: A Reader on Indian-White Relations in Canada*, edited by J.R. Miller, 215-40. Toronto: University of Toronto Press, 1991.

Tomlinson, Alan. "Olympic Spectacle: Opening Ceremonies and Some Paradoxes of Globalization." *Media, Culture and Society* 18, no. 4 (1996): 583-602.

Tough, Frank, and Erin McGregor. "'The Rights to the Land May Be Transferred': Archival Records as Colonial Text—A Narrative of Metis Scrip." *Canadian Review of Comparative Literature/Revue Canadienne de Littérature Comparée* 34, no. 1 (2007): 33-63.

Townsend-Gault, Charlotte, edited by "The Salvation Art of Yuxweluptun." In *Lawrence Paul Yuxweluptun: Born to Live and Die on Your Colonialist Reservations*. Exhibition catalogue. Vancouver: Morris and Helen Belkin Art Gallery, University of British Columbia, 1995.

"Traveller Types." Canadian Tourism Commission. 2012.

Troian, Martha. "20 Years since the Royal Commission on Aboriginal Peoples, Still Waiting for Change." *CBC News*. 3 March 2016. https://www.cbc.ca/news/indigenous/20-year-anniversary-of-rcap-report-1.3469759 (accessed 13 July 2020).

Troupe, Cheryl. "Mapping Métis Stories: Land Use, Gender and Kinship in the Qu'Appelle Valley, 1850-1950." PhD diss., University of Saskatchewan, 2019.

"Trudeau Changes Name of National Aboriginal Day." *CBC News*. 21 June 2017. https://www.cbc.ca/player/play/972885059738 (accessed 31 July 2020).

Truth and Reconciliation Commission of Canada. *Truth and Reconciliation Commission of Canada: Calls to Action*. 2015. Retrieved from the Truth and Reconciliation Commission of Canada website: http://trc.ca/assets/pdf/Calls_to_Action_English2.pdf.

Turner, Dale. "On the Idea of Reconciliation in Contemporary Aboriginal Politics." In *Reconciling Canada: Critical Perspectives on the Culture of Redress*, edited by Pauline Wakeham and Jennifer Henderson, 100-14. Toronto: University of Toronto Press, 2013.

———. *This Is Not a Peace Pipe: Towards a Critical Indigenous Philosophy*. Toronto: University of Toronto Press, 2006. UBCIC Aboriginal Rights Position Paper. https://kerrycoast.wordpress.com/2014/09/06/ubcic-aboriginal-rights-position-paper-1979/ (accessed 14 June 2020).

van Ham, Peter. "Branding Territory: Inside the Wonderful Worlds of PR and IR Theory." *Millennium: Journal of International Studies* 31, no. 2 (2002): 249-69.

Van Vleck, Jenifer. *Empire of the Air: Aviation and the American Ascendancy*. Cambridge: Harvard University Press, 2013.

VANOC. *Vancouver 2010 Bid Books: Volumes 1-3*. Vancouver: Vancouver Olympic Bid Committee, 2002.

"VOC1: 1723–Knit Hat, Licensed Merchandise, Four Host First Nations (FHFN), Kootenay Knitting Co., Vancouver 2010 Olympic and Paralympic Winter Game." Museum of Vancouver, 2010. http://openmov.museumofvancouver.ca/object/voc1-1723/%5Bfield_acquisition_object_name-raw%5D (accessed 13 March 2016).

Wamsley, Kevin B., and Mike Heine. "'Don't Mess with the Relay—It's Bad Medicine: Aboriginal Culture and the 1988 Winter Olympics." In *Olympic Perspectives: Third International Symposium for Olympic Research*, edited by Robert K. Barney et al., 173-78. London, ON: International Centre for Olympic Studies, University of Western Ontario, 1996.

Wang, Jiwu. *"His Dominion" and the "Yellow Peril": Protestant Missions to Chinese Immigrants in Canada, 1859-1967*. Waterloo: Wilfrid Laurier University Press, 2006.

Watts, Vanessa. "Smudge This: Assimilation, State-favoured Communities and the Denial of Indigenous Spiritual Lives." *International Journal of Child, Youth and Family Studies* 7, no. 1 (2016): 148-70.

Venne, Sharon. "Understanding Treaty 6: An Indigenous Perspective." In *Aboriginal and Treaty Rights in Canada*, edited by Michael Asch, 173-207. Vancouver: UBC Press, 1997.

Verboven, Will. "BC First Nation a Corporate Success . . . It All Started with a Vineyard." *The Bulletin*, 21 July 2021. https://brooksbulletin.com/bc-first-nation-a-corporate-success-it-all-started-with-a-vineyard/ (accessed 27 July 2021).

Wernitznig, Dagmar. *Europe's Indians, Indians in Europe: European Perceptions and Appropriations of Native American Cultures from Pocahontas to the Present*. Lanham, MD: University Press of America, 2007.

Werry, Margaret. *The Tourist State: Performing Leisure, Liberalism, and Race in New Zealand*. Minneapolis: University of Minnesota Press, 2011.

Wherrett, Barbara Jill. "The Struggle for Inclusion: Aboriginal Constitutional Discourse in the 1970s and 1980s." MA thesis, University of British Columbia, 1991.

White, John. *An Essay on the Indigenous Grasses of Ireland*. Dublin: Graisberry and Campbell, 1808.

"Whiteshell Blockade Threat Averted . . . for Now." *Winnipeg News*. 25 August 2010. http://www.cknw.com/Channels/News/Winnipeg/Story.aspx?ID=1269142 (accessed 13 August 2011).

Williams, Nicole, and Michelle Allan. "Celebrated Artist Says He's Indigenous and a Sixties Scoop Survivor: His Family Says He Isn't." *CBC Investigates*. 3 August 2021. https://www.cbc.ca/news/canada/ottawa/morris-blanchard-indigenous-claims-disputed-1.6117774 (accessed 12 August 2021).

Wilton, David. *Word Myths: Debunking Linguistic Urban Legends*. New York: Oxford University Press, 2008.

Wood, Stephanie. "'Dangerous Precedent': Pipelines, Land Defenders and the Colonial Policing of Indigenous Nationhood." *The Narwhal*. 22 December 2021. https://thenarwhal.ca/bc-coastal-gaslink-indigenous-identity/ (accessed 14 January 2022).

———. "Musqueam Shows Visitors 'Whose Territory They're Landing In' at Vancouver Airport." *Canada's National Observer*, 25 July 2019. https://www.nationalobserver.com/2019/07/25/features/musqueam-shows-visitors-whose-territory-theyre-landing-vancouver-airport (accessed 31 July 2020).

Woodsworth, J.S. *Strangers within Our Gates: Or, Coming Canadians*. Toronto: F.C. Stephenson, 1909.

"Working Effectively with Aboriginal Peoples." *Ian Tait stél'mexw siiyá'y* (The Peoples' Respected Friend). Blog, 2012. http://www.ictinc.ca/blog/ian-tait-stelmexw-siiyay-thepeoples-respected-friend (accessed 13 March 2016).

Wrigley, E.A. "The Mineral-Based Energy Economy." In *Continuity, Chance and Change: The Character of the Industrial Revolution in England*, 68–97. Cambridge: Cambridge University Press, 1988.

Yellow Bird, Michael. "Cowboys and Indians: Toys of Genocide, Icons of American Colonialism." *Wicazo Sa Review* 19, no. 2 (2004): 33–48.

YVR. "Past and Future." No date. https://www.yvr.ca/en/about-yvr/who-we-are/past-and-future (accessed 14 July 2020).

———. "Musqueam–YVR." No date. https://www.yvr.ca/en/about-yvr/musqueam (accessed 31 July 2020).

———. "Musqueam YVR Agreement." No date. https://www.yvr.ca/en/about-yvr/who-we-are/musqueam-yvr-agreement (accessed 31 July 2020).

YVR Art Foundation. "About." No date. https://www.yvraf.com/about (accessed 14 July 2020).

———. "The YVR Art Foundation." No date. https://web.archive.org/web/20100710124444/http://www.yvraf.com/ (accessed 28 July 2020).

Zalewski, Anna. "From *Sparrow* to *Van der Peet*: The Evolution of a Definition of Aboriginal Rights." *University of Toronto Faculty Law Review* 55, no. 2 (1997): 435–55.

Zaslow, Morris. *The Northward Expansion of Canada, 1914–1967*. Toronto: McClelland and Stewart, 1988.

Zhu, Lianbi. "National Holidays and Minority Festivals in Canadian Nation-building." PhD diss., University of Sheffield, 2012.

Index

A

Aboriginal, definitions. *see also* Aboriginal rights; Aboriginal tourism; the Indian Act: in the Constitution, 51-52; Ethel Deschambault's call for Métis inclusion, 39, 40; by Indigenous organizations, 55; people who were 'original' to a place, 33; by the Royal Commission on Aboriginal Peoples (RCAP), 61-62; by the Supreme Court of Canada, 53-55

Aboriginal as a word: as an adjective, 1, 2, 70; capitalization of the word, 70; David Wilton, 3-4; doesn't recognize diversity of Indigenous communities, 1, 3; Don Marks, 2; etymology, 1-3, 33, 180; as homogenizing, 179-80; as inclusive of First Nations, Métis and Inuit, 19; "Indigenous peoples: Terminology Guide" (Simeone), 1; #MakingIndigenousHistory (Animikii), 1; meaning not original, 2, 3, 179-180; meaning original inhabitants, 33, 37; as a noun, 1, 2, 70, 95, 180; popular with the public, 5; the prefix ab-, 2, 3, 179-80; in section 35 of the Constitution, 3, 4, 6

Aboriginal Congress of Alberta Association, 57

Aboriginal identity. *see also* self-identification: as binary with non-Aboriginal, 64; the census, 58-59; part of Canada's national brand, 19-20; Statistics Canada's category, 5-6, 19, 58-59

Aboriginal rights. *see also* the Constitution; the Indian Act; Supreme Court of Canada: "Aboriginal Rights Position Paper" (UBCIC), 42-43; based on ideas about Indianness, 35; Canadian government, 36; and Canadian Tourism Commission (CTC), 128; conceptualizing Aboriginal, 45-52; concern for leaving the definition to later, 50-51; defining Aboriginal descent, 45; defining Métis, 45, 56-57; defining non-status Indians, 45; Delia Opekokew, 50; Duff Roblin, 45-46; exclusion of guaranteed protections for women, 51-52; First Nations need time to research position, 40; Harry Daniels, 46-48; John Sinclair, 47; myth of embracement, 128; National Aboriginal Day, 60-61; Nellie Carlson, 45; *R. v. Sparrow* case, 52-55; raceshifting, 56; self-identification vs collective identification, 45; Wilton Littlechild, 51

Aboriginal title, 33-34, 36-37, 50, 186

Aboriginal tourism. *see also* Aboriginal Tourism Association of British Columbia (ATBC): Aboriginal as a corporate brand, 109; "Aboriginal Cultural Tourism: Checklist for Success" (ATTC and CTC), 130; Andaman Islands, 109; "Atiik Aski: Land of the Caribou" (Kelly), 130; authentic defined, 133-34; "Authenticity—What Do They (Tourists) Really Want?" (Laliberté), 134-35; Canadian Tourism Commission (CTC), 110, 123; colonial roots, 112-17; construction of the notion of authenticity, 28; definitions, 129-30, 135; Department of Tourism and Culture for the Yukon Territory, 133-134; Edward Roper, 109; *The Imaginary Indian* (Francis), 109; Indigenous Tourism Association of British Columbia, 110; Indigenous Tourism Association of British Columbia (ITBC), 129-30; to move away from the state's interests, 138-39; 2003 National Study on Aboriginal Tourism in Canada, 130-31; niche marketing, 129-35; non-traditional experiences, 130, 132,

135, 136; settler nostalgia, 27–31; as site of Indigenous possibility, 29–30
Aboriginal Tourism Association of British Columbia (ATBC), 110, 129–35, 139, 140, 189; Aboriginal Cultural Tourism Authenticity Program (of ATBC), 134, 135, 189–90
activism. *see* Indigenous activism
Adams, Howard, 28, 80, 113, 144
airports. *see also* aviation; Vancouver International Airport (YVR): art, 152–54, 155; Blatchford Field, 175; Denver International Airport "'Spirit of the People" (exhibit), 141; Department of Transportation (DOT), 147; dispossession of Indigenous peoples, 149–50, 175; land claims, 142; Macdonald-Cartier International Airport/ Ottawa International Airport, 142; Malton Airport, 150; Omàmiwininiwak, 150; the passenger terminal, 152–55; regional marketing, 154; removal of *Totem* (Yarwood), 153; Sea Island Airport (Vancouver), 150, 156; Toronto Pearson International Airport terminal, 141, 150; as tourism destination, 175; Winnipeg airport terminal, 153; xʷməθkʷəy̓əm territory, 150
Alfred, Taiaiake, 16, 17, 18, 128, 138, 139
Allen, George, 30
American imperialism, 113, 115
Anderson, Chris, 54–55, 58–59, 62
Animikii, 1, 2, 32, 179
Arctic sovereignty, 150, 153
assimilation: Aboriginality as marker, 111; "bad" Aboriginal people, 106; covered up in 1988 Calgary Winter Olympic opening ceremony, 85, 87; and disruption of British-Canadian hegemony, 12; Expo '67, 79; extension of the railway, 113; Gradual Enfranchisement Act of 1869, 200–201n20; impact on Indianness in colonial tourism, 115–16; multiculturalism policy, 80–81, 178; neoliberalism, 178; policies and actions, 20, 22–23, 65, 68; reconciliation, 6

Association of Métis and Non-Status Indians of Saskatchewan (AMNSIS), 38, 43, 47
"Atiik Aski: Land of the Caribou" (Kelly), 130
Atleo, Clifford, Jr., 136–37
Atleo, Shawn, 206n130
Australia, 34, 67. *see also* Māori resistance
aviation. *see also* airports: Aboriginalization, 29, 171–76; Arctic sovereignty, 150–51; colonization of the sky, 173–74; enabled population of remote regions, 147; First Nations participation in ceremonies, 156; frontierism, 149–50; golden age, 156–57; resource extraction, 173, 218n27; as symbol of national power, 151; technological colonization, 146; as technological nationalism, 143–46

B

"bad" Aboriginal people, 27, 91, 106, 168
"bad Indians," 14
Bargh, Maria, 8, 14, 196n39
BC Supreme Court, 184
Black Skin, White Masks (Fanon), 17
BNA Act (British North America Act). *see* British North America Act (BNA Act)
Borrows, John, 66–67, 200n11
Boykoff, Jules, 71
Britain. *see also* United Kingdom: British-Canadianness, 12, 20, 27; Canada's decolonization from, 43; colonial law, 33–34, 42; colonial policymaking, 34–35, 36; colonists, 9, 33, 114, 200n20; the Constitutional Express, 202–3n51; land, 174; Royal Proclamation of 1763, 37, 200n11; whiteness, 145
British North America Act (BNA Act), 39, 40, 200n8

C

Cairns, Alan, 22

Calgary Stampede, 80, 82

1988 Calgary Winter Olympics opening ceremony: attire of Indigenous peoples, 83; Bernard Ominayak, 88; Bruce Starlight, 86; Chief Fox, 82; countering Indigenous resistance movements, 86; Daniel Tlen, 83; Frank King, 82, 86, 87; Hudson's Bay Company's point blanket, 83, 84, 85; Jeanne Sauvé, 83; Julia Harrison, 89, 90; Leo Youngman, 86, 88; Lubicon Nêhiyawak peoples boycott, 88–90; the Mountie, Cowboy and Native, 81–82, 83–84, 86, 87–88; multiculturalism used to hide colonialism, 106; Native Participation Program (NPP), 85–86, 88, 208n41; Paddy Sampson, 83; promoting western hospitality, 81, 83, 87, 90; proposed 'Indian attack and wagon-burning,' 82–83, 87–88; racist tropes in, 73; Ralph Klein, 82; *The Spirit Sings: Artistic Traditions of Canada's First Peoples* (exhibition), 88–90; terminology choices reveal intent, 86–87, 90; Treaty 7 peoples, 81, 82, 83, 88

Canada's national brand identity. *see also* Canadian tourism: Aboriginal as symbol of forgiveness, 178; Aboriginal brand, 6, 111, 126, 140; Aboriginal multicultural brand, 19–27, 177; boosterism, 10, 12; branding, 9–13; Canada Vacations Unlimited, 11; corporate branding, 27–31, 140; experience-based tourism, 120, 122–124, 126–128; hiding paternalism, 15–16, 29, 80–81, 106, 107–108, 185; the imagineered national brand, 29, 60, 74, 128; Indigeneity as brand, 188–189; John A. Macdonald, 21; leveraging Indigenous peoples, 72, 90, 94–95, 98–105, 106, 128, 138, 140; marketing, 10–12, 11; multicultural, 140; multiculturalism, 75; neoliberalism, 9–10, 15, 67; the Olympic ceremonies as an opportunity for enhancement, 72; the Olympic games solidifying Canada's national brand, 74–75; rooted in assimilation, 87; *The Spirit Sings: Artistic Traditions of Canada's First Peoples* (exhibition), 88–89; success with using Aboriginal, 16; Tommy Douglas, 21; treaty federalism approach to Indigenous activism, 22

Canada's nation-building: image of Indigenous peoples as threat, 9–10; the Prairie expansion, 9–10, 83, 87–88, 113, 137, 143–144

Canadian Charter of Rights and Freedoms (CCRF), 44

Canadian federal government. *see also* Canadian Tourism Commission (CTC); Harper government; the Indian Act; residential schools; Trudeau government (Justin); Trudeau government (Pierre): Aboriginal Affairs and Northern Development Canada (AANDC), 68–69, 70; Andrew MacDougall, 69; assimilation policies, 22, 65, 68, 200–201n20; Carolyn Bennett, 181; Celebrate Canada, 188; Charlottetown Accord, 63; Coastal GasLink Pipeline, 183, 185, 187; commitment to United Nations Declaration on the Rights of Indigenous peoples (UNDRIP), 67, 183, 194; Crown-Indigenous Relations and Northern Affairs Canada (CIRNAC), 181–182; Department of Indian and Northern Affairs Canada (INAC), 58, 68–69, 130, 181; Department of Transportation (DOT), 147, 152; Federal Identity Program (FIP) policy, 68–69; the First Nations and Inuit Health Branch (FNIHB), 182; *Gathering Strength—Canada's Aboriginal Action Plan*, 63, 70; Gradual Enfranchisement Act of 1869, 200–201n20; High Arctic Relocation, 151; Indigenous Services Canada (ISC), 181–82; Jane Stewart, 64; John Borrows on Aboriginal rights, 66–67; Lubicon land claim settlement, 89; National Aboriginal Day, 70; Northwest Territories Act of 1875, 148, 149; payment to the Musqueam and the Tsleil-Waututh, 210n104; "Reward and Punishment" policy, 137; RIIRF ("Recognition and Implementation of Indigenous Rights Framework"),

186–87; Royal Commission on Aboriginal People's recommendations, 182; Royal Commission on National Development in the Arts, Letters, and Sciences, 153; Royal Proclamation of 1763, 37, 39; Statement of Reconciliation (1998), 26, 58, 64–68; Statistics Canada, 5–6, 19, 58–59; Vancouver International Airport (YVR), 157, 158; the 1969 White Paper ("Statement of the Government of Canada on Indian Policy, 1969"), 23, 186, 187

Canadian National Railway (CNR), 115

Canadianness: Aboriginal and non-Aboriginal, 66; Aboriginal defined, 128; Anglo-European, 118; anti-Black and anti-Asian racism, 145; British-Canadianness, 12, 20, 27; Cape Dorset Eskimo Cooperative, 153; Indianness as antithesis, 27, 111; in the Olympic ceremonies, 78, 98; pre-Canada, 124; tourism, 110, 111

Canadian Pacific Railway (CPR), 113–16, 118, 144–46

Canadian tourism. *see also* Canadian Tourism Commission (CTC): Aboriginal as corporate brand, 28, 110; brand defined, 120; Eurocentric views of Indigenous peoples, 128; experiencing Indigenous peoples' cultures, 124–125; Indigenous participation, 129, 212n23; language of frontier mythology, 120; marketed "authentic Indians," 123; railway, 113–14

Canadian Tourism Commission (CTC). *see also* Aboriginal tourism: "Aboriginal Cultural Tourism: Checklist for Success" (ATTC and CTC), 130; Aboriginality as brand, 140; Aboriginal peoples as symbol; based on colonial logic, 138; Canada's tourism brand defined, 120; experiencing Indigenous peoples' cultures, 124–126; experiential tourism in Canada, 120–22, 123–24; First Nations, 128; five unique selling points for experiential tourism, 120–22; hinges on racism, 135; Inuit, 128; portray of Métis, 127–28; selling diversity, 123–24;

a sense of destination deficiency, 120, 122–123; Statement of Cooperation, 27; types of travellers, 122, 124–25; website, 110, 120, 223n45; Whiteshell Provincial Park, 127

capitalism. *see also* celebration capitalism; resource capitalism: Aboriginality, 177; agreements related to the 2010 Vancouver Winter Olympics, 93–94; art acquisition for Vancouver International Airport (YVR), 164; and aviation, 147; desire for wilderness, 112; effect on Indigenous peoples life, 111; Indigenous communities threatened through commodification, 12–13; Osoyoos Indian Band, 137–38; resource extraction, 156; Yuxweluptun's critique, 171

Cardinal, Harold, 23

celebration capitalism, 71, 93

census, 56, 58–59. *see also* federal government: Statistics Canada

Charland, Maurice, 143, 144, 145

Chrétien, Jean, 26, 44, 64

City of Edmonton, 149–50

City of Vancouver, 99–100, 101. *see also* 2010 Vancouver Winter Olympics

Coalition of Aboriginal Peoples of Saskatchewan, 57

Coastal GasLink Pipeline, 15, 183, 184–86, 187

Coleman, Daniel, 122

colonialism. *see also* neoliberal colonialism; settler colonialism: affect on Indigenous peoples forms of livelihood, 111; airports, 30–31; "Being Indigenous: Resurgences against Contemporary Colonialism" (Alfred and Corntassel), 17; burying the legacy, 29, 32; covering up, 12; the Cowboy and the Indian, 86; expropriation of Indigenous cultural matters, 131–32; extension of the railway, 113–16; hidden via Aboriginalism, 126; impact of frontierism, 150; Indigenous homelands as *terra nullius*, 112; intergenerational effects of, 100, 101; mercantile colonialism, 65, 85; Métis resistance movements, 127-28; and neoliberal colonialism, 7, 16, 136, 177; tourism, 135, 138; treaty-making, 113, 114, 115; unwillingness to be accountable, 101

colonization. *see also* technological colonization: Aboriginalization and Indigenization, 32; aviation, 142, 147, 150; Call #47 (Truth and Reconciliation Commission), 183; Canadian Tourism Commission (CTC), 122, 129; neoliberalism as, 14; and Olympic narratives, 85, 87-88, 107; relocation of select communities to remote locations, 13-14; of the sky, 173-74; Vancouver International Airport (YVR), 168, 192

Committee for Original Peoples' Entitlement (COPE), 39

Congress of Aboriginal Peoples (CAP), 57. *see also* Native Council of Canada (NCC)

the Constitution. *see also* 1982 Constitution Act; section 35 of the Constitution: aboriginal as placeholder, 43-44; Association of Métis and Non-Status Indians of Saskatchewan (AMNSIS), 43; Christopher Lafontaine, 40; First Nations need time to research position, 40; Harry Daniels, 41; importance of expansive terminology, 41; Indigenous peoples advocating for entrenchment, 50-51; and Inuit, 39, 41, 42, 43, 45, 46, 51-52, 58, 61-62, 70; mass action campaign of Union of British Columbia Indian Chiefs (UBCIC), 42-43; Métis, 19, 35, 39-41, 43, 62-63; reason to use Aboriginal, 19; recognition politics, 38-45; Rob Milen, 43; section 37, 52; Special Joint Committee of the Senate and the House of Commons on the Constitution of Canada, 38, 39, 40, 43, 44, 55-56; Trudeau government (Pierre), 39-40, 43

1982 Constitution Act, 4, 62, 106, 110

Corntassel, Jeff, 16, 17, 18

Coulthard, Glen Sean, 17, 18, 26, 171

Courtwright, David T., 149-50, 173, 174

COVID-19 pandemic, 187, 193

D

Daschuk, James William, 145
Day, Richard, 17-18
Dewdney, Edgar, 137
Diabo, Russ, 186
Distant Early Warning Line, 150
Doctrine of Discovery, 146, 183
Dodek, Adam, 51
Døving, Runar, 152
dream catchers, 169

E

ecological genocide, 88, 90
ecotourism, 13, 29, 111, 135
environmentalism: Callaghan Valley Nordic Competition Venue for ski jumping, 93; ecological disasters, 170-71; pollution, 173; sustainability, 190; 2010 Vancouver Winter Olympics, 102
Eriksen, Thomas Hylland, 152
Eskimo, 35, 40, 127, 153. *see also* Inuit
Eurocentrism, 51, 128
experiential tourism: airports, 142, 154; Canadian, 120-26; defining experience, 130; history, 117-19; replication of the Aboriginal experience, 133
Expo 67, 79

F

Fanon, Frantz, 17
federal government. *see* Canadian federal government
Federation of Saskatchewan Indians (FSI), 37, 50, 51
Fetrow, Karla, 100-101, 102
Flaman, Bernard, 141, 153, 154
Forsyth, Janice, 74, 78, 80, 86, 92, 94, 105, 106
Foucault, Michel, 4
foundation myth, 32, 123

252 **Aboriginal™**

France, 124, 202-3n51
Francis, Daniel, 9, 85, 109, 113, 156
Francis, Jessica, 29
Furlong, John, 95-96, 210n85
fur trade, 83, 148, 149, 218n27

G

genocide. *see also* ecological genocide; neoliberal colonialism: aviation as tool, 151; economics, 137; and national brand narrative, 24, 25-26, 29, 32, 60, 65, 67, 99, 106; in nation-building, 106; *The Spirit Sings: Artistic Traditions of Canada's First Peoples* (exhibition), 89, 89; triumphant attitudes, 85
Germany, 82, 124, 202-3n51
global capitalism, 153-54
globalization, 12-13, 90, 134. *see also* neoliberal globalization
"good" Aboriginal peoples, 27, 74, 81, 91, 101, 106-7, 168

H

Hall, Stuart, 4
Harper, Elijah, 59
Harper, Stephen, 68, 181
Harper government, 68-69
Haudenosaunee, 15, 70
Hawthorn, Harry, 22
Heine, Michael, 90
Henderson, James (Sakej) Youngblood, 22
hiding colonial history, 15-16, 29, 80-81, 106, 107-8, 185; genocide, 24, 25-26, 29, 65, 67, 99
Hodge, Bob, 123
Howard-Wagner, Deirdre, 13
Hubregtse, Menno, 165
Hudson's Bay Company's point blanket, 83, 84, 85
Huhndorf, Shari, 127

human rights: Canada's history of infringement, 26; in Canadian Charter of Rights and Freedoms (CCRF), 44; the Indian Act, 21; and the state's agenda, 178

I

the Imaginary Indian, 109, 119, 156
imperialism: mining, 219n35; power, 171; temporal gap, 122
imperialism, American, 113, 115
imperialism, romantic, 140
imperialist nostalgia, 27, 122-23
Imperial Oil, 147-149
the Indian Act: ability to grant and deny, 136; definition of Indian, 35-36, 45, 201n28; dismantling, 182, 186; elected band council system, 81, 184, 200-201n20; inclusion of the Inuit, 20; National Indian Brotherhood's (NIB), 39; neoliberalism, 15-16; non-status Indians and Métis, 35, 37-38, 54; Paul Williams, 48-49; Pierre Trudeau's proposed dissolution, 23, 24; as reason for social issues in the Downtown Eastside (DTES), 100; rebranding Department of Indian and Northern Affairs Canada (INAC), 68; technologic nationalism, 144; women, 21-22, 35-36, 201n20
Indian as term: capitalization of the word, 70; defined in the Indian Act, 35-36; foregrounded in policymaking, 34-35; section 35 of the Constitution, 35
Indian Chiefs of Alberta, 23
Indianness: Aboriginal rights, 35; as antithesis of Canadianness, 27, 111; as antithesis to Canadianness, 27; colonial tourism, 115-116; compared to Aboriginality, 27-28, 111; and The Imaginary Indian, 109; as marketing ploy, 114, 116, 172
Indians of Quebec Association (IQA), 79-80
Indian title. *see* Aboriginal title
Indigeneity, 179-87, 188-90, 191-94

Indigenous: *An Essay on the Indigenous Grasses of Ireland* (White), 180; calls for self-determination ignored by Canadian government, 7; etymology, 2-3, 33, 180; as placeholder for diverse community, 190; as standing outside Aboriginal, 16; term comes from within Indigenous communities, 1; used in the Truth and Reconciliation Commission (TRC), 182-83

Indigenous activism: the Constitution, 18-19, 43, 50-51, 53, 67, 81; importance of terminology, 41-42; Métis, 21, 46, 50-51; National Aboriginal Day, 60-61; "No Olympics on Stolen Native Land," 102, 103; treaty federalism approach, 22; 2010 Vancouver Winter Olympics, 95

Indigenous peoples: challenging founding myths of settler nationhood, 25; corporatization as threat, 14; demand of self-determination, 6; as display of regionalism and nationalism, 101; economic development constrained by the federal government, 137; as signifiers of Canada's diversity, 124; stereotype of dying out, 113, 114

"Indigenous peoples: Terminology Guide" (Simeone), 1

Indigenous Peoples' Assembly of Canada (IPAC). *see* Congress of Aboriginal Peoples (CAP)

Indigenous theory, 17

International Union of Official Travel Organizations (IUOTO), 117

Inuit. *see also* Eskimo: and Aboriginal, 1, 3, 6, 7, 19, 20, 33, 178; air travel and the north, 147, 150, 151; artwork, 89, 153, 173; as Eskimo, 35; the First Nations and Inuit Health Branch (FNIHB), 182; High Arctic Relocation, 151; Indian and Northern Affairs Canada (INAC), 68; as Indians, 35, 200n8; self-determination, 72, 186-87; self-identification, 59; subjected to assimilation policies, 65; tourism, 123, 125-27, 128, 129, 130; 2010 Vancouver Winter Olympics, 96, 106

Inuit Tapirisat of Canada (now Inuit Tapiriit Kanatami), 38, 40

Ipperwash, 59-60
Irlbacher-Fox, Stephanie, 67

J

Jennings, Peter, 85
Jensen, Patricia, 112

K

Kanehsatà:ke, 59-60, 61
Kelly, Michael E., 130
Kelly, Robert, 119
Kulchyski, Peter, 148, 149
Kusugak, Michael, 151

L

Labrador Métis. *see* Nunatukavut (Labrador Métis)
Ladner, Kiera, 18
Laliberté, Michèle, 134-35
Lambertus, Sandra, 20, 23-24
land claims: airports, 142; Canada's claim to unceded land, 144; Inuit Tapirisat of Canada (now Inuit Tapiriit Kanatami), 38; Lubicon settlement, 89; The No Olympics on Stolen Native Land movement, 102-4, 103
Landriault, Mathieu, 181
Lawrence, Bonita, 65
League of the Indians of Canada, 38
Leblanc, Roméo, 60
Leddy, Shannon, 162-65, 220n82
Leroux, Darryl, 56
Lil'Wat: aboriginal rights, 70; involvement in bid for 2010 Vancouver Winter Olympics, 91-93, 104; return of land with strings attached, 93-94
Loft, F.O., 38
Louie, Clarence, 136

M

MacCannell, Dean, 117

Macdonald, John A., 21, 143

Manitoba Métis Federation, 39

Manitowabi, Darrel, 14

Manuel, George, 39, 43

Māori resistance, 196

marketing: Aboriginal as label, 4-5; Aboriginal tourism as niche, 129-135; boosterism, 9, 10, 12, 113-14; branding, 12, 27, 30, 111, 113-14, 122, 165; Canada's national brand identity, 10-12; Canadian Tourism Commission (CTC), 120-23, 135; Indianness as ploy, 114, 116, 172; Vancouver International Airport (YVR), 4-5, 154, 164, 192

Martinez, Doreen E. Martinez, 141-42

Mawani, Renisa, 25

McChesney, Robert, 8

Membean, 2

Merilees, Harold, 157

Métis. see also the Constitution; Métis Nation; self-determination; self-identification: as Aboriginal, 178; activism, 21, 46, 50-51; capitalization, 70; definition, 54, 55; did a Métis community exist as an Aboriginal community, 54-55; effects of aviation, 150; Ethel Deschambault, 39, 40; fight to be counted as Indian, 35; John Sinclair, 43, 47; multiculturalism, 20; recognized in British North America Act (BNA Act), 39; resistance movements, 10, 87-88, 126, 127-128, 137; the Royal Commission On Aboriginal Peoples (RCAP), 61-62; Tom Eagle, 39; in 2010 Vancouver Winter Olympics opening ceremony, 96

Métis Association of Alberta, 37

Métis Nation: as Aboriginal, 46-47, 55; the Constitution, 70; distinct political status, 42; 1992 Métis Nation Accord, 63; resistance as insurrection, 127-28; the Royal Commission on Aboriginal Peoples (RCAP), 61-63; self-identification, 46, 56; in 2010 Vancouver Winter Olympics opening ceremony, 96

Miller, J.R., 37

Milloy, John Sheridan, 174

Mishra, Vijay, 123

Mississaugas of the Credit First Nation (MCFN), 188

modernity, 112, 115-17, 118, 127

Mohawk, 80, 172

1976 Montreal Summer Olympics closing ceremony: Andrew T. Delisle, 76; Artur Takac, 77; attire of participants, 76-77, 80; Aurélien Gill, 76; *Danse sauvage* (Mathieu), 75; designed by Olympic organizers for Aboriginal peoples, 78-79; fear of demonstrations by Indigenous peoples, 77, 79-81; "good" Indians, 27, 81; Howard Adams, 80; Hugo de Pot, 75; Indian Days celebration, 79-80; Janice Forsyth, 78, 80; Kevin Wamsley, 78; Killanin, Lord, 77-78; Max Gros-Louis, 76; Michael Cartier, 75; Mike McKenzie, 76; Otto Shantz, 75; Queen Elizabeth, 77; recruitment of First Nations people to "play Indian," 72, 73; Sandra Henderson, 75; Stéphane Préfontaine, 75

Morton, Samuel, 34

multiculturalism. see also Canada's national identity; neoliberal multiculturalism: Aboriginal as, 4, 66, 178; Aboriginality and Indianness, 111; anchored in english/french duality, 75; as base for Aboriginal relations 2010 Vancouver Winter Olympics, 102; Canada's core brand identity, 19-20, 153; Canada's vision of, 7; Canadian Multiculturalism Day, 60; Celebrate Canada, 188; conceals colonialism, 105; National Aboriginal Day, 60; and Olympic narratives, 73-74, 75, 78-79, 80-81, 106-8; as pillar of Canadian identity, 60, 87; and reconciliation, 26; the Royal Commission on Aboriginal Peoples (RCAP), 63-64; selling diversity to transform the national narrative, 123-24

Musqueam, 210n104. *see also* Vancouver International Airport (YVR); xʷməθkʷəy̓əm

N

National Aboriginal Day, 58-61, 188

National Aboriginal History Month (now National Indigenous History Month), 1

National Committee on Indian Rights for Indian Women (NCIRIW), 38

National Gallery of Canada, 152

National Indian Brotherhood (NIB), 38, 39, 40, 41, 59

National Indian Council (NIC), 38, 79

Native Council of Canada (NCC), 38, 40, 41, 47-48, 57, 201n28. *see also* Congress of Aboriginal Peoples (CAP)

Native replaced by Aboriginal, 5, 7, 201n28

native title. *see* Aboriginal title

Native Women's Association of Canada (NWAC), 38, 44

neoliberal colonialism. *see also* colonialism: Aboriginal as acculturated inferiority, 18; Aboriginal as hallmark, 4, 6; Aboriginal tourism, 28; defined, 7-9; de-indigenized Aboriginality desired, 111; furthered by Aboriginal tourism, 23; genocidal function of aboriginalism, 128; and Indigenous peoples, 10-16; Project Civil City, 101; promises freedom to Indigenous peoples, 15-16; reconciliation, 185-86; refusal to give up "being" Indigenous, 107; results in poverty, 179; Safe Streets Act, 101; search for resources, 26; state relations, 68; transformed Indigenous peoples from liabilities to resource, 12-13

neoliberal globalization, 6, 7, 10, 13, 71. *see also* globalization

neoliberalism, 7-16. *see also* neoliberal multiculturalism; assimilation, 178; capitalism, 12-13; cuts to social spending, 8-9; defined, 7-8; economic thought, 179; the Indian Act, 15-16; Indigenous communities threatened through commodification, 12-13; Margaret Little, 8-9; market as only means to improve human well-being, 9; market solutions for colonial problems, 13-14; Mike Harris, 8; multiculturalism, 7; as new form of colonisation, 14-16; place-branding, 30; reframing of national identities, 10-12; search for resources, 26; as solution, 136-37; willingness to adopt new terminology, 90

neoliberal multiculturalism, 25

neoliberal settler colonialism, 7, 15. *see also* settler colonialism

New Brunswick Aboriginal Peoples Council, 57

New Zealand, 67

NIB (National Indian Brotherhood). *see* National Indian Brotherhood (NIB)

Nimijean, Richard, 124

Nisga'a nation, 36-37

North American Indian Brotherhood, 38

the Northwest Rebellion, 10, 126, 136

Nunatukavut, 55-56

Nunatukavut (Labrador Métis), 46, 62

Nye, Joseph S., Jr., 72

O

O'Bonsawin, Christine M., 74, 86

the Olympic games. *see also* 1988 Calgary Winter Olympics opening ceremony; 1976 Montreal Summer Olympics closing ceremony; 2010 Vancouver Winter Olympics: "bad" Aboriginal people, 27, 91, 106, 168; celebration capitalism, 71; Christine M. O'Bonsawin, 74; "good" Aboriginal people, 27, 74, 81, 91, 101, 106-107, 168; Indigenous people in ceremonies, 26-27, 72; Indigenous Youth Gathering, 178; International Olympic Committee (IOC), 76; motivations for Indigenous peoples' participation, 105; motives for Indigenous peoples' participation, 72-73, 79; move to Indigenous

terminology, 188; solidifying Canada's national brand, 74, 106; tokenism, 74, 85–86, 99; Vancouver's Bid for, 91–92, 93, 94
Omàmiwininiwak, 142, 150
O'Neil, John, 100
Osoyoos Indian Band, 136–38

P
Paull, Andrew, 38
Pierre-Aggamaway, Marlee, 44, 45
place-branding: airports, 30–31, 154; as extension of corporate branding, 30; Indigeneity as, 191–94; of Vancouver International Airport (YVR), 4, 30, 31, 142, 143
Point, Krista, 161
Point, Susan A., 160, 161–162, 163
Pointe, Shane A., 161–62, 163
political activism. *see* Indigenous activism
political correctness, 32, 86, 90, 195n13
politics of recognition, 16–19
postracial society, 217n148
poverty: context for acceptance of aboriginal, 17; in the Downtown Eastside (DTES), 99–100; economic development as antidote to, 178; as manifestation of neoliberal colonialism, 179; Mother's Allowance, 8–9; neoliberal colonialism leads to, 179; neoliberalism as solution, 14–15, 136; reason to change national narrative, 99; tourism as solution, 139
Powderface, Sykes, 81, 88, 208n41
Prentice, Richard, 118

Q
Queen's University, 189

R
racial neoliberalism, 101, 177
racism. *see also* scientific racism; systemic racism: anti-Asian, 144, 168; anti-Black, 144; anti-Indigenous, 173, 177; 1988 Calgary Winter Olympic opening ceremony, 86; Canadian Tourism Commission (CTC), 135; Indigenous people's humanity, 114; Inuit stereotypes, 127; in the 1976 Montreal Summer Olympics, 80; neutrality of words, 195n13; and Olympic narratives, 107–8; positioned as attitude, 65; representations of national identity, 101; role in technological nationalism, 145; of settlers, 178; stereotype of Indigenous peoples dying out, 113
Raibmon, Paige, 28, 134, 139
railway. *see* Canadian Pacific Railway (CPR)
Ranasinghe, Prashan, 100, 101
RCMP (Royal Canadian Mounted Police): action against Wet'suwet'en people, 184, 185, 186; colonial administration of the Northwest Territories, 148; represented in 1988 Calgary Winter Olympic opening ceremony, 81–82, 83–84, 86, 87–88; represented in 1976 Montreal Summer Olympics closing ceremony, 83; restricting Inuit travel, 20
"Recognition and Implementation of Indigenous Rights Framework" (RIIRF), 186–87
reconciliation: assimilation, 6; Call #47 (Truth and Reconciliation Commission), 183; dismantling the Indian Act, 182; Justin Trudeau on lack of advancement, 185; land acknowledgments, 193–194; and multiculturalism, 26; neoliberal colonialism, 185–86; Statement of Reconciliation (1998), 26, 58, 64–68; Truth and Reconciliation Commission (TRC), 173, 182–83, 191; use of Aboriginal to indicate, 177
#RECONCILIATIONISDEAD, 186
the Red Paper ("Citizens Plus") (Cardinal), 23

Red Skin, White Masks: Rejecting the Colonial Politics of Recognition (Coulthard), 17

Reid, Bill, 162–64

the reserve system, 100, 113, 115, 144

residential schools: effect on Indianness of colonial tourism, 115–16; exhibit at Expo 67, 79; Office of Indian Residential Schools Resolution Canada, 182; position as in the past, 6; as reason for social issues in the Downtown Eastside (DTES), 100; role of aviation, 151; in the Statement of Reconciliation, 66

resource capitalism, 147–49

Riel, Louis, 128

Romanticist-driven tourism, 112, 114, 140

Rorke, Rosalind Alix, 155, 156, 157, 168, 171, 173

Rosaldo, Renato, 123

Rosenbloom, Donald, 44, 50

Royal Canadian Mounted Police (RCMP). *see* RCMP (Royal Canadian Mounted Police)

Royal Commission on Aboriginal Peoples (RCAP): Aboriginal people (singular), 63–64; Aboriginal peoples defined, 62; aboriginal title, 33–34; capitalization of Aboriginal, 70; definition of Aboriginal, 61–62; definition of Métis defined, 62–63; Métis Nation, 61–63; politics of recognition, 18; recommendation to establish a national holiday as part of public education, 60; in the Statement of Reconciliation, 64–65

S

Sanders, Douglas, 24

the Saskatchewan Métis Society, 37, 40

Sawchuk, Joe, 56, 204–5n95

scholarship: acceptance of the aboriginalist voice, 143; on Canada's transportation infrastructure, 143; critiquing land claimed by Canada, 144; examining the term Aboriginal, 16–17; on role of racism in technological nationalism, 145

scientific racism, 34

section 35 of the Constitution, 51–52; Aboriginal as term, 3, 4, 6; capitalization of Aboriginal, 70; Indian as term, 35; interpreting who is Aboriginal, 53–54, 56, 57; rights entrenchment via, 13, 81, 186; waiting until after patriation, 44

self-determination: Aboriginal title, 50; Aboriginal tourism, 29; Canadian government, 7, 67; colonial power structures, 94; constitutional talks focused on, 42; First Nations as ethnic municipalities, 186–87; "good" Aboriginal people, 106; Indigenous peoples demand, 6; Métis, 186–87; neoliberalism allows, 13; potentially achieved through tourism, 109

self-identification: of communities, 63; to generate social capital and financial gain, 57; irrelevance of Aboriginal, 37; Joseph Boyden, 57; Métis, 45–46, 54, 56; Michelle Latimer, 57; qualifications for Indigenous, 189, 190; reflecting identity and not rights, 19; rise in, 189; self-identification vs collective identification, 45; Statistics Canada, 5–6, 19, 56, 58–59

settler anxiety, 122–23, 126–27

settler colonialism, 7, 12, 15, 16, 35, 60, 114, 115–16. *see also* neoliberal settler colonialism

settler nationalism, 27, 98, 101

Shantz, Otto, 75

Shell Canada, 88, 89, 90

Sheller, Mimi, 140

Simeone, Tonina, 1

Simpson, Audra, 184, 185

Simpson, Leanne, 180

Site C dam, 187

Skwxwú7mesh: aboriginal rights, 70; involvement in bid for 2010 Vancouver Winter Olympics, 91–93, 104; return of land with strings attached, 93–94

Slattery, Brian, 33–34

Slowey, Gabrielle, 13

Sparrow, Robin, 161, *163*

258 Aboriginal™

Squamish. see Skwxwú7mesh

Statement of Reconciliation. see Canadian federal government

stereotypes: Aboriginality, 178; Clarence Louie accused of pandering, 136-37; Inuit as happy, 127; Jim Crow Museum of Racist Memorabilia, 221n96; in the Olympic Games, 77-78, 79, 80, 99; performances to follow, 156

Stewart-Harawira, Makere, 12-13

Supreme Court of Canada: the *Calder* decision, 36-37; *Daniels v. Canada (Indian Affairs and Northern Development)*, 35; *Delgamuukw* decision, 185; did a Métis community exist as an Aboriginal community, 54-55; how it defined Aboriginal related to Aboriginal rights, 53-55; Indian and Aboriginal used interchangeably, 37; Indian and Eskimo as coterminous, 200n8; Inuit as Indians, 35; *R. v. Pamajewon*, 136; *R. v. Powley*, 53-54; *R. v. Sparrow* case, 52-54, 176; *R. v. Van der Peet*, 53-54, 135, 136, 176

systemic racism, 101

T

technological colonization, 146-49

technological nationalism: frontierism, 156; Indigenous homelands as uncultivated, 145-46; John A. Macdonald, 143; railroad, 143-46

teepees, 76-77, 83, 84, 125, 156

Tester, Frank, 148, 149

Tsleil-Waututh, 94

tokenism, 74, 85-86, 99, 188, 193

Toronto Aboriginal Support Services Council (TASSC), 179-80

totem poles: as markers of Otherness, 115, 116; in the Olympic ceremonies, 96-98, 97; tourism, 115, 116, 125, 131

tourism, 28. see also Aboriginal tourism; Canadian tourism; Canadian Tourism Commission (CTC); ecotourism; Romanticist-driven tourism; airports as destination, 175; appeal of Aboriginal linked Canada's national identity, 110-111; authentic Aboriginality, 4; Canada's worldwide ranking, 119; colonial tourism, 112-117; COVID-19 pandemic, 193; draw to Calgary, 106; engaging Indigenous peoples, 10; First Nations, 128; Indianness as marketing ploy, 114, 116, 172; mass tourism, 117-18; as means of economic development, 109; role in revitalization and preservation, 190; role in shaping Canada's national brand identity, 28; romantic imperialism, 140; romanticism, 114, 118, 122, 140; Skwxwú7mesh and Lil'Wat First Nations, 93; as solution for poverty, 139; sustainability, 135; types of Aboriginal people, 178; Vancouver International Airport (YVR), 30

Trans Mountain expansion, 187

Trask, Haunani-Kay, 139, 215n117

treaties. see also unceded land: Aboriginal title, 36; airports, 155, 175; Canada's change in desire, 148-49; cession, 144, 155; colonial logic, 114, 115; constitutional talks, 39, 40, 46, 48; Dene, 149; Gitxsan, 185; Lubicon, 89; Manitoba Treaty, 21; Métis identity, 46; Northwest Territories (NWT), 148-149; Omàmiwininiwak, 142; on the Prairies, 113; Reward and Punishment policy, 137; Treaty 4, 174, 217n13; Treaty 6, 174; Treaty 7, 81, 82, 83, 88, 208n41; Treaty 11, 149; Treaty at Niagara, 200n11; Treaty Land Entitlement Process, 127; United Nations Declaration on the Rights of Indigenous peoples (UNDRIP), 185; the White Paper, 23

treaty rights: "Citizens Plus" (the Red Paper) (Cardinal), 23; the Constitution, 48, 51-52, 64; in the Hawthorn Report, 23; in section 35 of the Constitution, 52; Whiteshell Provincial Park, 127

Trott, Christopher, 127

Trudeau, Justin, 31, 185, 188

Trudeau, Pierre: Indigenous policymaking and multiculturalism, 24; Jim Sinclair's lawsuit, 50; proposed dissolution of the Indian Act, 23, 24, 182, 186; the 1969 White Paper ("Statement of the Government of Canada on Indian Policy, 1969"), 23, 186, 187

Trudeau government (Justin), 31, 181–82, 183, 185, 186–87

Trudeau government (Pierre), 39–40, 43

Truth and Reconciliation Commission (TRC), 173, 182–83, 191

Tsleil-Waututh, 94, 210n104

tuberculosis, 20, 151

Turner, Dale, 63

Turtle Island, 3, 200n11

U

unceded land: British Columbia, 93, 168; Gitxsan peoples, 185; land acknowledgments, 193–194; Omàmiwininiwak land, 150; relationship to the sky, 173; Trudeau government (Justin), 185; Vancouver International Airport (YVR) on xʷməθkʷəy̓əm land, 31, 142, 155–56, 161, 164, 175, 191; Vancouver's Sea Island Airport, 150, 155–56; 2010 Vancouver Winter Olympics, 104; Wet'suwet'en lands, 184, 185

United Kingdom, 124. *see also* Britain

United Nations (UN) conference on tourism, 117

United Nations Declaration on the Rights of Indigenous peoples (UNDRIP), 67, 183, 184, 185, 194

United States: aviation as tool of hegemony, 151; frontierism, 149–150; railroad as "solution to the Indian problem," 217n13; triumphalist attitude towards genocide, 85; United Nations Declaration on the Rights of Indigenous peoples (UNDRIP), 67; Vancouver International Airport's identity aimed at travelers from, 165

universities, 5, 189

The Unjust Society (Cardinal), 23

Urry, John, 117

V

Vancouver International Airport (YVR): Aboriginalization in, 154–55; anti-immigration, 168, 173; authenticity and Aboriginal inclusion, 153; Basil Point, 156; Clive Grout, 159–160; controversial art, 168–71, 192, 193; Craig Richmond, 192; dispossession of xʷməθkʷəy̓əm, 155, 192; Frank O'Neill, 162, 164–65; gift shops, 167, 169, 172; *The Great Wave* (Haufschild), 165, 166; Howard Grant, 162–64; inclusion of First Nations art, 155, 157, 164–65; international terminal, 159–67; Joe David, 159; Lawren Harris, 159; marketing, 4–5, 154, 164, 192; Megan Stewart, 168–69; The Musqueam Indian Band –YVR Airport Sustainability and Friendship Agreement, 191–93; Musqueam Welcome Area, 161–62, 163, 164, 175–76; *Northwest Coast Killer Whale* (Yuxweluptun and Wood), 170; *Out of the Silence* (K. Point, R. Sparrow, D. Sparrow, Grant, Callbreath), 161; relationship to colonization of land, 142–43; relationship with xʷməθkʷəy̓əm, 142, 158, 173, 175–76; Rita Beiks, 168, 170, 171; Roy Henry Vickers, 159; *Spindle Whorl* (Point), 161, 163; *The Spirit of Haida Gwaii: The Jade Canoe* (Reid), 162–63, 164, 165, 165, 166; Tsimele'nuxw (Chief Jack Stogen), 156; on unceded xʷməθkʷəy̓əm land, 31, 142, 155–56, 161, 164, 168, 175, 191; Vancouver's Sea Island Airport, 150, 155; Waisman Dewar Grout Carter Inc., 159–60; Wayne Sparrow, 193; Wendy John, 193

Vancouver International Airport Authority (VIAA), 30, 158, 161, 165, 175

2010 Vancouver Winter Olympics. *see also* City of Vancouver; Sḵwx̱wú7mesh and Lil'Wat: Aboriginal as Canada's brand of liberal multiculturalism, 4, 106, 107; Aboriginal Sports Legacy Fund, 93; Bid Corporation, 86; boosted Aboriginal tourism, 131; costumes, 96, 98; David Atkins, 95–96; *The Economist*, 99–100; Four Host First Nations Society

(FHFN) Protocol agreement, 27, 94, 95, 102, 104-5, 171; Gord Hill, 102, 103; guerrilla-style surprise to participants of "Indigenous Youth Gathering," 96; hiding the city's problems, 99; host nations involvement as symbolic, 102-4; "Indigenous Youth Gathering," 96; Jody Broomfield, 94; logo of Four Host First Nations (FHFN), 94-95; opposition as politics of refusal, 106-7; *Patriot Hearts* (Furlong), 95-96; preventing demonstrations, 102-4; the problems of the Downtown Eastside (DTES), 99-101; resistance movement, 102, 103; Tewanee Joseph, 104; Vancouver International Airport Authority (VIAA), 30; Vancouver Organizing Committee (VANOC), 93, 95, 98, 111

2010 Vancouver Winter Olympics opening ceremony, 97; Aboriginal as Canada's national brand, 80-81; Aboriginal Participation Strategy, 92; financial legacies, 92-93; formal participation Sḵwx̱wú7mesh or Lil'Wat Nations not permitted, 91-92; Indigenous peoples as symbol of diversity, 73-74; "Landscape of a Dream" segment, 98; "Sacred Grove" segment, 98; a turning point in Canada's relationship with/to Indigenous peoples, 90-91

Van Ham, Peter, 123

Van Vleck, Jennifer, 151

Venne, Sharon, 174

W

Wamsley, Kevin, 78, 90, 105, 106

Watts-Powless, Vanessa, 180

Werry, Margaret, 29, 128

Wet'suwet'en, 15, 183, 184-86

"What's in a Name: Indian, Native, Aboriginal or Indigenous" (Marks), 2

Wherrett, Barbara Jill, 24, 41

White, John, 180

whiteness, 25, 83-85, 128, 145

white settler guilt, 107-8

white supremacy, 107, 111

"Why We Say 'Indigenous' Instead of 'Aboriginal'" (TASSC), 179-80

Williams, Paul, 40, 41, 48-49, 59, 70

2010 Winter Olympics opening ceremony: Adrienne Keene, 98-99; Bryan Adams, 96; Donald Sutherland, 98; Lisa Charleyboy, 99; Nelly Furtado, 96; Ryan McMahon (Clarence Two Toes), 99

Wood, Glen, 170

Wrigley, E.A., 147

X

xenophobia, 168. *see also* racism

xʷməθkʷəy̓əm. *see also* unceded land; Vancouver International Airport (YVR): Basil Point, 156; burial site, 164; Dominic Point, 156; Musqueam Cultural Committee, 161; The Musqueam Indian Band -YVR Airport Sustainability and Friendship Agreement, 191-93; Musqueam Welcome Area (YVR), 161-62, 163, 164; *Out of the Silence* (K. Point, R. Sparrow, D. Sparrow, Grant, Callbreath), 161; payment from Vancouver International Airport (YVR), 191; relationship with Vancouver International Airport (YVR), 18, 142, 156, 161, 164, 173, 175-176; *Spindle Whorl* (Point), 161, 163; *The Spirit of Haida Gwaii: The Jade Canoe* (Reid), 162-63, 164, 165, 165, 166; Tsimele'nuxw (Chief Jack Stogen), 156; Vancouver's Sea Island Airport, 150

Y

Yellow Bird, Michael, 81, 86

Yuxweluptun, Lawrence Paul, 170-71, 173, 192

YVR. *see* Vancouver International Airport (YVR)

Z

Zalewski, Anna, 53

Zhu, Lianbi, 61